WORLD'S BEST
CITIES

(previous) Sugarloaf Mountain looks over Rio de Janeiro's waterfront.

Prague's romantic perch along the Vltava River features graceful bridges and medieval spires.

WORLD'S BEST
CITIES

CELEBRATING 220 GREAT DESTINATIONS

Foreword by Annie Fitzsimmons,
National Geographic Travel's "Urban Insider"

NATIONAL GEOGRAPHIC
WASHINGTON, D.C.

Shopping in Shanghai's
fashionable Bund neighborhood

CONTENTS

*The majority of the population statistics come from the United Nations and represent the best estimates for each city's overall metropolitan area in 2015.

FOREWORD

By Annie Fitzsimmons,
National Geographic Travel's "Urban Insider"

People love Ping-Pong in Berlin. I had no idea. It is my first visit to this vast, constantly changing city 25 years after the wall fell. I have nabbed a coveted sidewalk table at Café Liebling, cappuccino in hand.

Across the way, in a grassy neighborhood square, I see a long line of people waiting for their turn at table tennis. I wander over, and although my flair for Ping-Pong is limited, I'm invited to join. With a huge dose of laughter, lobbing that little ball back and forth, new friends are made, even though they are part of my life for that moment only.

In cities we find ourselves right where we are meant to be, obsessed with a constant heartbeat of possibility, gifted with a greater license to take a leap of faith, have fun, and embrace irreverence in a place where the political, social, and cultural meet and often clash.

We have seen the great icons of cities—the Eiffel Tower, the Colosseum, the Sydney Opera House—so many times in movies or magazines that we often feel a familiarity before we get there. I love those icons, like the Brandenburg Gate here in Berlin—it makes me realize I am here, actually here! I still get butterflies when I see the Empire State Building at home in New York City.

But most of all, I am on the hunt for the daily rituals that connect locals to their cities because it connects me to them—the perfect cup of coffee in Rome, authentic tapas in Barcelona, a great bike path in Boston, a hidden bar in Siem Reap. And I've learned to create my own daily traditions, like always visiting dog parks, local libraries, and grocery stores. I climb to the great viewpoints in cities, like St. Paul's Cathedral in London, to see what feels like chaos on the ground reimagined as a perfect puzzle from above.

The daily rhythm, whether it is a warm baguette on the Île Saint-Louis in Paris or a late night walk on the Bund in Shanghai to marvel at the lights of Pudong, reveals a city's soul not found in an airport postcard or a hastily snapped selfie.

Flipping through these pages, I feel like I'm having coffee with a friend dishing about their home, their city. Armed with recommendations, I set off to find my own path. I sharpen my senses of wonder and connection. And I can't wait to see what happens next.

The Empire State Building:
a New York landmark and
Hollywood film darling

Portland
U.S.
p. 228

Seattle
U.S.
p. 214

Montreal
CANADA
p. 154

Toronto
CANADA
p. 116

Minneapolis, U.S., p. 218

Halifax, CANADA, p. 306

San Francisco
U.S.
p. 200

Denver, U.S.
p. 230

Chicago
U.S.
p. 96

Boston, U.S., p. 162

New York, U.S., p. 28

Las Vegas
U.S.
p. 274

Los Angeles, U.S.
p. 54

Asheville
U.S.
p. 320

Philadelphia, U.S., p. 128

Washington, D.C., U.S., p. 166

Honolulu
U.S.
p. 290

New Orleans
U.S.
p. 266

Miami, U.S.
p. 146

Mexico City
MEXICO
p. 18

Havana
CUBA
p. 220

NORTH AMERICA

Oslo
NORWAY
p. 286

Edinburgh, U.K.
p. 294

Amsterdam
NETH., p. 260

London, U.K., p. 84

Paris, FRANCE, p. 70

EUROPE

Geneva, SWITZ.
p. 316

Florence, ITALY, p. 246

Lisbon
PORTUGAL
p. 208

Barcelona
SPAIN
p. 120

Marrakech
MOROCCO
p. 282

Dakar
SENEGAL
p. 206

A F

Atlantic

Ocean

Pacific

Ocean

SOUTH

AMERICA

0   1,000 miles
0   1,000 kilometers

Rio de Janeiro
BRAZIL
p. 44

Santiago
CHILE
p. 112

Buenos Aires
ARGENTINA
p. 40

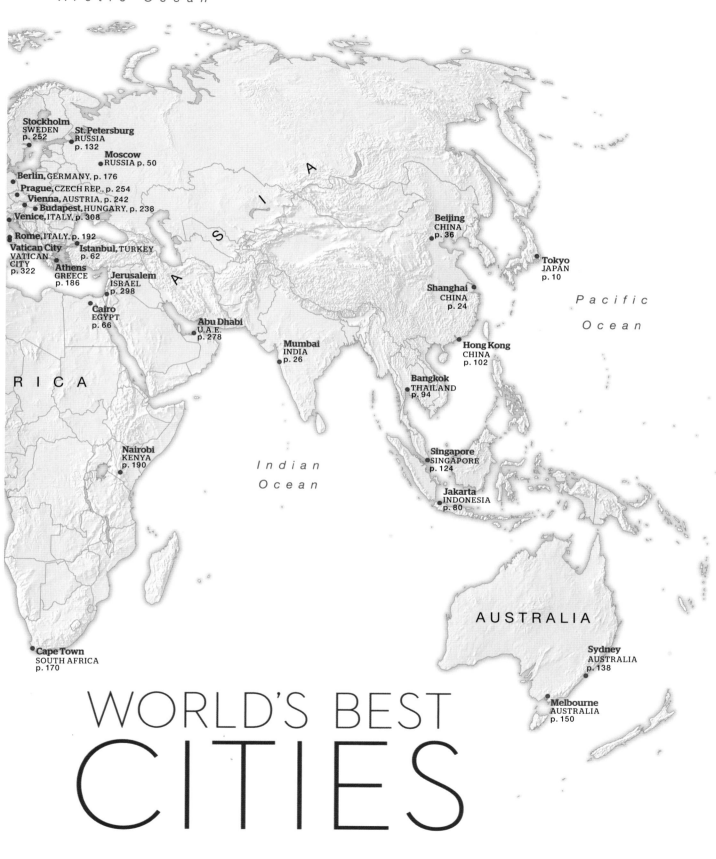

Arctic Ocean

Stockholm
SWEDEN
p. 252

St. Petersburg
RUSSIA
p. 132

Moscow
RUSSIA p. 50

Berlin, GERMANY, p. 176
Prague, CZECH REP., p. 254
Vienna, AUSTRIA, p. 242
Budapest, HUNGARY, p. 238
Venice, ITALY, p. 308
Rome, ITALY, p. 192
Vatican City
VATICAN
CITY
p. 322
Athens
GREECE
p. 186

Istanbul, TURKEY
p. 62

Jerusalem
ISRAEL
p. 298

Cairo
EGYPT
p. 66

Abu Dhabi
U.A.E.
p. 278

Mumbai
INDIA
p. 26

Beijing
CHINA
p. 36

Tokyo
JAPAN
p. 10

Shanghai
CHINA
p. 24

Hong Kong
CHINA
p. 102

Bangkok
THAILAND
p. 94

A S I A

Pacific

Ocean

RICA

Nairobi
KENYA
p. 190

Indian

Ocean

Singapore
SINGAPORE
p. 124

Jakarta
INDONESIA
p. 80

AUSTRALIA

Cape Town
SOUTH AFRICA
p. 170

Sydney
AUSTRALIA
p. 138

Melbourne
AUSTRALIA
p. 150

WORLD'S BEST
CITIES

TOKYO

A dazzling, towering capital where future and past converge

Mount Fuji towers over Yokohama on a rare fogless day.

VITAL STATS

- **Yearly passengers on Tokyo's subway** 3.3 billion, the world's busiest

- **Sushi-specialized restaurants** 3,635

- **Skyscrapers** 410, the third largest number in the world after first-place Hong Kong and New York

- **Typical size of a one-bedroom apartment** 248 square feet (23 sq m)

My City: Yoshiaki Takazawa

Working as a chef is a job that abuses your mind and body from early in the morning until late at night, so on days off it's very important to rest the body from its core. For me, the ultimate place to relax is in *onsen* hot spring spas. Since I cannot go to onsen outside of the city on every day off, I go in Tokyo to Niwa no Yu spa at Toshimaen theme park in the Nerima district (Toshimaen Station). *Niwa no Yu* means "garden spa," and it features a range of pools, onsen, and saunas set in a large Japanese garden. It's surrounded by greenery, so I can relax and spend leisurely time there just as if I were in an onsen in the country. It also has a casual restaurant on the second floor that often does theme months or days where they specialize in Japanese regional food. For example, there might be a Hokkaido food month or an Akita food day. It was a nice surprise to find, in a theme park, that I can enjoy bites from around the country with beer, even though I am still in Tokyo.

I like eating at friends' restaurants. Among my favorites are Sawaichi for Japanese food in Roppongi, and for sushi, Harutaka in Ginza and Shimizu in Shinbashi. With friends who know the restaurant business, I can share problems and also gain inspiration. These times are good for relieving stress. When you go many times, the chefs get to know your preferences, so you come to know even very old friends better. When the person in front of you is cooking especially for you, the food is definitely different from food at a restaurant that you are going to for the first time. Food made with the heart for others is delicious.

Much of my creativity comes from the atmosphere in the countryside, picking and choosing from nature and the seasons. Driving is very therapeutic. For instance, I go to Niigata where my parents' house is or around the wineries in Yamanashi. From these encounters I often come across new ingredients.

People always enjoy it when I take them to department store food courts. These are truly incredible in Japan. A good one to check out is Isetan in Shinjuku. These are easy and cheap ways for visitors to get a taste for Tokyo's food scene.

Midtown in the Roppongi District of Tokyo you'll find a range of cutting-edge products and made-in-Japan goods. One of my favorite shops is The Cover Nippon, which specializes in modern takes on traditional Japanese products like fabrics, pottery, and lacquerware. It has a huge range of shops, from a 24-hour supermarket to fashion boutiques and food outlets. I also like it because it's just five minutes from my house.

Chef Yoshiaki Takazawa was born in Tokyo and has lived there all his life. His eponymous restaurant, Takazawa, is regarded as one of Asia's 50 best restaurants, serving just ten diners per night and is one of the hardest places to get a reservation in Tokyo. ∎

"Tokyo Midtown" features top-notch shops, restaurants, and a hospital.

"Tokyo is too close up to see, sometimes. There are no distances and everything is above your head—dentists, kindergartens, dance studios. Even the roads and walkways are up on murky stilts. An evil-twin Venice with all the water drained away."

—British author David Mitchell, *number9dream*

Ginza

When a citywide fire in 1872 destroyed Ginza, Tokyo's iconic center, the new westward-looking Japanese government had the area redesigned by a British architect with broad avenues in a rational grid (above). The lure of the reborn Ginza was its department stores—originally kimono emporia that borrowed from France and England the idea of putting all sorts of goods under one roof. Stores like Mitsukoshi and Matsuzakaya were the Neiman Marcus and Bergdorf Goodman of their day. That's still the case today. Ginza, with showcase boutiques, from Armani to Harry Winston, and its smart restaurants, clubs, and art galleries, is Tokyo for grown-ups. Ginza is best on weekend afternoons, when Chuo-dori, the main north-south artery, is closed to traffic and parasols set out in the street invite lingering. ■

Ginza Finds and Anime Central

Swaths of kimono fabric at Gallery Kawano

Small Finds The massive NYC-style avenues of Ginza are famous for high fashion, designer boutiques, and big department stores, but they're also home to *Cha Ginza* (5-5-6 Ginza), where you can pick up premium teas to take home or just stop in for a cup. Want something stronger? *Shochu Authority* (1-8-2 Higashi-Shimbashi) has more than 2,300 varieties of the powerful spirit shochu, Japan's lesser known alcoholic beverage after sake. Elsewhere, in the Shibuya district near Omotesando Station, you can find vintage kimonos at *Gallery Kawano* (4-4-9 Jingūmae) or Hello Kitty toys at the Harajuku branch of *Kiddy Land* (6-1-9 Jingūmae).

Geek Out! The electronic stores that make up the *Akihabara district,* also known as Akiba or "electric town," took root with stalls selling radio parts after World War II. Today, the neon-lit area is also home to subcultures, including *otaku* (geeks), many coming for the manga and anime shops, such as *Tokyo Anime Center* (fourth floor, UDX Building, 1-18-1 Sotokanda) and *Mandarake Complex* (3-11-2 Sotokanda).

Cook's Heaven Stretching a half mile (800 m) with over 170 shops, *Kappabashi* is Japan's largest shopping street devoted to kitchen implements, the place to pick up anything from novelty fake-food key chains to chopsticks, elegant Japanese tableware, and teapots. Many locals come especially for the high-quality kitchen knives. ∎

Stock up on elegant tableware and foodie tchotchkes on Kappabashi's shopping street.

NOVEL INTRODUCTIONS

Norwegian Wood
Haruki Murakami (1987)
Named after the Beatles' song, the Japanese author's best-selling, purportedly autobiographical novel, set in 1960s Tokyo, is a nostalgic look back at sex, passion, loss, and friendship, against a backdrop of political change.

number9dream
David Mitchell (2001)
The *Cloud Atlas* author, who lived in Japan for several years, makes multifaceted and sometimes overwhelming Tokyo the star in a surreal coming-of-age tale of a young Japanese man, Eiji.

Tokyo Year Zero
David Peace (2007)
The first of two crime novels in an expected trilogy tells the story of Tokyo Detective Minami as he investigates the murder of two young girls. Set in 1946, Peace explores a country struggling to find its identity after World War II. ∎

The Eiffel Tower–inspired Tokyo Tower in the Minato district

Tokyo's Famed Cuisine: Where to Start

Slurp-worthy ramen is a staple of Tokyo's "fast" food scene.

• Some 160,000 restaurants serve up sashimi, noodles, tempura, teppanyaki, the renowned Kobe beef, the infamous fugu fish (poisonous if not properly prepared), and, of course, sushi, invented in Tokyo. Book an early morning visit to Tsukiji Fish Market (5-2-1 Tsukiji) to see the fishermen bring in their impressive hauls, available to sample in cafés through the market. Or, for a classically Japanese experience, allow expert sushi chef Masakazu Ishibashi to serve excellent tuna, sea urchin, and other wasabi-powered sushi in his intimate restaurant Sushi Ichi (1F, 4-4 Ginza 3-Chome), tucked away on a back-street away from Ginza's busy shops.

• Tokyo famously boasts more Michelin stars than any other city in the world, including Paris. See what the fuss is about at Michelin-starred restaurants like Narisawa (2-6-15 Minami Ayoyama), where chef Narisawa artfully fuses cutting-edge French and Japanese cooking techniques. But you don't need to spend a fortune to eat well in Tokyo. A few dollars will buy a delicious bowl of ramen noodles, and a visit to Tokyo isn't complete without stopping in at an *izakaya*, a laid-back "sake shop" or pub. Many chains around the city, including Watami, Murasaki, and Shirokiya, have picture menus with some English. ∎

Rare Eats and More

The top floor of the Tokyo Metropolitan Government Building #1 has a free, 360-degree observation floor, with excellent views across the sprawling metropolis. In the right weather you can see recently anointed UNESCO World Heritage site, Mount Fuji. But you have to be lucky: Mount Fuji is visible, on average, only 79 days of the year.

Mount Takao, a small mountain on the western edge of Tokyo, is easy to climb and very popular with the Japanese. A monkey park and numerous shrines are among the attractions, but another reason it's so popular has to be the fact that there's a beer garden on the summit during the summer.

Tokyo moves at a quick pace, so grabbing a bite to eat sometimes means not even taking a seat. Many small, counter-only food stalls and bars serve local delicacies. Find them in narrow alleys and on street corners at Omoide Yokocho in Shinjuku and Nonbei Yokocho (also known as Drunkard's Alley) in Shibuya, or in the smoke-filled tunnels under the train tracks at Yakitori Alley in Yurakucho. These are the places to grab some grilled meat on a skewer and wash it down with a cold beer. ∎

A Buddhist temple crowns the top of Mount Takao, an easy outing from Tokyo.

Shinjuku Gyoen Park is a popular picnic retreat, particularly in cherry blossom season.

Mexico
MEXICO CITY

A dynamic megacity sizzling with vibrant street life and irresistible cultural finds

The Old Basilica of Guadalupe, the city's most sacred shrine

- **Americans living in Mexico City** 600,000, more than in any other city outside the United States

- **Size of Chapultepec Park, the "lung" of Mexico City** 1,600 acres (647 ha), about twice the size of New York's Central Park

- **Museums** 150, second only to Paris

- **Miles of canals in the Xochimilco Floating Gardens** 50 (80 km), dating to the time of the Aztec

- **Size of the Zócalo** 14 acres (5.1 ha), the largest public square in Latin America

- **Rate the city is sinking** 6 to 8 inches (15 to 20 cm) a year, and more than 40 feet (12 m) in some areas over the last century

Today's Mexico City is a cultural hub and kaleidoscope of humanity. Its rich, 1,000-year history intermingles distinctly modern atmospherics created by contemporary art with irresistible crafts and street vendors hocking classic Mexican eats.

À LA CARTE

Beyond Tacos: Sublime Street Eats

• The city is filled with exquisitely fresh and flavorful street food. Among the tasty standards: Tlacoyos, oval corn masa patties, topped with sliced cactus, sour cream, onion, cheese, cilantro, or salsa. Try the masa at the stand at the corner of Francisco Pimentel and Joaquín Vázquez de León in Colonia San Rafael, or buy a big basket of plain patties to make your own at Mercado de Xochimilco. Another street vendor at the corner of Río Nilo and Paseo de la Reforma serves especially tender and savory deep-fried flautas, corn tortillas filled with chicken, pork, or potato.

• Look for pambazos, sandwiches made with white bread rolls soaked in guajillo chili sauce, then filled with potatoes, chorizo, lettuce, sour cream, and mild queso fresco cheese, at weekly street markets like Sullivan, at the intersection of Altamirano and Sullivan.

• And listen for the piercing whistle of a pressure cooker letting off steam. It's the sweet sound of a roving vendor, cooking up piping-hot camotes, or sweet potatoes, drizzled with condensed milk and cream. ■

Carne de res tacos

Flat-bottomed trajineras
navigate the canals of
Xochimilco's floating gardens.

Metropolitan Cathedral

In this undated photo, published in the July 1922 issue of *National Geographic,* Mexico City's Metropolitan Cathedral stands proudly in the heart of the city. Begun in 1573 and completed in 1813 it is the largest and one of the oldest cathedrals in Latin America. It blends a wide range of eras and architectural styles, from baroque to neoclassic to Spanish Churrigueresque, and was built using stone from the nearby Aztec Templo Mayor. For centuries the massive edifice (it weighs 161,000 tons/146,000 metric tons) sank into the soft lake bed underlying Mexico City, and was considered one of World Monuments Fund's most endangered sites, until the city's $33 million restoration of the building's foundation. The cathedral dominates the Plaza de la Constitución, better known as the Zócalo, the city's pulsing center of cultural events, civic demonstrations, and riotous celebrations. Diners at the terrace at the square's southwest corner get a spectacular view of the action. ■

All Kinds of Crafts

Handwoven baskets at the Jardín del Arte Sullivan

Homemade and Haggle-Free Avoid the endless bargaining that comes with market shopping. *The National Fund for Promoting Arts and Crafts (FONART)* offers high-quality, local artisan merchandise at fixed prices. Look for hand-painted ceramics, embroidered clothing, glassware, and papier-mâché. For the best selection, head to the historic district location (Av. Juárez 89, Col. Centro) or the main store and warehouse, which occasionally has sales (Av. Patriotismo 691, Col. Mixcoac).

Bargain-Hunter Hubs Often, the best prices for made-in-Mexico goodies are found at *Mercado de Artesanías de la Ciudadela* (Plaza de la Ciudadela at Balderas), which sells traditional Talavera pottery, hammocks, and rugs. Each Sunday more than 400 local artists, mostly painters, exhibit and sell their work at prices from $30 on up in the tree-filled city park, *Jardín del Arte Sullivan* (Plaza Sullivan; Calle Sullivan near Serapio Rendón y Río Neva), billed as the world's largest outdoor gallery. For excellent antiques and rare coins, check out the Sunday *Mercado de Antigüedades la Lagunilla* (Allende and Juan Álvarez). ∎

Find everything from dried peppers to loose candy at Mexico City's sprawling markets.

THE BEST
Olympic Cities

After the crowds leave, these host cities open the games' world-class venues to all.

Sochi, host of the 2014 Winter Olympics

St. Moritz, Switzerland

This Alpine host of the 1928 and 1948 winter games bustles in every season. Snow lovers come for the skiing and to bobsled. Come summer, chairlifts connect trails that welcome hikers and mountain bikers. But for other visitors, the main sport hasn't changed for more than a century: shopping the glittering designer emporiums lining Via Serlas.

Calgary

Calgary, Canada

Every winter, Canada Olympic Park opens its downhill runs, ski jumps, and bobsleigh track, where in 1988, a dark-horse team from Jamaica captured the world's heart.

Nagano, Japan

Japan showcased its athleticism—and its ultramodern architecture—in the 1988 winter games. Venues like the White Ring speed skating rink and the Big Hat hockey arena still add a contemporary look to this historic city.

Sochi, Russia

With buildings like the asymmetrical Fisht Olympic Stadium, the glass Iceberg Skating Palace, and the Bolshoy Ice Dome, topped with 38,000 LED lights, this built-from-scratch Olympic creation makes an indelible mark on this Black Sea coastal town.

Sochi 2014 logo

Helsinki, Finland

A soaring observation tower marks the Olympic Stadium, home to the 1952 games. Its height—72.71 meters (239 feet)—has an Olympic connection: That's the length of a gold medal–winning javelin throw by Finn Matti Järvinen in 1932.

Turin, Italy

This Alpine city still uses its stunning Olympic Palasport steel-and-glass stadium. Once the hockey arena, it has since welcomed concerts by Pearl Jam, REM, and Bruce Springsteen.

The velodrome at the 1972 Summer Olympics, Munich

Salt Lake City, Utah

The Utah Olympic Oval has been called the fastest ice in the world. The high-altitude cuts wind resistance, accounting for the record number of speed-skating firsts set here. The ice also hosts curling classes and nighttime skating under a giant disco ball.

Munich, Germany

Visitors can feel like champions themselves, clipping on carabiners for a sky-high stadium climb on the Olympic Stadium roof and then ziplining across the field. On a more somber note, a memorial plaque remembers the terrorist attack on the Israeli team in September 1972.

Antwerp, Belgium

Antwerp Zoo saw wildlife of another sort in 1920, when it hosted the boxing and wrestling competitions. Today, it's one of the world's oldest animal parks, with novel exhibits like Hippotopia, where hippopotamuses take center stage.

Lillehammer, Norway

History remembers Lillehammer for the notorious Nancy Kerrigan–Tonya Harding face-off, but sports lovers flock to the town's five winter Olympic venues. Norway's obsession with cross-country skiing centers on Birkebeineren Ski Stadium, which links to 280 miles (451 km) of trails.

Norway's ski town of Lillehammer was host to the 1994 Winter Olympics.

SHANGHAI

A beguiling city where past, present, and future overlap, and quirky surprises abound

The hypervertical skyline of Shanghai's Pudong district

VITAL STATS

- **Population growth** About 10 percent a year for the past two decades

- **Skyscrapers** 15 of world's tallest, including Shanghai Tower with 121 stories

- **Language** 97 percent of the population speaks Mandarin, more than those who can speak the Shanghai dialect (80 percent)

- **Maximum speed of the Maglev Train** 267 mph (430 kph), making it the world's fastest

China's most cosmopolitan city blends sparkling modernity with traditional culture and a foreign-influenced heritage, making it a place of fascinating contrasts. Glamorous, energetic, and lots of fun—get ready to be dazzled by the Pearl of the Orient.

SHOPPING CART

From Shanghai Silks to the Finest Teas

Stylish Souvenirs Gift hunters should head to a clutch of boutiques near The Bund selling locally made wares. *Song Fang Maison de Thé* (19 Fuzhou Rd.) sells a range of premium Chinese teas packaged in appealing aqua blue tins emblazoned with Mao-era propaganda designs. *Suzhou Cobblers* (Rm. 101, 17 Fuzhou Rd.) is a wardrobe-size shop showcasing chic, hand-embroidered silk slippers by Shanghai designer Denise Huang. *Blue Shanghai White* (Rm. 103, 17 Fuzhou Rd.) features the traditional porcelain creations of ceramist Hai Chen. Around the corner behind a lacquer-red door, *Annabel Lee's* exquisite silken accessories and leisure wear with hand-sewn Chinese motifs make coveted Shanghai gifts (No. 1 Lane 8 Zhongshan East, 1st Rd.). ■

Shanghai Feasts—Street Fare and Secret Gourmet

Xiaolongbao, **a Shanghai specialty**

• From local street eats to glam fine dining, Shanghai is an emerging foodie destination. Be sure to try the two famed varieties of Shanghai dumplings: *xiaolongbao,* delicate steamed dumplings filled with pork or crabmeat and a rich broth; and the heartier *shengjianbao,* filled with pork and broth then shallow-fried until their bottoms are toasty. The tastiest xiaolongbao is served upstairs at Nanxiang (85 Yuyuan Rd.), while Yang's Dumpling (2/F, 54–60 Wujiang Rd.) is the place for shengjianbao.

• For sophisticated local cuisine, head to one of Tony Lu's celebrated "Fu" restaurants. There are three of them: Fu1015, Fu1088, and Fu1039, all in the same Yuyuan Road neighborhood. For expense account dining, Fu1015 (1015 Yuyuan Rd.) is the pick; Fu1039 (1039 Yuyuan Rd.) is more affordable. Next door, Lu's latest creation Fu He Hui serves creative Chinese vegetarian fare.

• One of the world's unique gourmet experiences resides at a "secret" Shanghai location (diners are chauffeured there). Ultraviolet is the brainchild of French chef Paul Pairet. Seating just ten guests around a single table, the restaurant's 20 whimsical courses are accompanied by a choreographed interplay of light, sound, scent, and imagery designed to elevate the experience. It gets booked out months in advance, so reserve online at *www.uvbypp.cc.* ∎

The multimedia dining experience at Ultraviolet

City of Speed

The Chinese Grand Prix in Shanghai is a popular fixture each April on the Formula 1 motor racing calendar. The purpose-built Shanghai International Circuit in Jiading district was constructed over swampy marshland, and is shaped like the Chinese character *shang,* which stands for "high" or "above."

Shanghai High

The 100th-floor Sky Walk of the Shanghai World Financial Center, aka "The Bottle Opener," stretches across the top of the trapezoid aperture at the building's apex. The 1,555-foot-high (474 m) viewing corridor has glass-inset floors enabling visitors to look directly down over Shanghai from almost a third of a mile (0.5 k) in the sky.

Street Smart

One of the most inventive ways to tour Shanghai's colorful side streets and lanes is in the sidecar of a vintage Chang Jiang motorcycle, a replica of Russian Ural sidecars once used by China's People's Liberation Army. Shanghai Insiders *(insidersexperience.com)* provides sidecar tours narrated by an expert guide. ∎

India
MUMBAI

An unstoppable, high-octane sensory tsunami of breathtaking extremes

Over a century old, the Taj Mahal Palace and Tower Hotel is the jewel of Mumbai's harbor.

VITAL STATS

- **Year Bombay was renamed Mumbai** 1995

- **Height of the Gateway of India** 85 feet (26 m)

- **Films produced a year by Mumbai-based "Bollywood"** An estimated 1,000, about double the number of Hollywood

- **Number of plant species at Sanjay Gandhi National Park** Some 1,000

India's most populous city emits a nonstop, infectious energy. Like its seven islands merged into one megalopolis, the city is a combo of different places, a mind-bending mix of tastes, architectural styles, world-class restaurants, shops, vehicles—and humanity.

À LA CARTE

Tastes of Mumbai

• Mumbai, right on the water, tempts the palate with its wide array of fabulous, fresh seafood. Try the prawns at Trishna (Sai Baba Marg, Kala Ghoda), whose variations include butter pepper, tandoori, and ginger garlic. Trishna serves up plenty of other seafood options, too, including crab and lobster.

• Mumbai has *chaat*, or savory snacks, galore. *Panipuri* are small, hollow, fried spheres, filled on the spot with vegetables and dipped into spiced water. *Bhelpuri*, another favorite, is spiced puffed rice with veggies and chutney. Both are on hand from vendors at Chowpatty Beach, where you can also get a break from hectic city life with a stroll along the sands. ∎

Kindle Redux and Crafts with Conscience

A local Mumbai craftswoman

Bombay Bibliophilia With the largest number of English speakers—and readers—outside the United States in the world, the Indian publishing industry, centered in Mumbai, is booming. Find scores of books by Indian authors you may not find overseas at *Strand Book Stall* (Cawasji Patel St./Sir PM Rd.), an intimate shop that has been a literary institution since 1948. You can get lost in the stacks at the flagship store of *Landmark,* the country's largest bookseller, in the Palladium Mall. Or search for out-of-print treasures at *New & Secondhand Bookstore* (526 Kalbadevi Rd.), in its second century of existence.

Conscientious Handcraft Bypass mass-manufactured kitsch and seek out ethically made souvenirs. *Creative Handicrafts Shop* (Bandra Homeland Co-op Housing Society, Hill Rd.) sells home décor and accessories made by women in Mumbai's slum communities. *Soul FUEL* (288 Perry Cross Rd.) dedicates most of its space to products like mugs, cushions, and bags made via various nongovernmental organization (NGO) projects. At *Shrujan: Threads of Life* (Sagar Villa, 38 Bhulabhai Desai Rd.) buy gorgeous saris, shawls, skirts, and other wears hand-embroidered by women from rural villages. Women's India Trust, or *WIT* (Shop No. 23, Bombay Market, Tardeo), offers a vast selection of items crafted by women in need whom the organization has trained. ∎

It's browsing paradise at Mumbai's Strand Book Stall.

NEW YORK

The city of superlatives where you can lose yourself and find the best of anything

Times Square, New York's unofficial epicenter

My City: Douglas Rushkoff

I was raised in Whitestone, Queens, in the 1960s, across the highway from the incomparably heavenly Adventurer's Inn. It was a hamburger place with an amusement park in back, just a stone's throw from the 1964 World's Fair, Shea Stadium, and everything else that meant "city" to me.

It wasn't until we began to travel that I realized New York was different from other cities. It had an intensity, an honesty, and a sense of origin to it. This was not a town even money could make a dent in if it wasn't native.

The city, the real city, has receded in the years since its new prosperity. Starbucks and Gaps and condominiums now occupy the blocks where one used to find shoemakers, die cutters, and delightfully greasy diners.

But if you know the nooks and crannies and outer boroughs well enough, you can still find New York just around the corner from the generic brands that characterize pretty much any downtown in the Western world.

It means going out to Astoria or Long Island City, where you can still get a real cup of espresso in a joint that's actually been there since the 1920s, or get the soles of your shoes replaced by the son of a guy who replaced your grandfather's. I can't give you their names; if I did I'd have to, well, you know the drill. Just walk down 30th Avenue in Queens and look for old Italian men or Arabic signs, and you'll end up somewhere that's so authentic no one has to tell you so.

Or stroll through the East Village on a weekday afternoon, looking for a bunch of strangely dressed people on a rehearsal break outside La MaMa or one of the other experimental theaters.

Better yet, head out past Williamsburg and Fort Greene, all the way to Bushwick, where kids put pop-up art galleries in storefronts. Can't give you an exact location for that, either, because they're changing by the week.

In a sense the New York I love is the New York of those who survived these so-called better times. New York that remains a center of industries like pattern making, printing, or meatpacking. Luckily, anyone willing to venture off the Google map will find it in the faces, the bodegas, and the public school playgrounds that really define the character of this place.

That's the magnet of this city. Not Wall Street or the banks that may own it, but the characters who aren't even on anyone's radar. It's the late-night arguments about philosophy over cheap wine at the Kiev, the guy at the donut shop on the corner of 23rd and 8th, the racks of 25-cent books on the sidewalk outside the Strand. They attest not to history, but to resilience.

Somehow, these places and people survive. That's the lesson of New York.

Douglas Rushkoff, the author of books including Present Shock: When Everything Happens Now, Life Inc, *and* Program or Be Programmed, *was raised in Queens and lived in Greenwich Village.* ∎

Brooklyn's Peter Luger Steakhouse, one of the outer borough's many local draws

ODDITIES

Hot Dog!
The city's famed, ubiquitous hot dog carts come at steep price—for the vendors. You'll find the most expensive pushcart at Fifth Avenue and E. 62nd Street, near the entrance to the Central Park Zoo. The annual license fee: $289,500.

Headline Wars
In sharp contrast to the *New York Times,* nicknamed the "gray lady," the morning *New York Daily News* and afternoon *New York Post* vie daily for most outrageous headline. Many consider this 1983 *Post* classic the standing champ: "Headless Body in Topless Bar."

Naked Cowboy
Sophistication and kitsch are two sides of the Gotham City coin, and nowhere is the latter more in evidence than in Times Square. Amid the bright lights and flashing billboards, the Naked Cowboy, sporting only cowboy boots and hat, strategically placed guitar, and white briefs, has been holding his own for over a decade. Tap your inner tacky and pose for a Naked Cowboy selfie. ∎

"[New York] is harsh, dirty, and dangerous, it is whimsical and fanciful, it is beautiful and soaring—it is not one or another of these things but all of them, all at once, and to fail to accept this paradox is to deny the reality of city existence."

—New York architecture critic Paul Goldberger

Central Park, an oasis in the middle of Manhattan

ICON

The Statue of Liberty

It's hard to even think the word "liberty" without conjuring an image of this grand, verdigris lady. For a century and a quarter, she has stood resolute, with outstretched arm and gold-leafed torch, inviting generations of dreamers, drifters, and defectors to the nation's shores—and to New York. • The 1886 statue was a goodwill gift from France,

but the United States chipped in with funds from auctions and prize fights. • Total height from the base of the pedestal to the tip of the torch is 305 feet, 6 inches (93 m, 15 cm). • Her face measures more than 8 feet (2.4 m) tall. • The statue was originally shiny and brown before 30 years of natural oxidation turned the copper exterior bluish green.

• The statue is said to have been modeled after Charlotte Bartholdi, the sculptor's mother. • The rays on her crown represent the seven continents, and each weighs as much as 150 pounds (68 kg). • Following the September 11 attacks of 2001, the statue remained closed for almost three years. ■

The Best of Brick-and-Mortar

Dylan Candy Bar's new JFK branch

Better Than Amazon New Yorkers don't need to shop online. They just walk around. You name it, there's a store for it, from a shop dedicated just to buttons (*Tender Buttons,* 143 E. 62nd St.) to a boutique that sells only hoodies (*The Hoodie Shop,* 181 Orchard St.). *Dylan's Candy Bar* (1011 Third Ave. and JFK Airport) is a Disneyland of just confections, while fashion meets reading at Marc Jacobs' only bookstore, *Bookmarc* (400 Bleecker St.), with titles like *Little Black Dress* and *Les Girls. Korin* (57 Warren St.) carries only Asian cookware and its knife master can help you choose the perfect cutting tool.

A Browser's Paradise Save your dollars and savor New York's signature pastime: ogling. Browse the *Strand Bookstore*'s (822 Broadway) 18 combined vertical and horizontal miles of new, used, rare, and out-of-print titles, from the $1 preowned books lining the sidewalks outside to rare editions on the third floor. Then stroll famed Fifth Avenue where inspired creations are on view year-round at flagship stores like *Tiffany & Co.* (725 5th Ave.) and *Louis Vuitton* (1 E. 57th St.), and a block over at *Barneys New York* (660 Madison Ave.). ∎

All hoodies all the time at The Hoodie Shop

Big Apple Does It Best: Bagels, Pizza, and Deli

Patsy's Pizzeria has been serving up crispy pies for generations.

• A New York bagel is a Gotham must-eat. Among the crunchy-chewy best: the spare and small Bagel Hole in the Park Slope section of Brooklyn (400 7th Ave.), where it's hot-out-of-the-oven-and-into-your-mouth heaven, and Murray's Bagels in Greenwich Village (500 6th Ave.), with 15 varieties and a slew of fillings to go with.

• For thin-crusted, cheesy, authentic New York pizza, hit Patsy's Pizzeria in East Harlem (2287 First Ave.), serving up slices since 1933. BYOB and make a pizza pilgrimage to Di Fara in Brooklyn (1424 Avenue J) for a thicker crust topped with fresh basil leaves and olive oil.

• The world is littered with deli imposters but, for the real deal, midtown's Carnegie Deli (854 7th Ave.) and downtown's Katz's (205 E. Houston)—the site of Meg Ryan's legendary movie orgasm—top the list. Both are kosher down to their Jewish pastrami on rye, with two-inch-thick, hand-cut corned beef sandwiches accompanied by the perfect dill pickle. ■

PG Raves and Uptown Retreats

Brooklyn, the famed epicenter of all things hipster, continues to captivate with new storefronts and surprises. Join the outdoor party and bring the kids (if you want) for empanadas and dancing at Mister Sunday, a weekly family-friendly rave in Brooklyn's Gowanus Grove, right along the banks of the Gowanus Canal; discover local talent at artist-run 440 Gallery (440 Sixth Ave.) in Park Slope; or take in sweeping views of Manhattan and an eclectic cocktail at The Ides rooftop bar in Williamsburg's cool Wythe Hotel (80 Wythe Ave.). Unplug and wonder why even lifelong New Yorkers don't know about sprawling, 67-acre (27 ha) Fort Tryon Park, nestled uptown and not too far from the madding crowds you'll find in Central Park. For lunch, step through the stone archways of its New Leaf Restaurant & Bar for an upscale burger or salmon with grapefruit; nab a table on the airy, tree-lined patio in good weather. Then spend the afternoon at the park's magnificent Cloisters, actually part of the Metropolitan Museum of Art. Immerse yourself in the city's otherworldly anti-Brooklyn of tapestry-lined convents and meticulously maintained medieval gardens (check the website for directions, fees, and hours at *metmuseum.org*). ■

The Cloisters art museum nestles within Fort Tryon Park.

The iconic Empire State Building rises over Midtown.

China

BEIJING

A dynamic Chinese capital steeped in history and charging toward the future

Dazhalan Jie, the famous pedestrian shopping street, bursts with centuries-old shops.

VITAL STATS

- **Metro rider** More than 10 million riders a day, the busiest in the world

- **Bicycles** An estimated 10 million

- **Residents with the surname "Wang"** Approximately 2 million

- **Couples who married in Beijing on August 8, 2008, on the opening day of the Beijing Olympics** 15,646. The number eight is considered lucky in China.

- **Rooms in the Forbidden City** Nearly 10,000

- **Population growth between 2000 and 2010** 42 percent, double its previous rate of increase

- **Size of Tiananmen Square** 109 acres (44 ha), about the size of Vatican City

With Olympian arenas, hulking skyscrapers, and an ancient palace that's a city unto itself, Beijing is a Brobdingnagian capital in its own league. Like the country it leads, this open-air museum of traditions and treasures is an economic, political, and artistic powerhouse that is changing by the minute.

SHOPPING CART

Beijing's Best: Toys to Teas

Made in Beijing The "Made in China" label needn't have a stigma—many shops sell quality-crafted items. *Bannerman Tang's Toys & Crafts* (38 Guozijian Jie) stocks intricate handicrafts made by a family that's been manufacturing toys for over 150 years. Master shoemaker Yu Qigong at *Lao Yu* (37 Gulou Dong Dajie) cobbles together leather footwear that conforms exactly to your feet. Celebs like Jackie Chan wear custom-made silk finery from *Ling Xi* (46 Fangjia Hutong), whose owner Xu Dong makes traditional qipao fitted dresses as well as modernized changshan shirts to measure.

All the Tea in China Befitting the capital of the nation that gave the world tea, Beijing offers a number of excellent tea shops. From oolong to pu'er, every Chinese variety finds its way to the four-story *Maliandao Tea Market* (Maliandao Lu), which also sells pots, cups, and other paraphernalia that make great gifts. Chains like *Zhang Yiyuan* (22 Dazhalan) and *Wu Yutai* (44 Dongsi Beidajie) also boast excellent selections. ■

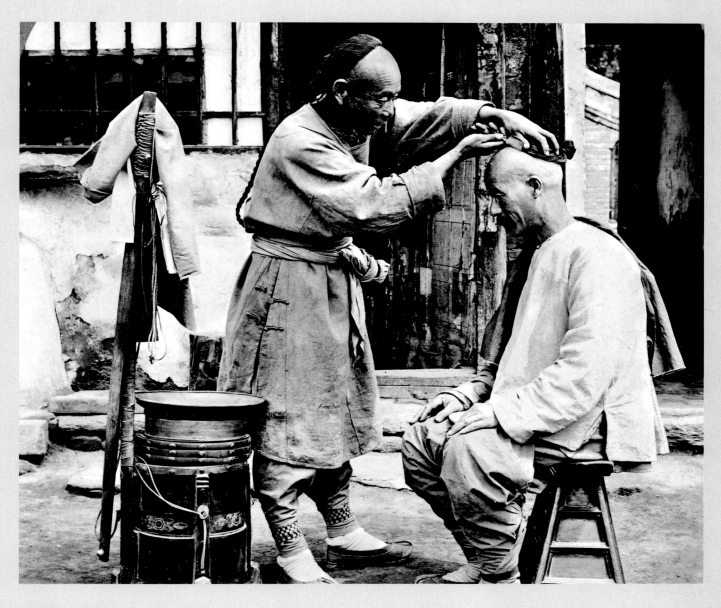

THEN & NOW

Street Barbers

As it was the case a century ago, some barbers in Beijing work on the sidewalks today. But similarities end there. The haircutter photographed in 1902 carried his kit on his back and coiffed clients with a straight blade. At the turn of the 20th century, Chinese men still wore the queue, or braided pigtail, with shaved forehead, forced on the Han ethnic majority as a sign of submission to their Manchu rulers.

Queues went out of fashion when the Qing dynasty ended in 1912, and they were no longer required. Today's barbers wield scissors and comb to create fashionable hairstyles. Brick-and-mortar salons have encroached their territory, but itinerant haircutters won't disappear just yet. "When Chinese tourists arrive from the countryside to visit the Forbidden City and other important sites," photographer Macduff Everton says, "they often visit a street barber so they will look their best when having their picture taken in front of a shrine." ∎

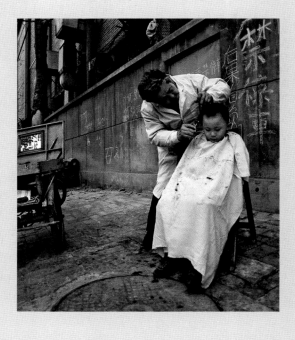

Beijing's exquisite "Lama Temple" and Tibetan Buddhist monastery

Back Alleys and Hidden Cities

A frenzy of silks in a Hutong shop

Beijing's growth has eaten up the hutongs, or back alleys, formed by the outer brick walls of traditional homes. But a central neighborhood of one-story dwellings has not only dodged the wrecking ball, but has also reinvented itself as a trendy destination. Find stylish furniture and accessories at Good Design (52 Baochao Hutong), or score wearable art at Triple-Major (81 Baochao Hutong), a clothier inside a former apothecary. Mercante (8 Fangzhuanchang Hutong), a ten-table trattoria run by a Bolognese expat, shares the alley with hand-pulled carts selling produce. Great Leap (6 Doujiao Hutong) has stamped the hutongs with the ultimate seal of hipster approval: a microbrewery.

There's more to Beijing than meets the eye. Subterranean city Dixia Cheng is 33 square miles (85 sq km) of catacombs built directly underneath central Beijing. Created in the 1970s as a Cold War bomb shelter, the underground city has countless halls designed to serve as schools, restaurants, movie theaters, and even a roller-skating rink. We are lucky no nuclear apocalypse put the basement city to work, and the entire complex faded into obscurity. Currently under renovation, the complex is slated to reopen to visitors in the near future. ∎

Hutongs, or alleys, offer a glimpse of Beijing before modern development.

Dream of the Red Chamber
Cao Xueqin (18th century) This epic comedy of manners traces the rise and fall of a wealthy clan in Qing dynasty Beijing.

Rickshaw Boy
Lao She (1937) A haunting account of a young rickshaw driver in the 1920s, by a great modern writer who was driven to suicide during the Cultural Revolution.

Please Don't Call Me Human
Wang Shuo (1989) The government will go to any length to humiliate its citizens in order to win a bizarre Olympic event in this political satire banned in China.

Beijing Coma
Ma Jian (2008) A man who has been unconscious since 1989 emerges from a coma and recounts the Tiananmen protests in this allegorical tome. ∎

Argentina
BUENOS AIRES

A city of old European charms and new Latin chic

The pedestrian-only Puente de la Mujer draws foot traffic to the revitalized Puerto Madero neighborhood.

VITAL STATS

- **Number of barrios (neighborhoods)** 48

- **Population of Italian descent** More than 50 percent

- **Jewish population** An estimated 250,000, one of the world's largest

- **Age of subway** 101 years old, Latin America's oldest

- **Width of Avenida 9 de Julio** 361 feet (110 m), likely the world's widest avenue

- **Length of Avenida Rivadavia** 23 miles (37 km), said to be the world's longest avenue

- **Psychologists** Some 37,260, or 46 percent of those in Argentina; the world's highest per capita rate of therapists

One of the most vibrant metropolises on the South American continent, Buenos Aires is a cauldron of cultures serving up modern cuisine, a pulsing nightlife, and plenty of chic. Wander its café-lined grand boulevards, watch a street tango, and soak up its singular spirit.

SHOPPING CART

Local Luxe: Leather Goods

Leather Lovers With so much beef on the plate, it's no wonder leather is an Argentine specialty. *Murillo 666* (Murillo 666) in the Villa Crespo neighborhood anchors the Murillo Leather District, with everything from women's coats and accessories to probably the continent's largest men's leather coat selection. *Rossi & Caruso* (Posadas 1387) in Recoleta has offered upscale leather duds since 1868 to the likes of royalty, including Spain's Queen Sofia and Britain's Prince Philip. Head to *El Nochero* (Posadas 1245) inside of the Patio Bullrich Mall in Recoleta for fine quality Argentine leather crafting in shoes, boots, and belts. ■

Buenos Aires's renowned Rossi & Caruso

Calle Florida

Calle Florida in downtown Buenos Aires, or Microcentro, has been at least partly pedestrianized since 1913. Now strictly verboten for vehicles, it's one of the city's biggest tourist attractions, with shops and arcades selling leather, jewelry, books, and souvenirs. Distinctly Argentine with its chaotic stream of bargain-hunting locals and lunching workers from The City, the nearby financial district, it's also where British influence comes alive. Here is the long-empty Harrods, sung about in *Evita,* along with the Galerías Pacífico mall, named for the British-owned Buenos Aires and Pacific Railway company, whose offices for a railway service linking Argentina to Chile were here. Before that, it had been a shopping arcade, with dozens of international boutiques and Centro Cultural Borges under one roof. Mixing highbrow and lowbrow, Calle Florida is literally and figuratively pedestrian and uplifting all at once. ■

Buenos Aires's magnificent
Teatro Colón opera house can
hold 2,478 people in the seats and
120 musicians in the orchestra pit.

Deluxe Steaks, Infinite Feasts, and—Pizza!

Fresh breads at steakhouse Cabaña Las Lilas

• Few places in the world beat Argentina when it comes to a great steak. El Obrero (Agustín R. Caffarena 64) is a family-run steakhouse with great prices and a local ambience in the La Boca neighborhood. Mixing casual with formal, Cabaña Las Lilas (Alicia Moreau de Justo 516 in Dock 3) overlooks the Puerto Madero renovated waterfront.

• *Cuisine d'Auteur*, where chefs create hours-long tasting spectacles, is a signature dining experience in Buenos Aires. Tegui (Costa Rica 5852) is a modern chic dining space with an open kitchen and intriguing taste combinations. The exquisite Hernán Gipponi Restaurant (Soler 5862) in the Fierro Hotel sports a wide-ranging, three-hour, seven-course feast that includes Incan quinoa dishes, all with wine pairings by Andrés Rosberg, the Argentine Sommelier Association president and hotel co-owner.

• With more than half the country tracing its roots through Italy, Italian food is Argentine food— TripAdvisor lists 159 Italian restaurants in Buenos Aires. For decades, Las Cuartetas (Corrientes 838) has served up some of the city's most satisfying pizzas, heaped with creamy mozzarella and large green olives. Amici Miei (Defensa 1072) offers generous portions of traditional dishes in its airy brick dining room. ∎

The posh barrio of Palermo Viejo is home to dozens of restaurants, including the upscale Tegui.

NOVEL INTRODUCTIONS

Santa Evita
Tomás Eloy Martínez (1996) The book recounts in truth and fiction the journey of Evita's corpse as it makes its way through secret hiding places throughout Buenos Aires, as the military caretakers go mad.

The Story of the Night
Colm Tóibín (1997) The story of Richard Garay, a gay Argentine with an English mother treated as an enemy during the Falklands War. His coming of age coincides with descriptions of how privatization under President Menem changed the city.

Collected Fictions
Jorge Luis Borges (1999) The translated short stories of Argentina's most important writer are a great way to learn about the city, especially the tumultuous dark underworld of the *compadritos,* gangsters, of the 1920s and 1930s. ∎

Brazil
RIO DE JANEIRO

A beach-flanked urban beauty where passion defines the moment

The girls (and guys) of Ipanema beach

VITAL STATS

- **Average annual temperature** 75°F (24°C)

- **Miles of beach** 45 (72 km)

- **Years it was a French colony** 5, from 1555 to 1560

- *Botequim,* **or neighborhood bars** Approximately 12,000

- **Number of favelas (shantytowns)** 750

- **Vertical climbing routes to the top of the city's famed Pão de Açúcar mountain (Sugarloaf)** 270

This sultry Atlantic coast city moves to the rhythms of its own drummer. It's not just the samba that sways at Carnival time—an inviting swagger marks nearly everything resident Cariocas undertake, from playing soccer to wearing a bikini.

LOCAL SECRETS

Stars, Steps, and Stadiums

Raised in Lapa district, singer and actress Carmen Miranda (1909–1955) was known for her saucy manner and flamboyant fruit-laden hats. Once the highest-paid actress in Hollywood, she starred in more than a dozen musicals including *That Night in Rio* (1941) and *Copacabana* (1947). The Museu Carmen Miranda (Ave. Rui Barbosa, across the street from 560) showcases her life with film clips, photos, posters, and several of her over-the-top stage costumes.

Urban art lovers consider the bright Escadaria Selarón, a series of 250 steps decorated with colorful glazed tiles, a must-see. The stairs rise from Rua Joaquim Silva to Santa Teresa Convent. The giant artwork was created as a labor of love by Chilean-born Jorge Selarón, who constantly worked on the steps from 1990 until his death in 2013. ∎

Grand Rio Eats: On a Spit and at the Bar

Caipirinha

• Carnivorous cravings are sated at Rio's scores of *churrascarias,* or Brazilian barbecue restaurants, including Porcão (Rua Barão da Torre, 218) in Ipanema, where roving waiters dispense meals from humongous spits of meat. In addition to an endless supply of beef, chicken, pork, and seafood, diners can continue gorging at all-you-can-eat buffet spreads. Located just off Copacabana Beach, Churrascaria Palace (Rua Rodolfo Dantas, 16) also offers grilled specialties like lamb chops, beef ribs, and Argentine shoulder steak, while upscale Pampa Grill (Av. das Américas, 5150) mixes it up with eclectic sides like sushi, a salad buffet, and black rice with mango.

• *Pestiscos* (the Brazilian version of tapas) is best sampled at a *botequim,* a neighborhood bar where locals gather for a drink and bite to eat. Over a *chopp* (draft beer) or Caipirinha, Brazil's national cocktail, munch on grilled sardines, cod fish balls, meat skewers, or *pastéis* (turnovers filled with all sorts of things). Among the most renowned are the art deco–infused Bar Lagoa in Ipanema (Av. Epitácio Pessoa, 1674), Bar do Adão in Botafogo (Rua Dona Mariana, 81), and Aconchego Carioca (Rua Barão de Iguatemi, 379). ∎

Brazilian steakhouses known as *churrascarias* are a meat lover's paradise.

The sprawling Tijuca National Park flanks Rio's urban center and favela-dotted hillsides.

THE BEST
Festival Cities

Splendid celebrations of everything from steamy love and icy splendor to local delectables and the dead.

A typical July morning in Pamplona

Pamplona, Spain

The running of the bulls is only the best known part of the weeklong San Fermín festival (July 7 through 14). After witnessing—or testing your luck in—the daily morning bull run, stay for the traditional sports, art, folklore, fireworks, and nonstop partying.

SXSW

Austin, Texas

South by Southwest (SXSW, in March) has mushroomed into a sprawling, ten-day extravaganza of music, film, technology, celebrity sightings, and barbecue attracting thousands hoping to discover the next big thing. (Twitter first gained traction here in 2007.)

Chiang Mai, Thailand

The Songkran festival (April 13 through 15) began as a purification ritual in preparation for the Thai New Year. Today, it's the world's largest water fight. Expect to be doused.

Oaxaca, Mexico

The city of Oaxaca is the capital of Mexico's countrywide Día de los Muertos, the Day of the Dead (November 1 and 2). Paint your face, tour the graveyards, remember the dead, and celebrate life, all to the soundtrack of a mariachi band.

Des Moines, Iowa

The 11-day Iowa State Fair (August) is practically a national treasure. More than a million people a year flock to the fair for the midway, the livestock, the famed butter sculptures, deep-fried Snickers, bacon-wrapped pork riblets, and much more.

Yogyakarta, Indonesia

Residents of this Javanese city celebrate the Prophet Muhammad's birthday with Sekaten, a weeklong festival preceding his May 2 birth with gamelan music, dance troupes, and parades.

Day of the Dead

Galway food and drink

Galway, Ireland

The Galway Oyster Festival (last weekend of September) celebrates the bounty of the sea. But oysters are the stars here: At last count, festivalgoers had consumed more than three million of the mollusks since the event began in 1954.

Jerez de la Frontera, Spain

Each September this southern Spanish city celebrates the Fiestas de la Vendimia, a week of outdoor dancing, prancing horses, and sherry sipping that revolve around the annual grape harvest. More than 10,000 revelers descend on Jerez to sample the sweet wine and sultry flamenco.

Porto, Portugal

Festa de São João (June 23) is Porto's wild, elaborate festival of love. Celebrants "beat" their sweethearts with leeks or plastic hammers, and the city is alight with floating lanterns and beach bonfires. Revelers dance in the streets until dawn, and then take a dip in the ocean.

Harbin, China

Even temperatures that plunge as low as minus 30°F (-35°C) cannot keep oglers away from the winter Snow and Ice Festival (January and February), the largest of its kind in the world. Harbin's icescape transforms into a wonderland of massive, glowing frozen sculptures, from life-size replicas of ruins to "glass" buildings towering 14 stories into the air.

Harbin shimmers during its annual snow and ice festival.

Russia
MOSCOW

Colossal ambitions fuse with modern vitality in a city where change is the new mantra.

The Moscow River reflects an ever evolving skyline.

VITAL STATS

- **Size of Metro system** 2.5 billion passengers a year, the most heavily used public city transportation system in Europe

- **Height of Ostankino Tower** 1,772 feet (540 m), the tallest free-standing structure in Europe

- **Age of the Bolshoi Ballet Company** 238 years, one of the world's oldest ballet companies

- **Weight of the Tsar Bell** Over 223 tons (202 metric tons), the world's largest. It has never been rung.

- **Number of billionaires** 77, second only to New York, which has 84

Change is no stranger to Muscovites, whose city has glided into the new millennium following a century of upheaval. Bohemian galleries and cafés, world-class art collections, glitzy nightclubs, and innovative eats are popping up all over this fast-growing city of billionaires.

À LA CARTE

Paper-Thin *Blinis* and Pickled Everything

• Russian pancakes, *blini*, can be eaten for breakfast, lunch, or (and!) dinner. The paper-thin, crepe-like delicacies are equally as popular when stuffed with savories like mushrooms, fish, or cheese as with chocolate. Try blini on the go from the popular chain of street-side stands called Teremok, located throughout the city.

• In Slavic culture, a pickle isn't just a preserved cucumber—it's a way of life. Russian cuisine embraces an array of pickled and marinated foods, including tomatoes, garlic, beets, beans, and herring, the traditional chaser to a vodka shot. For an introduction to Moscow's breadth of pickled delicacies, head to Taras Bulba (30/7 Ulitsa Petrovka), a popular restaurant serving traditional Ukrainian and Russian cuisine. Don't forget to wash it down with their home-brewed kvass, a beverage made of fermented brown or rye bread that's been popular throughout Eastern Europe for a thousand years or more. ∎

Blini with salmon roe

Red Square/Krasnaya Ploshchad

Red Square, Russia's famed political symbol, has been the front yard of rulers from Ivan the Terrible to Vladimir Putin. Along with Moscow's great architectural jewels, including the crenellated Kremlin walls and St. Basil's onion domes, Red Square remains the beating heart of Russia. • Although its name evokes the color of communism, *krasnaya,* or "red," means "beautiful" in Old Russian. • Red Square is actually a rectangle sprawling 785,765 square feet (73,000 sq m). • The Beatles were banned, but Paul McCartney performed in Red Square in 2003. • The square's Victorian Gosudarstvenny Universalny Magazin mall (GUM) opened in 1893 with more than 1,000 shops. Today it's an outlet for luxury goods. • The body of Vladimir Lenin, the Soviet Union's first leader who died in 1924, has been on display since 1930 in the granite tomb that flanks the square. His mummy is swabbed regularly with bleach to fight discoloring and mold. ■

The Moscow River

The Moscow River has always been a magnet for development, even though the nature of the skyline soaring above it has changed drastically over the last century. The famed onion-shaped domes of Orthodox churches that define Moscow for so many now stand in the shadows of modern skyscrapers. Hotel Ukraine, the beige, wedding cake–shaped building in the photo at right, is one of seven white towers scattered throughout the city—the "seven sisters"—built by Stalin in the late 1940s and early 1950s. The sleek skyscrapers behind it are Moscow's most recent architectural endeavors set to include four of the five tallest building in Europe. Some things remain the same, though. The pointed tips of the Kremlin around the farthest river bend in the first photo still maintain a dominant spot on the riverbank. ∎

Behind—and Beyond: Red Square

The Donskoy Monastery Cathedral

Moscow's deepest history hides just behind the multi-colored domes of Red Square, along Ulitsa Varvarka. On the city's oldest street and historic center of medieval life, you cannot walk more than a few feet in any direction without bumping into a cluster of centuries-old onion domes. Highlights include the pink facade of St. Barbara's (2 Ulitsa Varvarka); the medieval English Embassy (4a Ulitsa Varvarka); and the 16th-century Romanov Residence (10 Ulitsa Varvarka).

Originally built to defend against intruders, today Moscow's thick-walled monasteries block the ambient drone of traffic and provide an antidote to urban din. Climb the hill up Ulitsa Zabelina for a bowl of hot soup, made and served by the nuns who live at Ivanovsky Convent (4 Ulitsa Zabelina). Or wander through the quiet cemetery behind the red-and-white-walled Donskoy Monastery (Donskoya Ploshad, 1–3).

Though Moscow has become a brand-name city, there's a growing counterculture in the art of antiquing. The entire back section of Izmailovsky Park (73 Izmailovskoe Shosse), one of Moscow's largest outdoor flea markets, is devoted to vintage antiques straight from grandma's attic. Baboushka (1 Kudrinskaya Pl.) is another store whose five rooms are stuffed with Soviet-era antiques, from toy robots and women's hats to old Christmas ornaments. ◾

Left to ruins for decades, Tsaritsyno Park today draws crowds to its manicured lawns and restored palace turned museum.

ODDITIES

Soviet-Style Celebrations

During the Soviet days, Christmas, tradition-ally celebrated January 6 to 7, was effectively removed from the cal-endar and merged into secular New Year's. Today, December 31 to January 1 is still the main winter holiday. Muscovites celebrate loudly with fireworks over the Kremlin, all-night family dinners, and gift exchanges.

Walks in All Weather

Muscovites love to get out and walk, no matter how cold it is. Partake in a Sunday stroll at a former estate turned park like **Tsaritsyno** (1 Dolskaya Ulitsa), among the Gothic spires of Catherine the Great's palace. Or try sprawling **Izmailovsky Park,** a favorite of young Peter the Great. If it's winter, don your fur hat like a local!

Russian Sushi

Sushi restaurants are the Starbucks of Moscow—found on nearly every street corner in the city. What started as a fad has quickly become a main-stay of Moscow cuisine. As most restaurants—Japanese or not—have a sushi section on the menu, you'd better add *palochki* (chopsticks) to your list of essential Russian words. ◾

LOS ANGELES

Glamorous and global Los Angeles's newest sequel: embracing its urban side

Echo Park Lake offers scenic views of the Los Angeles skyline.

VITAL STATS

- **Average sunny days** 292 a year

- **Length of the coastline (in L.A. County)** 75 miles (121 km)

- **People working in the entertainment industry** Approximately 130,000

- **Time commuters are stuck in traffic** 72 hours a year

- **Residents of Latino heritage** 49 percent

My City: Roy Choi

Los Angeles is my home. The freedom is what I love. You can be anyone, anything, anybody you want out here—or just be yourself, even if you are still figuring yourself out. You can just see us for the surface, or you can look deeper and discover that we've got a lot of inside culture here. Also, the weather can't be beat.

We may be famous for our car culture, but you need to walk to experience all the different vibes of L.A. Take a stroll on any of our piers, walk the stairs in Echo Park, or explore the streets of downtown, from Chinatown to Boyle Heights and Koreatown—they're all so different, but at the same time they're all quintessentially L.A. I also like to see people walking dogs all over the city. Runyon Canyon and the tree-lined streets of Hollywood are always great.

If you want to feel L.A., then there's nothing like a picnic or a nap under a tree in a park: Elysian Park, Griffith Park, Silver Lake, Venice, Commerce, El Dorado . . . the list goes on and on.

If you feel like watching pretty people, head to 3rd Street, Larchmont, Silver Lake, or Abbot Kinney, where all the stores are so eclectic and cool. I cannot afford a lot of that stuff on the daily. (But I want to!) Once in a while I'll even shop in malls. I know it ain't sexy in a hipster sense, but the Glendale Galleria is straight L.A.

We've got bars that are so new that you never knew they opened, and we have some with lasting power, too. Some of my favorite watering holes are La Descarga, Alibi Room, The Roger Room, and Jumbo's Clown Room. I don't go out to clubs much anymore, but if I do, I'll go to a Korean one. Vibe on Western is popping.

For music, the Greek Theatre, an outdoor performance space at Griffith Park, and The Hollywood Bowl, a 1920s amphitheater, are L.A. at its finest. The El Rey and the Roxy are two other classics. Pantages Theater is so dope—I have an affinity for the place because I performed there one night.

In addition to the Los Angeles County Museum of Art and the Museum of Contemporary Art, I always take people to the Griffith Observatory in Venice, where we can eat outside and catch great views of the city. If we can hit Koreatown in between, then I'm good. To be honest, that's where I spend a lot of my time. I shop, go to the dentist, mail packages, eat, drink, think—it's where the city never blinks. You can find me at Sizzler and Myung In Dumplings, just like on that Anthony Bourdain show.

Roy Choi is a chef who shot to fame with his gourmet Korean-Mexican food truck Kogi. He runs three restaurants, Chego!, Sunny Spot, and POT, and is the author of the memoir L.A. Son: My Life, My City, My Food. ∎

Roy Choi dishes up rice bowls at his restaurant Chego!

"People cut themselves off from their ties of the old life when they come to Los Angeles. They are looking for a place where they can be free, **where they can do things they couldn't do anywhere else."**

—Former mayor Tom Bradley

ICON

The Hollywood Sign

This iconic landmark perched on one of Los Angeles's tallest peaks has lured dreamers since 1923. Visible from throughout the city and famous around the world, the bold sign is not a mere geographic moniker. It is a symbol of ambition, glamor, and reinvention—which is to say, it's quintessentially L.A. • Originally the sign read "Hollywoodland," to promote a real estate development. • After the original wooden sign fell into disrepair, nine benefactors came to the rescue in 1978. *Playboy*'s Hugh Hefner sponsors the letter Y; Alice Cooper dedicated the final O to the memory of Groucho Marx. • An estimated 60 million people tuned in to watch the televised unveiling of the restored sign. • The letters measure about four stories both tall and wide. • Over the years pranksters have altered it to spell various messages, including HOLLYWeeD (after marijuana was decriminalized in 1976). A security system was installed in 1999 to prevent further tampering. ■

From Boho Chic to Industrial Cool

A gallery in Downtown's Arts District

One-of-a-Kind Forget the valley girl shopping mall cliché. Angelenos in the know head to **Abbot Kinney Boulevard** in Venice for its boho chic boutiques and galleries. You won't find any mass-market chains, though Gap designers are said to roam this breezy street in search of next year's fashion inspirations. Standouts include the designer accessory shop **Mona Moore** (1112 Abbot Kinney Blvd.), the carefully curated clothier **Heist** (1100), the quirky home furnisher **A+R Store** (1121), and the olfactory funhouse **Strange Invisible** (1138) that stocks high-end, organic perfumes.

Where the Lights Are Bright L.A.'s downtown is undergoing a dazzling renaissance. Head east of Little Tokyo and City Hall, and you'll find young creative types transforming the industrial district into the newfangled Arts District. Find cool stationery and design goodies at **Poketo** (820 E. 3rd St.) or hunt for vintage home furnishings at **Hammer and Spear** (255 S. Santa Fe Ave.). An haute couture shop has taken over a garage at **Guerilla Atelier** (821 E. 3rd St.), and across the street you'll find **Apolis: Common Gallery** (806 E. 3rd St.), which brings together preppy clothes with gallery exhibitions and film screenings. ■

ODDITIES

Gourmet Food Trucks
Long before the other cities caught on, Los Angeles kicked off the trend of elevating lowly food trucks to eating destinations. In southern California, the humble purveyors of greasy food have evolved into high-end eateries boasting eclectic menus and celeb chefs. Serving everything from gourmet grilled cheese to handmade ice cream sandwiches, the food trucks roam the city, trailed by discerning diners who stalk them on Twitter.

Flight of Fancy
At 298 feet long (91 m), the landmark funicular railway of Angels Flight in downtown's Bunker Hill was the world's shortest incorporated railway when it operated from 1901 to 1969. The original orange wooden cars resumed traveling in 1996, and the three-minute ride now costs 50 cents. ■

The lifestyle boutique Poketo frequently hosts workshops and art exhibitions.

Authentic L.A. Tacos, Thai, and Pacific Eats

Son of a Gun's nautical-themed décor is almost as good as its seafood.

• Los Angeles takes its tacos seriously—and frequently. Foodies praise Guisados (2100 E. Cesar Ave. and 1261 W. Sunset Blvd.) for its slow-stewed meat. My Taco (6300 York Blvd.) is noted for its lamb fare while Ricky's (1400 N. Virgil Ave.) serves perfectly fried fish tacos.

• With the largest Thai population outside of Thailand, L.A. is the place for authentic Southeast Asian cuisine. Head to Thai Town in Hollywood and sample tongue-searing beef salad at Yai (5757 Hollywood Blvd.), boat noodle soup at Sapp Coffee Shop (5183 Hollywood Blvd.), and pork jerky and sticky rice from Isan Province at Ruen Pair (5257 Hollywood Blvd.).

• Los Angeles's coastal setting is finally paying off with great seafood. Michelin-starred chef Michael Cimarusti's new West Hollywood venture Connie & Ted's (8171 Santa Monica Blvd.) celebrates fresh Pacific fish with its raw bar and stew specialties. Shrimp toast and fish and chips take the center stage at Son of a Gun (8370 W. 3rd St.). And you can probably guess what to order at Blue Plate Oysterette (1355 Ocean Ave., Santa Monica). ■

Unexpected L.A.: Bike Rides and Walks

For decades Los Angeles seemed to be in complete denial that a river ran right through its center. Today, rehabilitating the Los Angeles River's wildlife is more than just a pipe dream. The seven-mile (11 km) stretch known as the Glendale Narrows is already popular with fishermen and bird-watchers, who congregate to spot the great blue heron, American white pelican, cinnamon teal, and other avian Angelenos. You can even go on guided kayak expeditions.

Outsiders imagine L.A. to be a dystopian maze of highways, but it's actually a collection of highly walkable neighborhoods. Take the Metro and experience the city at a slower pace, and you'll happen upon surprises like a Sunday farmers market at Hollywood Boulevard (near Hollywood/Vine Station) or El Pueblo de Los Angeles, a preserved remnant of the oldest section of the city where the city's Mexican heritage is honored (near Union Station). CicLAvia plans pedestrian- and bike-friendly events that take over major thoroughfares. (See *ciclavia.org* for the next happening.) ■

A great blue heron on the Los Angeles River

Venice Beach, the iconic fun-in-the-sun hub for skaters, bodybuilders, and beachgoers

THE BEST
Silver Screen Cities

Holly- and Bollywood aren't the only places where cinematic dreams are born.

The inspirational hills of Salzburg, Austria

Salzburg, Austria

The hills were indeed alive with the sound of music when the much beloved movie was shot on location in and around Salzburg in 1964. Filming took place at the city's Mirabell Gardens, Nonnberg Abbey, and Felsenreitschule.

Naples, Italy

Naples, Italy

Naples's long love affair with cinema started in 1915 with the silent classic *Assunta Spina*. A century later, hundreds of movies have been shot or set in this southern Italian city and surroundings, from the action-packed *The Bourne Supremacy* (2004) to the volcanic disaster epic *Pompeii* (2014).

Atlanta, Georgia

Atlanta blazed to fame in the epic *Gone with the Wind* (1939). In recent years the state capital has bloomed into a TV hub where shows like *The Walking Dead* and *The Vampire Diaries* are filmed.

Monte Carlo, Monaco

The Riviera city-state has served as a backdrop for many memorable movies, from the Alfred Hitchcock classic *To Catch a Thief* (1955) to several James Bond 007 spy flicks. Not to mention its Hollywood royalty: Princess Grace.

Johannesburg, South Africa

The South African metropolis has appeared as both itself (2009's *Invictus*) and other places (2004's *Hotel Rwanda*). Even though it pitted aliens against humans, the 2009 sci-fi hit *District 9* was a metaphor for Johannesburg under apartheid.

Fargo, North Dakota

The dark comedy and cult classic *Fargo* (1996) turned this sleepy Dakota city into a household name. Though the look and feel of the movie say Fargo, in reality only a few exterior shots were filmed in the city.

Lights, camera, action!

Wellington, New Zealand

New Zealand's seaside capital has been host to a slew of movies and TV shows, but it was hometown boy/director Peter Jackson who put the city on the map. He shot all three *Lord of the Rings* here, plus *The Hobbit* (2012) and *King Kong* (2005). Among other "Wellywood" productions, both from 2009: blockbuster *Avatar* and *The Lovely Bones*.

Wellington, New Zealand

Albuquerque, New Mexico

Breaking Bad (2008–2013) and *In Plain Sight* (2008–2012) are among dozens of TV shows filmed in the New Mexico metropolis. With eight giant sound stages, Albuquerque Studios now rivals the major L.A. studios in the number of movies and series that were shot there.

Baltimore, Maryland

Baltimore-born director Barry Levinson shot several steeped-in-nostalgia films in the Raven City including *Diner* (1982) and *Avalon* (1990). The city's grittier side is center screen on TV's *The Wire* and *Homicide*. Fun fact: Baltimore doubles for Washington, D.C., in much of the hit TV series *House of Cards*.

Casablanca, Morocco

A 1942 movie with Humphrey Bogart and Ingrid Bergman transformed Casablanca from an obscure North African seaport into a global cinematic icon. Visitors still arrive in the Moroccan city expecting to find the fictional Rick's Café and Blue Parrot.

Modern-day Casablanca doesn't look anything like the movie version.

Turkey
ISTANBUL

An irresistible intersection of civilizations and continents

Istanbul's architecture is a blend of Byzantine, Ottoman, and modern Turkish styles.

VITAL STATS

- **Shops in the Grand Bazaar** 5,000

- **Mosques** 3,028

- **Public toilets during the Ottoman Empire** 1,400, a point of great pride

- **Year founded** Around 660 B.C.

- **Muslim population** 99 percent

- **Churches and synagogues** 56

- **Length of the Bosporus** 19 miles (31 km)

From its ancient mosques and bazaars to blooming neighborhoods of chic cafés and boutiques, Istanbul pulsates with change and contrasts. The Bosporus Strait, which splits the hilly urban landscape between Europe and Asia, provides the sparkle.

À LA CARTE

Bites on the Bosporus—Dumplings and Kebabs

• Don't miss the popular dish *manti*, meat dumplings served with garlic yogurt (sometimes nicknamed "Turkish ravioli"). At Gönül Abla (Bostan Sokak 50) in Moda, on the Asian side, the *manti* is made to order. For a more central option with a great view, head to the restaurant at the Istanbul Modern (Meclis-i Mebusan Caddesi Liman işletmeleri Sahası Antrepo 4) in Karaköy overlooking the Bosporus. (While you're there, see some top-notch 20th-century Turkish art.)

• Turkish kebabs come in endless varieties. Try the *çöp şiş*, or lamb kebab at Adana Ocakbaşı (Ergenekon Caddesi, Baysungur Sokak 8), a small restaurant with an open stove, or one of 17 kinds at Hamdi Restaurant (Kalçın Sokak 17, Eminönü), also a spot with spectacular vistas. ■

Upstarts and Easy Riders

One of Istanbul's many hammams

To get a sense of Istanbul's contemporary art scene beyond the well-known Modern, seek out the lesser known gems, Istanbul's upstart galleries. See photographs at Elipsis Gallery (Hoca Tahsin Sokak, Akce Han 10, Karaköy) and emerging artists' work at Galeri NON (Tomtom Mahallesi Nur-i-Ziya Sokak 16, Beyoğlu).

In Istanbul, taxis are for tourists. To get around cheaply and easily, join the locals on the city's comprehensive public transportation system. Buy an Istanbulkart card at one of the major transportation hubs, and hop on a bus or tram. The Zeytinburnu-Kabataş Tram Line crosses the water from Istanbul's modern half to its historic one, running along the gleaming Bosporus.

Istanbul is famous for its hammams, or bathhouses, where you can relax in the steam and get a soothing scrub or a massage. To avoid the throngs of tourists at the well-known Çemberlitaş and Cağaloğlu, head to the minimalist Kılıç Ali Paşa (Kemankeş Mah. Hamam Sokak 1, Tophane Karaköy) or to Ayasofya Hürrem Sultan Hamami (Cankurtaran Mahallesi Ayasofya Meydani 2, Fatih), both of which date to the 1500s. ∎

The Museum of Modern Art is housed in a former warehouse.

The 17th-century "New Mosque" dominates the waterfront along Istanbul's European side.

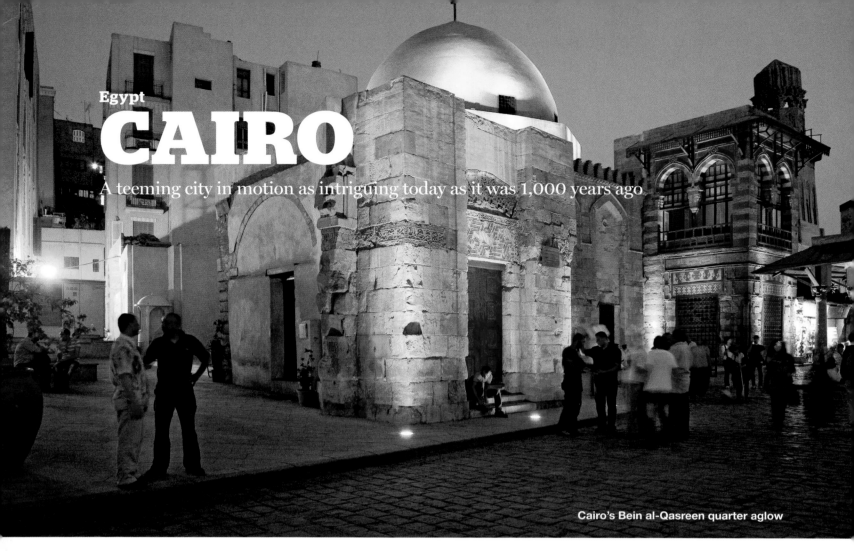

Egypt
CAIRO
A teeming city in motion as intriguing today as it was 1,000 years ago

Cairo's Bein al-Qasreen quarter aglow

Home to the Pyramids of Giza and the Sphinx, few cities match Cairo in mixing modern energy with a timeless history. It might be in the throes of revolution, but that is just a blip in time for this metropolis.

LOCAL SECRETS
Ancient Pharaohs and Distant Views

If you're visiting during the summer, when the Saharan sun and daytime temperatures are at their highest, see the pyramids and the Great Sphinx during the evening sound-and-light show. The program bathes the ancient wonders in all-too-modern colors as a narrator relays their history.

Everyone knows the pyramids, but often overlooked even in guided tours is the Solar Boat Museum, next to the Great Pyramid. This ugly, oblong shed of a building contains the intact 4,500-year-old cedar wood boat, discovered in 1954, that was to transport Pharaoh Khufu into the spiritual afterworld.

The Grand Nile Tower, set on the Nile at Corniche El Nil in Garden City, just outside of downtown Cairo, has a revolving rooftop restaurant—it's one of the highest eating spots in the Middle East, with one of the best views of the city and the pyramids, day or night. ∎

Pharaoh Khufu's divine dinghy

The Great Sphinx

The Sphinx's greatest riddle is who built it. Tall as the White House with paws bigger than city buses, the limestone statue was erected during the Old Kingdom, likely by Pharaoh Khafre, circa 2558–2532 B.C. The crouching lion with a man's head was ancient when Cleopatra gazed upon it in 47 B.C. and retains its allure to this day. • The Sphinx is an alias created by the ancient Greeks. The Egyptian name was Hor-em-akhet, meaning "Horus in the horizon," for Horus, god of the sky. • Of the seven wonders of the ancient world, only the Giza Pyramids and the Sphinx are still standing. • Contrary to popular history, Napoleon's cannonballs did not shoot off the Sphinx's nose. The evidence suggests the nose was intentionally cleaved off at least 300 years before the Little Corporal invaded Egypt in 1798. • You might not solve all its mysteries, but you can friend the Great Pyramid on Facebook. ■

Intricate Islamic architecture, as in the Al-Azhar Mosque, is sprinkled throughout the city.

Cairo Classics: Bedouin Duds and Decorative Smokes

Desert motifs adorn a rug for sale in Cairo.

Moveable Feast Straight from the desert, gorgeous Bedouin-made jewelry, dresses, shawls, and decorative items are the forte at *Nomad Gallery.* The wares are crafted throughout Egypt, including the Sinai Peninsula. The main branch is in the Zamalek neighborhood (14 Saray Elgezira), with another nearby in the Marriott.

Dream Puffs Even if you're not a shisha smoker, hookah pipes are iconic Egyptian handicrafts as well as keepsakes that are bound to arouse discussion when displayed on your coffee table back home. The *Sheesha Shop* (41 Syria St., Mohandiseen) hawks a wide variety of brass-and-glass hookahs, from traditional designs to contemporary water pipes that can easily double as modern art. For those who don't wish to toke the real thing, the shop also sells new "e-shisha" in flavors like peach and grape.

Recycled Riches *Gezazy* gallery brings Egyptian handicraft into the 21st century with a range of decorative arts fashioned from recycled glass and other castoffs. The collection ranges from candleholders and light fixtures to vases and bottles refashioned into miniature planters. Every Thursday, Gezazy throws a bazaar featuring modern creative items from other Cairo artists and artisans. The shop is on Street 250 in Maadi district right behind the Grand Mall. ∎

Unwind at one of Cairo's myriad hookah bars.

PARIS

Alluring, accomplished, externally romantic, and always true to itself

As appropriate as the City of Light moniker is to Paris, its name actually stems from its central role in the Age of Enlightenment.

VITAL STATS

- **Museums** 134

- **Michelin-starred restaurants** 95 (at time of publication)

- **Street markets** 94

- **Arrondissements** 20 neighborhoods, numbered clockwise in a spiral around the city

- **Per capital yearly wine consumption** Approximately 15 gallons (57 L), declining at a rate of 5 percent a year

My City: Alexander Lobrano

As a teenaged tourist on a first visit to Paris, I became besotted with the city. I loved the olfactory punch-in-the-nose of the cheese shops, the cafés where the waiters would serve a shy 16-year-old a glass of red wine without batting an eyelash, and the relentless but nonchalant elegance of the city. When I moved to the city to take a job as an editor, however, I warned myself that it couldn't possibly be as wonderful as it had been during that initial, hopelessly romantic interlude.

I was right. It wasn't the same; it was even better.

Walking home from work, I'd cross the Tuileries, watch the Bâteaux-Mouches on the glittery Seine, or glimpse a peach-colored sunset through the glass domes of the Grand Palais. I could stop at the Musée d'Orsay to see its spectacular collection of Impressionist paintings, treat myself to a kir on the terrace of the famed Café de Flore, or catch a movie at La Pagode, the spectacular Japanese pagoda cum movie theater just around the corner from my apartment.

Imagine being able to spend 40 minutes browsing in a cheese shop as good as Quatre-homme while your clothes are drying in the self-service laundry around the corner. And imagine a city where eating a meal is held in such esteem that it's considered perfectly normal to dine out on your own. Daring myself, I went to Chez Georges on Boulevard Pereire, now one of my favorite bistros, alone. I was babied by an older waitress who served me the rest of a bottle of Meursault another table had left behind.

I learned both food and better French at my favorite street markets on the Avenue du Président Wilson and the organic one in Les Batignolles. And as a resident, I had time to visit all the great small museums: the splendid Musée Carnavalet (on the history of Paris), the elegant Musée Jacquemart-André, and the Musée Marmottan Monet (with superb Monets). I could spend hours browsing the accoutrements of French daily life in Le Bon Marché or Le BHV department stores' curiously formal caverns of commerce.

Eventually I made friends and took lovers, who shared their Paris with me, too. I admired the roses in the Bagatelle gardens, walked hand in hand in the park of the Château de Versailles, ate onion soup and oysters in the middle of the night at Au Pied de Cochon, and learned that bread isn't generic, but a profoundly distinctive product that varies from one bakery to another.

A fresh *baguette tradition* is never far away.

Then one day I reached that point when the first sight of the Sacré-Coeur from a cab coming in from the airport made my heart flutter, not just because it was beautiful, but because I knew I was home, back in the city that groomed me into the man I wanted to become.

American writer Alexander Lobrano has lived in Paris for almost 30 years and is the author of Hungry for Paris *and* Hungry for France. ■

> **"If you are lucky enough to have lived in Paris as a young man, then wherever you go for the rest of your life, it stays with you, for Paris is a moveable feast."**
>
> —American author and Parisian resident Ernest Hemingway

The heart of artsy Montmartre

ICON

Eiffel Tower

It's France at its best: confident, brilliant, putting on a show for the world. The Eiffel Tower was the centerpiece for the 1889 World's Fair. Built to last only 20 years, it was originally considered an eyesore by French critics. But the more they looked, the more Parisians saw they had created an accidental masterpiece, an eternal symbol for France. • At first, most of France's artists and intellectuals denounced the project in near-hysterical terms; it was called a "carcass" and a "factory chimney." • The tower can lean up to 7 inches (18 cm) in summer heat. • Until the Chrysler Building appeared in 1930, it was the world's tallest structure at 1,023 feet (312 m). • The tower is built of 18,038 metal pieces and some 2,500,000 rivets.• Since New Year's Eve of 1999, 20,000 flashbulbs sparkle up and down the tower for five minutes every hour after dark until 1 a.m. ∎

Gift-Worthy Eats to Second-Hand *Trésors*

Antique silverware, a fine flea market find

Gourmet Gifts Buying noshes from *traiteurs*, purveyors of specialty foodstuffs, is a quintessential Parisian experience—and you can bring the food home. Charming *Hédiard* (21 place de la Madeleine, 8e), dating back to the 19th century, is a temple of French gourmet treats, including foie gras from Strasbourg. *Fauchon* (26 place de la Madeleine, 8e), famous for gorgeously packaged Gallic gift items, is a popular source of preserves and sweets including macarons.

Temples of Fashion At historic department stores, where belle epoque grandeur meets contemporary style, the experience of shopping is the very souvenir you'll take home. The two best are neighbors: *Le Printemps* (64 Blvd. Haussmann) and the glass-domed *Galeries Lafayette* (40 Blvd. Haussmann). Over on the Left Bank is one of the world's first department stores: *Le Bon Marché* (24 Rue de Sevres 7e), founded in 1852 and still *très chic.*

Trash and *Trésors* A Parisian's trash is your treasure. No trip to Paris is complete without a day at the 17-acre, some 3,000-stall *Marché aux Puces de Saint-Ouen* on the city limits (along Rue des Rosiers in Saint-Ouen). You might score vintage French cookery or antique tomes at centrally located *Marché aux Puces d'Aligre* (place d'Aligre, 12e). A visit to the intimate and friendly *Vanves flea market* (Av. Marc Sangnier & Georges Lafenestre, 14e) is like rummaging through the attic of the French grandparents you never had. ∎

Galeries Lafayette, a belle epoque marvel, draws foodies and fashionistas from around the world.

Spécialités de la Maison

Debauve and Gallais, purveyors of fine Parisian chocolates

• *Brasseries* are dear to Parisian hearts; originally Alsatian and offering lots of sauerkraut and charcuterie, now they also serve other hearty traditional dishes, and usually oysters and other seafood. Bofinger (5–7 Rue de la Bastille, 4e) is likely the city's oldest. Two other classics are Mollard (115 Rue Saint-Lazare, 8e) and Chez Denise la Tour Montlhéry (5 Rue des Prouvaires, 1e).

• Parisians have taken *pralines and truffles* to new artistic heights. Mad artist Patrick Roger (108 bd. Saint-Germain, 6e) creates realistic (and delectable) cocoa sculptures. Intricate ganaches from Richart (258 bd. Saint-Germain, 7e) deserve their jewel box–like packaging, and Jean-Paul Hévin (231 Rue St. Honoré, 1e) surprises and delights with his cheese-filled chocolates. The precious and many-flavored caramels take center stage at Jacques Genin's stylish Marais shop (133 Rue de Turenne, 3e), while the confections at Debauve et Gallais (30 rue Saints-Pères, 6e) have been making Parisians happy for more than 200 years. ■

Underground, Under Glass, and Around the Canal

Glass-roofed shopping arcades are a Paris invention from the 18th century. Once the city had over 100; the ones that survive, mostly around the old Bibliothèque Nationale, are utterly charming: some packed with old bookstores, doll hospitals, and curiosity shops, others with chic galleries and boutiques.

Tourists haven't found them yet, but the long-neglected neighborhoods around the tree-shaded Canal Saint-Martin, made famous in the 1930s film *Hôtel du Nord* (and again in the 2001 movie *Amélie*) are becoming Paris's hipster headquarters, full of offbeat shops and cafés, a great place for a stroll or bike ride.

There's more to the Paris underground than just the Metro and the famous sewers. Paris *souterrain* is like Swiss cheese, with more than 180 miles (290 km) of tunnels, old gypsum mines and quarries, medieval crypts, bunkers, and even mushroom farms. Not to mention the underground lake (actually a huge water tank) where the Phantom of the Opera lived (it's real), and the Catacombs, which hold the bones of some six million Parisians. ■

The Canal Saint-Martin neighborhood's working waterway

The foyer of the Paris's Palais Garnier (aka l'Opèra) glows with beaux arts opulence.

THE BEST
Food Cities

What makes an urban legend? A dish so unforgettable it becomes just as famous as its birthplace.

Louisville's Brown Hotel

Louisville, Kentucky

Invented as a midnight snack for revelers at the Brown Hotel (335 W. Broadway), Hot Brown, an open-faced turkey sandwich on Texas toast with bacon, tomatoes, and a cream sauce, gives eaters plenty to get excited about, day or night.

Buffalo wings

Buffalo, New York

Spicy, tangy buffalo wings, a favorite of bar crawlers the world over, owe a debt to the city's Anchor Bar Restaurant (1047 Main St.), where the chicken finger food was born in 1964.

Chennai, India

Chicken 65 is to India's restaurants what buffalo wings are in the United States. It is widely believed India's spicy, deep-fried chicken starter was invented at Chennai's Buhari Hotel by the hotel's founder and possibly named after the number of chilies in the original recipe.

Ho Chi Minh City, Vietnam

Saigon, now called Ho Chi Minh City, became the hot spot for the popular Vietnamese crispy bread sandwich *bánh mì*, originally served on a French baguette, after gaining independence from France in 1954.

Sammy from Saigon

Lyon, France

In a country whose cuisine is arguably the world's finest, Lyon is considered its foodie epicenter. It seems only *juste* the city has a dish named after it: famed Lyonnaise potatoes, sliced and pan-browned spuds with onion and parsley.

Cincinnati, Ohio

Famed for their chili, Cincinnatians chow down on two million pounds of the city's spicy stew (beans optional) a year. Order like a local: three-way (on spaghetti topped with cheddar), four-way (add onions or beans), or five-way (all of the above).

Takoyaki, classic Japanese street food

Osaka, Japan

Street food *takoyaki* is so beloved in its birthplace of Osaka that there's even a theme park–like museum dedicated to the grilled balls of octopus batter, topped with seaweed flakes and served with sweet takoyaki sauce.

Bologna, Italy

Spaghetti with meat sauce is a staple of college students everywhere. But the real deal is pasta Bolognese, named after the city where it was created. To reestablish its authenticity, the city's chamber of commerce staged a cook-off in 1982 to choose an official version. (Rule No. 1: It's served with flat tagliatelle, not skinny spaghetti.)

Edam, The Netherlands

For centuries the most popular cheese in the world, still eponymous Edam is named for the town harbor where it was sold. In summer months, you can still watch farmers navigate the ancient canals and ferry taking rounded hunks of the cheese to the market.

Ensenada, Mexico

When the Ensenada market opened in 1958 and began selling fresh, local seafood, the fish tacos became the stuff of legend. Today, foodies flock to Ensenada's many street stands serving the classic combo of fried mako shark and shrimp topped with mayo, salsa, and cabbage.

Frutos del mar, Baja style

JAKARTA

An island nation simmering with an intoxicating brew of cultures

Indonesia's capital, one of the world's most populated urban centers

VITAL STATS

- **Previous city names**
  4—Sunda Kelapa
  (before 1527), Jayakarta
  (1527–1619), Batavia
  (1619–1942), and Dja-
  karta (1942–1972)

- **Percent of city below
  sea level** 40

- **Number of islands
  in the Thousand
  Islands** 128

- **Capacity of Istiqlal
  Mosque** 120,000
  worshipers, the largest
  mosque in Southeast
  Asia

- **Number of tweets**
  254 million over three
  months, making Jakarta
  the world's most active
  Twitter-using city

- **Number of motorbikes**
  Approximately 2 for
  every car

Amosaic of dynamic modern Indonesia and bygone Javanese traditions, Jakarta is a melting pot with a rich and complicated history that converges in a seemingly endless web of high-rise towers and shantytowns, superhighways and bucolic back streets.

SHOPPING CART

Jakarta Checklist: Batik and Handmade Crafts

To Dye For Indonesia is known internationally for its textiles, especially popular Javanese batik. *Plaza Indonesia* (Jalan M.H. Thamrin Kav. 28-30) has four stores devoted to Indonesian fashion and gifts, including *Batik Keris.* If you're on the hunt for antique batik or other flea market finds, try *Jalan Surabaya* (Menteng district), a multiblock outdoor market with everything from Old Dutch pottery to bargain-drenched souvenir puppets. Just be cautious for fakes and bargaining scams.

Handicraft Heaven Jakarta's gifted artisans create a vast array of handicrafts from *wayang kulit* puppets and hand-painted ceremonial masks to intricate basketry and brass- and metalwork. Several department stores have dedicated entire floors to handicrafts, including *Sarinah* in central Jakarta (Jalan M.H. Thamrin 11) and *Pasaraya* in Blok M (Jalan Sultan Iskandarsyah 2). ∎

Brass Buddha

The Canals of Jakarta

Dozens of canals built for transportation and flood control by the Dutch from the 17th to 19th centuries wound their way through Jakarta. The historic photo was taken when the city was known by its colonial name Batavia in 1941, toward the end of Dutch rule; Indonesia declared independence four years later.

In the modern picture, the colonial-era buildings lining the central canal of Kali Besar in Jakarta's Old Town stand as a contemporary reminder of the city's tumultuous colonial history. The Dutch created the "Big Canal" in 1632. By the 20th century, its importance had waned, following the opening of the northern port Tanjung Priok in 1885. Today, many of Jakarta's canals are plagued by heavy pollution and are a major cause of frequent flooding in the low-lying metropolis. A waterway cleanup is under way and has begun to show signs of improvement. ∎

Colonial-era Batavia (now Jakarta) was a hub for tea trade between China and the West.

City Staples: Tasty Stews and Street Satay

Spicy beef rendang

• Though it's a city of diverse eats, Jakarta has one ubiquitous go-to cuisine: *Padang* cuisine originated with the Minangkabau people of Sumatra. Try *rendang*, a staple, slow-cooked meat stewed in coconut milk with a pungent mix of ginger, turmeric, lemongrass, chili, and galangal. Until your stomach adjusts to extreme spice, a sit-down restaurant is best. Try Marco's Bofet (Jalan H.R. Rasuna Said Kav. 62 Kuningan), where many ingredients are sourced directly from the city of Padang, or the popular chain Garuda Padang (181 Orchard Road).

• Considered the national dish of Indonesia, *satay*— a skewer of grilled chicken, beef, or other meat—is everywhere. You'll find the most authentic versions from street vendors. Pick one along Jalan Sabang (just north of Plaza Indonesia), one of the more popular and central spots for inexpensive meals. Or sample the succulent *ikan* (fish) satay served at the temple-like Lara Djonggrang restaurant (Jalan Cik Di Tiro No.4, Menteng).

• Chinese cuisine is woven into the fabric of Jakarta, and the city's Chinatown, Glodok, is one of the world's biggest. For authentic, spicy Szechuan and the chance to try turtle or frog, check out Hunan Kitchen (Jalan Mangga Besar 1 St. No. 61). For a variety of Hakka-style dishes, Angke (Jalan Zaenal Arifin) is one of the most highly rated Indonesian Chinese restaurants. ∎

Street meat skewers or satays are a national treat.

LONDON

An international hub pulsing with new takes on everything from theater to food

At once regal and humble,
London is a city of
Lords and Commons.

VITAL STATS

- **GDP** $730 billion
  a year, larger than
  Belgium, Sweden, or
  Switzerland

- **Theater attendance,
  2013** 14,587,276 on
  300 stages

- **Number of pubs** 4,390

- **Number of universities**
  45, the greatest number
  in Europe

- **Number of times city
  has hosted the Olym-
  pics** 3, in 1908, 1948,
  and 2012

My City: Sharon Ament

London is a world city. I believe it's the world's greatest city, for many reasons, but one in particular, often hinted at but rarely heralded, is that London is in fact the food capital of the world.

If, like me, you're mad about food, you can eat your way round the globe here, courtesy of a two-zone bus pass. A double-decker is still a great way to get about. Go for an upstairs seat at the front. Take it all in.

Oyster transportation card in hand, you can enjoy a cornucopia of culinary offerings, including fare from many of the globe's greatest chefs. For me, nothing beats a biryani in an East End curry house, though dim sum at Sunday lunch at the Harbour City restaurant in Chinatown comes a close second. Oh, and everyone has to visit M. Manze's traditional Cockney eel and pie shop, in Peckham, at least once.

Exploring the city is an adventure of global proportions. I love hearing the multilingual chatter of Londoners. This is particularly handy when the Parisian businessman, sitting in the bus seat behind you, helps correct your French homework after a lesson at the Institut Français.

The world really is in London, and this is reflected in our great institutions, from restaurants, beautiful shops, and top museums. London is like some enormous living organism. It has always repurposed itself, adapting to the changing demands of the times.

In the past few years, the regeneration of King's Cross has transformed a no-go area into a destination in its own right. Emerge from King's Cross tube station now and you get an immediate sense of that vibrancy—with cafés, bars, a world-class concert venue, a fashion college, and beautiful outdoor spaces created around the Regent's Canal and the capital's former grain store.

In the south, I love Brixton, with its market by day, exotic food emporium by night. Up the road is the Ritzy cinema. You can enjoy a reconditioned classic film with glass of wine (or tea and biscuits) in hand.

Given I'm such a food lover, it's good that I'm enthusiastic about exercise. I love Bayswater's Porchester Spa, with its icy plunge pools and saunas. If you like to take a dip closer to nature, there are the ponds on Hampstead Heath. Feeling the pondweed wrapping round your ankles in the murky depths is a rare delight. Trust me. If you fancy something in between, there's always the Lido, in South East London's Brockwell Park, which has a new gym and lovely café.

I love the bus. But I love my bike too. We're not quite Copenhagen yet but provision for London cyclists is certainly getting better. Heaven for me is my annual ride through an empty London on Christmas morning—and sipping hot chocolate on a silent Tower Bridge.

Sharon Ament is director of the Museum of London, and was previously head of public engagement at the Natural History Museum. She lives in East Dulwich in London, not far from her birthplace in Peckham. ∎

The Brixton district embodies street art and ethnic eats.

"**London always reminds me of a brain. It is similarly convoluted and circuitous. A lot of cities, especially American ones like New York and Chicago, are laid out in straight lines . . . But London is a glorious mess.**"
—London-based American journalist James Geary

Centuries of architecture line the River Thames.

Tower of London

Fortress, prison, place of execution—the Tower of London has packed a lot into the past millennium. Confusingly named, this formidable complex on the River Thames was built to guard London and assert Norman control over the capital. • William the Conqueror began work on a "White Tower" fortress in the 1080s, soon after he invaded Britain in 1066. • In 1389 a clerk named Geoffrey Chaucer—author of *The Canterbury Tales*—oversaw construction of Tower Wharf. • In the 16th century, three English queens (including "Nine Days Queen" Lady Jane Grey) were executed on Tower Green. • The last execution at the tower took place during World War II, when German spy Josef Jakobs met a firing squad. • Don't miss the Ceremony of the Keys, a 700-year-old tradition. Every evening, the chief yeoman locks the main gate and brings the keys to the resident governor. ■

From Vintage Finds to High Design

Elegant eats at Daylesford Organic

Art Artery On Cork Street, the galleries are a good bet for modern British art, from Richard Boardman's animal sculptures at the *Medici Gallery* (#5) to Debbie Urquhart's still-life oils at *Redfern Gallery* (#20).

Go-To Source Cleaner and less overrun than Camden Lock, the *Portobello Road Market* (Notting Hill) turns up vintage clothes and antiques you won't find anywhere else. On Saturday, over 2,000 stalls hawk everything from Victorian settees to Gary Glitter wigs.

Designs on You London is a mecca of British design, and one of its most lauded ambassadors is *Thorsten Van Elten* (22 Warren St.). Quirky gifts include Perspex pigeon lights, wood and felt doily place mats, and chopping boards shaped like Ping-Pong paddles.

Sole Food Possibly the best shoemaker in town is *Tim Little* (560 Kings Rd.). Drawing on half a dozen exquisitely crafted models, Little has clad the heels of Robbie Williams, Jeremy Irons, and Elton John, not to mention the entire Chelsea soccer team. ∎

Portobello Road, prime hunting grounds for vintage treasures

Gourmet London: Hot Curries and Hotter Chefs

Find butchers and bakers at Borough Market.

• When in London, you must "do" an Indian curry—it's practically the law. Tourists still flock to Brick Lane, but more discerning grazers prefer Tooting. At Dosa n Chutny (68 Tooting High St.), the house specialty is *dosa*, a crisp pancake rolled and stuffed with fiery concoctions. Lahore Karahi (1 Tooting High St.) produces some of the best seekh kebabs and a formidable *karahi*, a spicy Pakistani pot dish.

• London's palate now ripples with trendsetting flavors. Some of the hippest new "no-booking" hot spots are in Soho, including 10 Greek Street, where you might stand in line an hour to enjoy the fireworks of Australian chef Cameron Emirali. Koya (49 Frith St.) is a stripped-down temple devoted to springy udon noodles kneaded by foot (!).

• Locavores are in their element at "London's Larder," Borough Market (8 Southwark St.), known for its bounty of beautifully displayed gourmet goodies. Foodies linger over the rare-breed meats (Wild Beef) and fine farm cheeses (Neal's Yard Dairy). Daylesford Organic (44b Pimlico Rd.) is an impossibly upscale "farm shop," café, and wine cellar spanning three floors, where every loaf of crusty bread and jar of organic chutney looks too perfect to eat. ■

A Taping at BBC and More

Plan ahead and join the BBC mailing list on its website *(bbc.co.uk)*, where you can apply for a roster of free tickets to tapings of radio *(Hear and Now*, BBC Symphony Orchestra) and television *(Up the Women, Strictly Come Dancing)* shows. Drop by Langham Hotel (1c Portland Place) for traditional afternoon tea, a stone's throw from BBC Broadcasting House (Portland Place).

Its high street in southwest London has been a thoroughfare for more than 500 years, but few natives know you can learn about Wandsworth Town on free, 30-minute cultural heritage walks. The town center walk includes a stop at a 1908 cinema (the oldest in London) and venerable Young's Brewery, opened in the 16th century.

Near the British Museum and Russell Square Tube station, family-friendly Coram's Fields (93 Guilford St.) has picnic areas, a wading pool, sports fields, a petting zoo (with chickens, sheep, and goats), and many organized activities for kids. No adult can enter the park without a child. ■

BBC's revamped Broadcasting House

The 30 St. Mary Axe skyscraper, known colloquially by Londoners as the Gherkin for its pickle-like shape

THE BEST
Haunted Cities

These notoriously frightful cities are beset with ghastly, ghostly close encounters.

Madrid's Linares Palace is suitably atmospheric for hauntings.

Madrid, Spain

Ghosts haunt all walks of life in this capital city, appearing in museums, like the Centro de Arte Reina Sofia, whose central building was formerly a hospital, and even the imposing Linares Palace, once wracked by family scandal. Join one of many ghost tours and you'll discover an urban trove of paranormal haunts.

Mud fort, Bahla

Glasgow, Scotland

Glasgow is home to the sprawling Southern Necropolis ("City of the Dead"), the resting place of approximately a quarter of a million souls and maybe even one child-eating vampire with iron teeth.

Drammen, Norway

In folklore, Nøkken is a shape-shifter who lures his prey to a watery death with beautiful music. Alongside Drammen's Ypsilon bridge stands a tribute to the Nøkken: Two round River Harp sound sculptures tempt you toward the water.

Bahla, Oman

This desert oasis on the Arabian Peninsula is said to be home to djinns, or genies, who live in the palm groves and empty stone houses in the city center. Legend has it that one of these spirits built a city wall in one night. Tread carefully; they can also bring misfortune.

Baguio, Philippines

You cannot stay at Baguio's now abandoned Diplomat Hotel, but who would want to when its purported residents are the noisy spirits of nuns and priests said to have been beheaded here during World War II?

Glasgow's Necropolis

Zanzibar City, Tanzania

A legendary shape-shifter called Popobawa haunts this East African island city and the surrounding countryside. The one-eyed creature is said to resemble a bat. Some believe he acts like a poltergeist, creating mischief, but others report more menacing attacks on entire households.

A ghostly Ben Chifley

Canberra, Australia

Meet the former Australian Prime Minister Ben Chifley at the Hotel Kurrajong. He is a dapper gray-suited ghost pointing from the hotel's room 214, where he suffered a fatal heart attack in 1951, toward the Old Parliament House, another of Canberra's haunted spots.

San Antonio, Texas

Who can forget the Alamo, especially given the hundreds of fatalities at the gory 1836 battle for Texas independence? Groundskeepers and visitors alike say they've encountered the spirits of soldiers led by James Bowie and William Travis that still haunt the former Mexican mission.

Salem, Massachusetts

In 1692, Massachusetts was gripped by hysteria: Witches are among us! Now Salem embraces the paranormal—if not the curse of Giles Corey, a victim of the witch trials who is still blamed for tragedies in "Witch City." More than 20 Salemites were executed for witchcraft that fateful year.

Sighişoara, Romania

The Transylvania birthplace of the man who inspired Dracula has embraced its bloody connection to Prince Vlad III. A torture museum regales visitors with the horrific tools of "Vlad the Impaler's" trade, and only the bravest will set out after dark to climb the long, creaky covered stairway to the medieval city's church.

Bran Castle, Count Dracula's fictional feeding grounds

BANGKOK

An exotic metropolis serving up great food, cheap luxuries, and feel-good *sà·nùk*

Wat Sai floating market,
Bangkok, Thailand

VITAL STATS

- **Number of registered taxis in Bangkok** More than 100,000

- **Average morning humidity** 87 percent

- **Floor space of downtown shopping malls** Well over 370 acres (150 ha)

- **Length of reclining Buddha at Wat Pho** 151 feet (46 m), the largest in Thailand

- **Typical price for a bowl of noodles at a street stall** $1

This sprawling, clamorous, and sweaty capital is a world hub of affordable luxuries: foot massages, bargain five-star hotel rooms, and sumptuous meals at food stalls or cloth-napkin restaurants. All to be savored with the city's innate sense of *sà·nùk,* Thai for fun.

À LA CARTE

Sticky Rice and Surprising Fruits

• Mango sticky rice, a sweet-savory combination of coconut sticky rice with slices of mango, is technically dessert. But it's so filling it feels like a full meal. It's found all year-round, but is best eaten during mango season (roughly March through June). Sample mango sticky rice in the stalls along Sukhumvit Soi 38 or the aromatic Mae Varee (1 Soi Thong Lor Rd. Sukumvit 55).

• Or Tor Kor Market is a showcase for the highest-quality Thai fruit, including many obscure varieties not available outside of Southeast Asia. Across from Chatuchak weekend market, Or Tor Kor features exotic taste treats like durians (April through July), mangosteens (May through September), and custard apples (June through August). ∎

Stylish Siamese Ceramics and Silks

Ceramic oil diffusers at Chatuchak

Divine Design Give your house an extreme make-over Thai style with ceramics, lacquerware, wooden furnishings, statues, and other exotic home décor from the markets and "antique" stores in Bangkok. Start at *Chatuchak,* the giant weekend flea market, and browse the eclectic selection at *Papaya Vintage* (Soi Lat Phrao 55/2, Lat Phrao Rd.). Finish at the upscale *Silom Galleria* (Soi Silom 19) or elegant *OP Place* (30/1 Soi Charoen Krung 38), and be aware most of the "antiques" sold at both places are high-quality reproductions.

Siamese Silk *Jim Thompson* (9 Surawong Rd.) was an American intelligence officer who arrived in Thailand during World War II and stayed on to revive the Thai silk industry. Thompson disappeared in Malaysia and was never found, but the company he founded has blossomed. Choose from silk scarves, ties, shirts, and cushion covers at the flagship store. JT has plenty of competition, including the Bangkok branch of northern Thailand's *T Shinawatra* (94, Sukhumvit 23 Rd.) and the contemporary designs at *Anita Silk* in the Siam Paragon Shopping Center (991 Rama 1 Rd.). ■

Thai silks at the Jim Thompson House

CHICAGO

The City of Broad Shoulders sports a proud, midwestern swagger.

Public art and picnickers mingle at Millennium Park.

VITAL STATS

- **Number of elevators in Willis Tower (formerly known as the Sears Tower)** 104, which can reach a speed of 1,600 feet (488 m) a minute

- **Age of Soldier Field** 90 years. The Chicago Bears football stadium is the oldest in the NFL.

- **Miles of elevated "L" train track** 36 miles (58 km)

- **Lakefront** 26 miles long (42 km)

My City: Maria Pinto

To me, whatever the season, a perfect Chicago Sunday afternoon is a walk through Lurie Garden in Millennium Park. The flowers are brilliant in spring and summer, but as fall takes over, the skeletons of the plants remain, equally lovely for their interesting shapes and muted shades. Piet Oudolf, who designed the perennial plantings, says, "Those who see beauty only in bright colors . . . must learn to look differently at plants, at the forms and structures beneath."

All of Millennium Park is a feast for the eyes and ears. The floating steel of Frank Gehry's Pritzker Pavilion houses fantastic, free performances year-round, and Anish Kapoor's Cloud Gate (affectionately known as "The Bean") is a marvelous, cheeky sculpture that reflects the city skyline. For more art, meander down to the Modern Wing of the Art Institute.

As a designer, I have a bit of an obsession with bones and the human form, so you can also find me at the Field Museum, wandering among the giant dinosaur skeletons and anthropology collections, or taking in dance performances at the Joffrey Ballet and Hubbard Street Dance.

Michigan Avenue is known for its shopping, but it's worth a trip farther west for more interesting finds. In River North, Elements is decked out with unique home accessories and gorgeous flatware, china, and crystal, and I always get into trouble at Haute Living showroom. They sell wonderful modern furniture from the United States and Europe—check out the sexy, curvy sofa by Vladimir Kagan. Nearby Blake has a beautiful mix of some of the greatest fashion designers in the world, but for truly avant-garde pieces, visit Robin Richman in Bucktown. She has an incredible eye, and the Goti jewelry she carries is killer.

To get out of the city—at least mentally—the Old Town florist Green is like walking through an enchanted garden overflowing with exotic plants and flowers. It takes my breath away, and gives me a brief respite from the hustle and bustle outside.

Dining is an exceptionally enjoyable experience in Chicago, and my favorite places are off the beaten path. In the West Loop, Sepia and Embeya have exquisite food and atmospheres. Logan Square and Ukrainian Village are both cool neighborhoods on the rebound that reverberate with eclecticism and creativity—Lula Cafe (Logan Square) and Bite Cafe (Ukrainian Village) are gems. And for the perfect after-dinner drink, I love Wicker Park's The Violet Hour—the ever changing graffiti outside belies the chic, speakeasy interior and delicious cocktails.

I see our "bright color" beauty shine in the lakefront, the parks, the charming neighborhoods, and the shimmering skyline. But there's also real beauty in the old industrial warehouses, the rumbling L trains, the underbelly of Lower Wacker Drive, or the rundown boulevards of Logan Square. Chicago's soul lingers in all these spaces, high and low; it's a sight to behold.

Native Chicagoan Maria Pinto is an award-winning fashion designer and artist. She recently launched a new women's wear collection, M2057 by Maria Pinto ∎

Hubbard Street Dance's modern moves

"My first day in Chicago, September 4, 1983. I set foot in this city, and just walking down the street, it was like roots, like the motherland. I knew I belonged here."
—Media star Oprah Winfrey, Chicago resident

Chicago's skyline glows over the Lake Michigan shorefront.

From Frango Mints to Frank Lloyd Wright

Lego's Farnsworth House kit

Made in Chicago There's nothing bad about getting the blues in a place famed for its soulful version of the music. Visit *Jazz Record Mart* (27 E. Illinois St.), which has ties to the famed Delmark Records, and pick up vinyl recordings from legends like Buddy Guy and Junior Wells. Fashionistas will want to visit *Southport's Cerato Boutique* (3451 N. Southport Ave.), stocking Chicago-based fashion lines such as *Henry & Belle* and *Kristin Hassan*. Although locals mourned when the city's beloved retailer Marshall Field's merged with Macy's years ago, the downtown flagship store (111 N State St.) still sells Field's famed *Frango chocolate mints*, a sweet tradition that dates to 1918.

Landmarks To-Go The *Chicago Architecture Foundation Shop* (224 South Michigan Ave.), sells items based on the works of local giants Frank Lloyd Wright (a trivet), Ludwig Mies van der Rohe (Farnsworth House Lego set), and other Chicago architects. ■

Find your groove in the aisles upon aisles of jazz, blues, and soul at Jazz Record Mart.

When in Chicago: Subs, Dogs, and Deep-Dish Pizza

A slice of Chicago heaven

• You can order your *Italian Beef*—thinly sliced, medium-rare roast beef stuffed in a long roll—hot (with giardiniera peppers), sweet (with sweet peppers), dipped (in the beef *jus*), double dipped, or even triple dipped. Even more outrageous: the "combo," adding an Italian sausage to the sizeable sandwich. Al's Beef (original location: 1079 W. Taylor St.) claims to have invented this Chicago standard.

• The Chicago-style hot dog piles it on: an *all-beef frank* in a poppy seed bun with yellow mustard, chopped white onions, tomato wedges, a dill pickle spear, pickled sport peppers, and celery salt, plus the signature neon-green relish—and no ketchup. Get your dog done right at Superdawg (6363 N. Milwaukee Ave.) or Redhot Ranch (2072 N. Western Ave.), two Chi-town favorites.

• *Chicago deep-dish pizza* is like no other version of the pie you've ever had. A butter-and-cornmeal crust is loaded with cheese, then a chunky tomato sauce for a knife-and-fork dish towering as high as a Loop skyscraper. Pizzeria Uno (29 E. Ohio St.) is the original. Lou Malnati's, Gino's East, and Pizano's (multiple locations for each) are also icons. ∎

From Flying Mascots to Fly Balls

The comfortable neighborhood of Hyde Park has an unusual mascot: wild monk parakeets. The colorful blue-and-green tropical birds were discovered in 1973. No one knows how they arrived or why they have thrived despite the harsh Chicago winters. Late mayor Harold Washington considered the birds a "good luck talisman."

While Wrigley Field's general admission outfield bleacher seats are hard to beat for a Cubs baseball game, the best seats in the house may not actually be in the house. For an only-in-Chicago experience, watch the game from the rooftop of a nearby Wrigleyville building. The experience was once reserved for area apartment dwellers, but now an enterprising company, Wrigleyville Rooftops, sells space on its rooftop to watch the game like a local (*wrigleyvillerooftops.com*).

If you aren't from Chicago, you've probably never heard of Jeppson's Malört. After you've tried the Second City's unique, shockingly bitter liquor, you may wish that you never had. But Chicagoans acquired a taste for the Swedish spirit made of wormwood and botanicals in 1930s, and it is now experiencing a resurgence in the city's cocktail bars. ∎

Wrigley Field, home ballpark of the Cubs

Chicago's Gold Coast

Grin and bare it? Not in 1921 Chicago, where a local beach-goer scowls at a policewoman checking for violations of bathing suit length laws, intended to preserve women's modesty. Back in 1921, the jazz age was starting to roar, but Victorian prudishness still held sway. Along Lake Shore Drive today, swank high-rises overlook Lake Michigan here along Chicago's Gold Coast. When temperatures rise, clothes vanish. A tiny ruler would be needed to measure the bikini tops that are standard beach attire. "It was July, and it was hot," recalls photographer Landon Nordeman. "The neat thing about Chicago is that right next to downtown are the beaches, so if you are sweating through your shirt in the middle of a sweltering day, a five-minute walk will get you to the cooling water of Lake Michigan." ∎

HONG KONG

A global hub of products, ideas, and entrepreneurial spirit

An escape from the center's vertiginous heights is just a boat ride away.

VITAL STATS

- **Number of million-aires** 601,000, or one in every 9 adults

- **Annual amount of tea consumed** 21.6 million pounds, triple the world average

- **Number of skyscrap-ers** More than 1,300, the most of any city in the world and double that of no. 2, New York

- **Number of islands that make up the city** 263

My City: Eddie McDougall

Hong Kong is the city that erupts with energy that passes through my body daily. With the hustle and bustle of Hong Kong streets and city living, I often find it difficult to sleep, let alone find time to eat. The energy is so fierce that you must learn to control yourself and find your home away from home. Mine is on the water, often training or racing in the annual dragon boat races. This is great way to explore true local culture and the outer islands of Hong Kong.

The most exciting thing to do in Hong Kong is to experience a Star Ferry cruise. It's just magical, nostalgic, and a great way to soak up the modern skyline of Hong Kong. The ferries are two-story re-creations of the originals from the 1920s colonial era. The views are stunning, especially if you sail from Kowloon to Hong Kong Island.

Eating in Hong Kong is epic. I am sucker for all Asian food, as it is great for sharing with family or friends. The most exciting place to eat locally is definitely local Cantonese food prepared at a *dai pai dong,* a dingy wet market. You can get the freshest of seafood, meat, and vegetables all in the one place. Tasty, fast, and cheap, I never go home hungry. But the best thing about these places: They don't charge a corkage fee for wines. Just be prepared to drink yours out of a bowl or plastic cup.

I'm not a regular gambler, but Hong Kong is home to one of the greatest horse racing scenes. In season, there are races twice a week. One racecourse, Sha Tin, is in the New Territories. The other, in Happy Valley, smack dang in the city, is my favorite track; the races are mostly held at night under glowing lights. The atmosphere is electric, and going once is never enough. Upon arriving, I love watching the thousands of people rushing to make bets, cheering, drinking jugs of beer, meeting new faces, and listening to some local cover bands bash out Bon Jovi. All this happens on a Wednesday night, so you can imagine my Thursdays are a little blurry.

Though I am not much of a shopper—there are just too many people around to shop in peace—there are some great brands and big stores in places like Ocean Terminal, Harbour City, IFC mall, and Pacific Place. For my part, I am a one-stop shopper, so department stores like Lane Crawford or Harvey Nichols are my answer. When I have to, I also shop our local mecca for sneakers and sportswear, a district called Mong Kok, which is super and accessible via the subway.

Highly chic, culturally diverse, and incredibly efficient, this city is the gateway to gastronomical experiences, entertainment, and home to some of the greatest professionals anywhere. This is the best city in the world!

Eddie McDougall is a Hong Kong–born TV host, owner of the store The Flying Winemaker, and an award-winning winemaker, judge, and commentator. ■

The Happy Valley horse track

"**Hong Kong is astonishingly beautiful. It is made so partly by its setting, land and sea so exquisitely interacting, but chiefly by its impression of irresistible activity.**"
—Jan Morris, *Hong Kong* (1988)

Beyond Hong Kong's glitz and glamour awaits Dragon's Back trail—one of many trails offering dizzying views.

Pre- and Post-Colonial Hong Kong

Between world wars, turmoil in mainland China drove migration to Hong Kong, Britain's crown colony off the South China coast. In this photo, published in *National Geographic* magazine in 1934, vendors sell cigarettes and traditional Chinese medicines; at the top of the steps awaits a sedan chair. The colony was a thriving seaport filled with commodity traders and off-duty servicemen. Across the harbor was the Kowloon Peninsula, also under British rule, but largely rural.

Today, Kowloon also bustles with commerce, as seen in this photo of hotel-lined Nathan Road. When Britain's lease on Hong Kong ran out in 1997, communist China reclaimed the territory but agreed to leave its economy and political system alone for 50 years. "Hong Kong has always been competitive and ambitious," says photographer Steve McCurry. "Now the sleeping giant next door has awakened. Economically, the rest of China will eventually surpass Hong Kong." ∎

From Cantonese Catches to Colonial Curries

Classic Hong Kong dim sum

• Hong Kong is justly known for its Cantonese-style seafood, freshly caught fish, and other deep-sea delicacies. One of the more evocative places to sample steamed fish or black pepper and chili prawns is Ming Kee Seafood on tiny Po Toi Island. Seafood restaurants on other outlying islands include Shum Kee and Rainbow Seafood on Lamma and Cheung Kee fish ball noodle house on Cheung Chau.

• Dim sum reaches a delectable peak at gourmet restaurants like Tin Lung Heen on the 102nd floor of the Ritz-Carlton (1 Austin Rd. W., Kowloon). But purists gravitate toward more traditional places—like Lin Heung Teahouse (160–164 Wellington St., Central District) or Saam Hui Yaat (11 Pokfulam Rd., Western District)—where the noise, chaos, and indifferent service complement the delicious dishes.

• One of the tastier legacies of British colonial rule in the territory is great Indian food, courtesy of South Asians who immigrated to Hong Kong in the 19th century. Among the best is the Michelin-listed Jashan (23 Hollywood Rd.), with its Bollywood-style floor shows and regional specialties from around India. Other top-notch Indian eateries include the Everest Club in backpacker haven Chungking Mansions (36–44 Nathan Rd, Kowloon) and Indian Village in Mid-Levels (31 Mosque St.). ■

Fresh seafood is the star attraction at Lamma Island's Rainbow Seafood Restaurant.

Custom Threads, Gadgets Galore, and Jade

Suit up at one of the city's many custom tailors.

A Cut Above Hong Kong's bespoke tailors are scattered across the city, ranging from edgy couturiers like *Cuffs* in Causeway Bay (27 Lee Garden Rd.) to more traditional thread-and-needle maestros like *A-Man Hing Cheong* in the Mandarin Oriental hotel (5 Connaught Road Central). Between multiple fittings and manufacture time, it takes about a week to produce a custom-made suit.

Electric Avenue Anchored by the "Digital Hub" statue near the Sham Shui Po metro station, this crowded Kowloon neighborhood is the best place on the planet to buy computers, electronic gadgets, and cyberaccessories. *Apliu Street* is renowned for an electronics flea market where vendors hawk both used and new computer parts, while the multistory *Golden Computer Arcade* (corner of Fuk Wa and Yen Chow Streets) is celebrated for its deep discounts on laptops, cell phones, and video games.

Green with Envy Hong Kong is famed for its abundance of all things jade. More than 400 vendors sell a wide variety of inexpensive stones and jewelry at Kowloon's *Jade Market*. Pricier purchases should be left for bona fide jewelry stores that can guarantee authenticity. *Edward Chiu* in the IFC Mall (1 Harbour View St.) creates a range of jade jewelry. ■

Kung Fu and Quiet Hong Kong

Chinese martial arts may have originated on the mainland, but it was Hong Kong's kung fu movies that brought them to world attention. The Hong Kong Shaolin Wushu Culture Centre (Shek Tsai Po St.) in bucolic Tai O village offers one-, two-, and three-day martial arts camps that include traditional *wushu* training combined with Shaolin-style Zen philosophy, accommodation, and vegetarian meals.

Despite its record-breaking population density, Hong Kong boasts myriad parks. Among the lesser known green spaces is the Kowloon Walled City Park, which replaced an infamous tenement demolished in 1994, and Penfold Park, in the middle of the Sha Tin Racecourse oval. Protected Cape D' Aguilar Marine Reserve on Honk Kong's southern tip is one of five underwater parks.

Launching their attack on the same day as Pearl Harbor, the Japanese had to fight fiercely for 18 days to capture Hong Kong from the British. Remnants remain of the Gin Drinker's Line, a series of redoubts, tunnels, and machine gun posts in the mountains north of Kowloon. War cemeteries in Chai Wan and Stanley contain the graves of those who died defending the colony. ■

Study martial arts with a master on Lantau Island.

The Avenue of Stars
honors Hong Kong film legends.

THE BEST
Island Cities

These unique, water-bound metropolises redefine urban living.

The historic city of Trogir, a UNESCO World Heritage site

Trogir, Croatia

Take an afternoon stroll with gelato in hand through the medieval maze of streets. Blessed with stunning nature and an easygoing pace of life, this immaculately preserved Adriatic fort may just be a perfect microcosm of Croatia.

Stone Town, Mozambique

Island of Mozambique

The UNESCO World Heritage site may be tiny, but it has a big history. Its cobbled streets and 16th-century convents hark to its past as the trade center and capital of colonial Portuguese East Africa.

Lübeck, Germany

This handsome city may have lost some of its might as a medieval capital, but Lübeck's immaculately preserved center, enveloped by the River Trave, stands as a timeless testament to its dazzling history.

Male, Maldives

The capital of the Maldives may share the same turquoise water as the country's famed all-inclusive resorts, but that's where the similarities end. The bustling hub of commerce and politics, Maale has seen its population double to 105,000 in 20 years.

Mexicaltitán, Mexico

This tiny island of tile-roof houses, navigable only by boat during the summer rainy season, has been called Mexico's Venice. Some consider the picturesque, man-made town one of the birthplaces of Mexican identity: It was from here the Aztecs are said to have launched for Tenochtlán, later to became Mexico City, in the 11th century.

Key West, Florida

Relaxed and eccentric, this enclave is the epitome of an island city's do-as-it-pleases independent spirit. Tin-roofed conch houses and fairy-tale mansions share the palm-fringed streets where Tennessee Williams once strolled and bars where Ernest Hemingway drank.

The Conch Republic

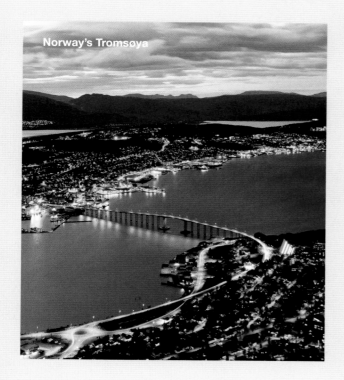
Norway's Tromsøya

Tromsø, Norway

This stunning Arctic Circle town is set against snow-capped fjords. In addition to spectacular northern lights views, it's called the "Paris the North" for its fashionable denizens, while the city center boasts an impressive number of charming old wood houses.

Lindau, Germany

Floating in the cobalt Lake Constance, Lindau boasts centuries-old streets and beautifully aged gables that soar into the sky. The best way to enter is as seafaring merchants once did—through the harbor with its iconic Bavarian lion statue.

Santa Cruz del Islote, Colombia

This Caribbean outpost—not Manhattan—is believed to be the most densely populated island in the world. If urbanness is defined by proximity, Santa Cruz del Islote is its essence: Here, 1,200 people in single-family homes share just 2.5 acres (0.01 sq km).

Florianópolis, Brazil

With 42 beaches and verdant wilderness harmoniously merged with urban sophistication, surfers and business moguls feel equally at home in this southern Brazilian city, dubbed the Island of Magic.

A beach-lovers paradise, Florianópolis is affectionately nicknamed Floripa.

Chile
SANTIAGO
Colonial charms mix with a modern vibe against a grand, Andes mountain backdrop.

Stroll along Santiago's Paseo Bulnes.

VITAL STATS

- **Year founded** 1541

- **Pieces in the National Museum of Natural History** 70,000

- **Highest peak visible from the city** Cerro El Plomo at 17,795 feet (5,424 m)

- **Height of Gran Torre Santiago, tallest building in Latin America** 984 feet (300 m)

- **Age of San Francisco Church** 396 years, the oldest surviving colonial building in Chile

- **Length of subway** 64 miles (103 km), the largest in South America

- **Local female winners of the Nobel Prize in literature** 1—Gabriela Mistral in 1945, the only Latin American woman to be so honored

An infusion of economic vitality is re-creating this colonial capital city. Hidden among its gleaming towers and quieter side streets are dazzling modern art centers and trendy, restaurant-filled neighborhoods. The Andes Mountains form the majestic backdrop to this South American capital, tracing a linear route as it hugs the course of the Mapocho River.

À LA CARTE

Santiago Specials—From Fresh *Pescado* to Pisco

• With that long coast, *seafood* is everywhere in Santiago. Ceviche, raw fish "cooked" with lemon juice, is a highlight of Astrid y Gaston (Antonio Bellet 201), among the city's best restaurants. For more than four decades, Jorge 'Coco' Pacheco's Providencia restaurant Aqui esta Coco (La Concepcion 236) has been a must for Chilean seafood. La Mar (Avenida Nueva Costanera 4076), in the Vitacura neighborhood, has a ceviche sampler, along with saucy pasta and seafood concoctions.

• Pisco, a form of brandy, is the Chilean national drink and the main ingredient in popular *pisco sours*, served with lemon, egg white, and sugar. For live music and to sample an array of pisco sours, few places in Santiago beat Liguria Manuel Montt (Avenida Providencia 1373) in Providencia. ∎

Tangy ceviche

Santiago Skyline

From his vantage point on Cerro Santa Lucía, Spanish conquistador Pedro de Valdivia saw the snowcapped Andes Mountains looming over the valley surrounding the Mapocho River. Here, he chose to found Santiago de Chile on February 12, 1541. Over centuries, the city grew along the river, long and narrow like its mother country. It became the capital of Chile in 1818 following the War of Independence from Spain. By the time this photograph was taken of downtown Santiago in 1916, the landscape was distinctly neoclassic.

Today, the skyline of Santiago, Chile's financial center and the most affluent city in the country, screams economic prosperity. Modern skyscrapers dominate the skyline, from the Movistar Tower in Providencia on Plaza Italia, shaped like a giant cell phone, to the business parks with their glittering hotels and offices reaching to the skies along the wide boulevards of upscale Las Condes. The Andes remain a looming presence over the city, though often through a cloud of haze. ∎

The telecommunications Entel Tower offers visitors spectacular views of the Andes from its observation deck.

Lovers, Warriors, and Sisters

Fresh snow in Portillo backcountry

NOVEL
INTRODUCTIONS

100 Sonnets of Love
Pablo Neruda (1959)
Dedicated to his wife, Matilde Urrutia, this book of poems by Chile's most famous author and part-time Santiago resident uses Chilean and other settings for his words of love.

History dictates that Cerro Santa Lucía was where Santiago de Chile was founded in 1541. Once the hill was developed in the 1800s into a palm tree- and fountain-studded park with hideaways and lookout points to the city down below, a new tradition developed: Today the hill is a place where young lovers escape, away from the prying eyes of family.

The only indigenous group never conquered by the Spanish was the Mapuche, the largest ethnic group in Chile. Visit the Plaza de Armas where a Mapuche statue commemorates this powerful warrior tribe. The statue was quite controversial when it was installed in 1992 because it depicts the broken face of a Mapuche man.

The name of the upscale, residential neighborhood Las Condes contains an apparent grammatical "mistake": It uses the feminine *las* to describe *condes,* or "noble male counts." But locals understand that one apparent explanation lies in its history: Two sisters with the last name Conde are believed to have once owned land there. ■

House of the Spirits
Isabel Allende (1982)
The book that launched the famed author's career tells the tale of three generations of the wealthy and powerful Trueba family through the tumultuous coup that took out her father, President Salvador Allende, and brought dictator Augusto Pinochet into power.

The Neruda Case
Roberto Ampuero (2012) Private inspector Cayetano Brulé meets the famous Pablo Neruda at a cocktail party in this wild chase throughout Chile, other parts of Latin America, and Berlin, where a mix of deadly left- and right-wing politics of the 1970s form a backdrop. ■

Sample local wines from Haras de Pirque vineyards

Ontario, Canada
TORONTO
An urban hub of worldly sophistication and progressive Canadian spirit

Ferry rides afford views of downtown Toronto's skyline and the CN Tower.

VITAL STATS

- **Length of waterfront on Lake Ontario** 29 miles (47 km)

- **Revenue of film and TV industry** $1.28 billion a year, with 273 productions

- **Nails in City Hall's "Metropolis" mural** 100,000

- **Animals in the Toronto Zoo** 16,000 representing more than 500 species, making it the largest zoo in Canada

- **Average annual days of sunshine** 305

- **Languages and dialects spoken other than French or English** 140

- **Outdoor skating rinks** 52

Buzzing with energy and innovation, Canada's biggest city balances an intriguing mix of European sophistication and North American informality. Progressive, globally focused residents follow their own path in art, architecture, and urban living.

À LA CARTE

Blissful Bites—From Bacon on a Bun to Butter Tarts

• Toronto is the home of peameal bacon, a cured slice of pork loin edged in cornmeal, best consumed in a peameal bacon sandwich. Carousel Bakery (St. Lawrence Market, 93 Front St. E.) serves a traditional sandwich with a half dozen slices of porky goodness and a choice of five mustards. At newcomer Rashers (948 Queen Street E.), the standby gets dressed up with a fried egg, cheddar cheese, and an English-style brown sauce.

• Butter tarts provoke challenges, smackdowns, and even a "Butter Tart Trail" through Ontario. In Toronto, the hunt for the best of these messy and delicious little sugar pies studded with raisins can take you from Leslieville's Bonjour Brioche (812 Queen St. E.) to Wychwood's Leah's (621 St. Clair Ave. W) to Little Portugal's OMG Baked Goodness (1561 Dundas St. W.), where the sweets get a kick of maple. ■

Butter tarts

The CN Tower

The CN Tower defines the ever changing Toronto skyline. The Canadian National Railway Company ("CN") built the structure as a communications tower in 1976. Today, it's a popular destination for visitors who want to view the city from the one of the highest observation decks in the world. • The tower is 1,815 feet (553 m), or about 181 stories high. • The extreme EdgeWalk puts you on a narrow ledge outside the tower, 116 stories above Toronto. • On a clear day, you can see nearly 100 miles (161 km). • Every night, 1,330 LED bulbs turn the tower into a colorful beacon, with a light show at the top of each hour and a different pattern of colors to mark events from a Maple Leafs hockey victory to the birth of the newest member of the British royal family (both blue). ∎

Serene Marina Quay West lies just
minutes from the downtown core.

Safaris, for Starters

A cheetah at Canada's largest zoo

Wake to the sound of African drums at the Toronto Zoo's Serengeti Bush Camp (2000 Meadowvale Rd.), where you can see rhinos, elephants, and hippopotamuses at leisure. Guests sleep in safari tents and wake early for a morning hike to see zoo animals when they're the most active.

For a century, supplies for Toronto's finest buildings like Casa Loma and the Ontario Legislative Building came from locally quarried clay bricks, and materials from the Don Valley Brick Works. The site now houses the Evergreen Brick Works park, a funky hidden green space amid the city sprawl. Paths and boardwalks lace quarry gardens, a farmers market, and the Centre for Green Cities promoting eco-conscious living.

Although far from the Caribbean, Toronto refines sugar in a wharf-side factory. It houses a little-known museum, with no-holds-barred exhibits about the role slavery, child labor, and exploitation played in the industry. The Redpath Sugar Museum's (95 Queens Quay E.) water-side location often allows a chance to see island sugar boats unloading their sweet cargo. ∎

ODDITIES

For the Record
Toronto is home to the world's largest underground shopping mall, with 1,200 stores stretching over 19 miles (31 km). The retailers are part of Toronto's PATH, a subterranean (winter-proof!) walkway that connects more than 50 of the city's buildings.

Little House on the . . .
The big city of Toronto loves its littlest house— a one-story abode about seven feet (2 m) wide by 47 feet (14 m) long. Built in space planned as a driveway, the century-old house remains an occupied private dwelling that has been described as "remark-ably roomy" (128 Day Avenue).

Red Light, Green Light
Atop the Canada Life Building (330 University Ave.), a beacon glows, sometimes red, some-times white, sometimes flashing. Introduced in the 1950s, light telegraphs the city's weather forecast. For the uninitiated, there is a guide to the colors in the building lobby. (Hope for steady green.) ∎

The Evergreen Brick Works, a center for green space and eco-conscious businesses

BARCELONA

A Catalan capital brimming with regional soul and European grace

Plaça de Catalunya in the city's heart

VITAL STATS

- **People walking La Ramblas pedestrian street daily** 150,000

- **Picasso works in his namesake museum** 4,249

- **Miles of beachfront** 2.8 (4.5 km), none of which was readily accessible before 1992

- **Official languages** 2, Spanish and Catalan

- **Number of annual bullfights** 0; the practice was banned January 1, 2012

A city both stylish and ancient, Barcelona proudly embraces its Catalan culture. It has long reveled in its creative side, welcoming eccentrics and modern masters alike, and the philosophy that life can be lived artfully.

À LA CARTE

Catalan Treats: Small Bites and Bubbly

• The Catalan capital is the perfect place to sample the region's famed "Spanish Champagne," its sparkling cava. Sample some of the best at Can Paixano (Carrer de la Reina Cristina 7), a legendary hole-in-the-wall restaurant with an extensive list, or tour famed producers Freixenet and Codorníu in Spain's cava capital, Sant Sadurní d'Anoia's, just outside the city.

• Barcelona also has a sweet tooth, which it gleefully indulges in its *chocolate restaurants,* called *granjas,* specializing in *churros y chocolate,* a fried sweet cake served with a cup of thick hot chocolate. Simply dip the cake in the steaming cup for a Spanish-style sugar rush. ∎

Where the Locals Dance and Play

Traditional Catalan sardana dancing

The city kicks up its heels every Sunday afternoon when hundreds of women converge on the Plaça de la Seu in front of the cathedral to join in the region's famous *sardana circle dancing.* The symbol of Catalan heritage, said to have been banned under Franco's long dictatorship, draws crowds who come to watch the intricate steps and hear the bands that urge the dancers on.

Long before Walt Disney had dreamed up a theme park, Barcelona families were boarding a funicular to visit Tibidabo, a mountaintop funfair, one of Europe's oldest. Although the park has a modern roller coaster, it's the old-fashioned rides like The Plane, which offers sweeping city views, which make the trip worthwhile.

The neoclassical Parc del Laberint D'Horta (Labyrinth Park) provides a romantic retreat, with a waterfall, fountains, swans, and canals. The city even limits the number of daily visitors to preserve the historic atmosphere. But the highlight, a formal labyrinth, provides a real-life puzzle. Once you step in, even GPS cannot route your way out—it will take trial and error. ∎

Morning, noon, and night, *churros y chocolate* are the perfect treat.

ODDITIES

Human Skyscrapers

Castellers, people who climb atop each other to build human towers, perform at festivals and in city squares. Human heights can soar ten stories high. UNESCO named the Catalan competitions part of the globe's "intangible cultural heritage."

Walk on Art

Joan Miró's whimsical sculptures and paintings fill an airy, hilltop museum. But you don't have to pay admission to see the modern artist's colorful work. Just head to an ATM from La Caixa bank, which uses a Miró design as its logo, or find the artist's mosaic in the middle of La Ramblas, trod over by throngs of unsuspecting tourists every day.

Look Both Ways

Architect Antoni Gaudí, the master of modernism, died when a Barcelona streetcar struck him in 1926. He was poorly dressed and without identifying papers, so he was assumed to be a beggar and didn't receive immediate care. ∎

The Gaudí-designed Parc Güell

SINGAPORE

A confluence of cultures bursting with surprising flavors and finds

The pedestrian-only Cavenagh Bridge drapes across the Singapore River.

VITAL STATS

- **Height of Bukit Timah Hill** 537 feet (164 m), the highest natural point that is dwarfed by at least 40 of the city's skyscrapers

- **Lowest temperature ever recorded** 66.9°F (19.4°C), in 1934

- **Islands that make up the city** 63, most which are uninhabited

- **Official languages** 4—Malay, English, Mandarin, and Tamil. The national anthem may only be sung in Malay.

Scratch the shiny surface of this Southeast Asian nation and you'll find an exciting potion of Malay, Indian, Chinese, and Western traditions. You might even say Singapore is a microcosm of our globalized world.

À LA CARTE

Malay Breakfast and Roti Prata

• Hawker Food   To taste Singapore at its most authentic, head to its many mom-and-pop street vendors for a delicious array of snack treats. Try chili crab, flash-fried in a tangy chili sauce, or *laksa*, a rich coconut-based curry noodle soup heaped with seafood. The Malay breakfast *nasi lemak*, coconut rice with deep-fried side dishes, is an all-day favorite, as is *roti prata*, flat bread dunked in fiery curry. Some of the popular hawker centers, the open-air street food courts that you'll find all over town, include Makansutra Gluttons Bay (Esplanade Mall 01-15), Maxwell Road Hawker Centre (11 S. Bridge Rd.), and Newton Circus (500 Clemenceau Ave. N.). ■

Fantasy Island Getaways

Island time on Pulau Ubin

For all its ultramodern and high-tech veneer, Singapore is still a tropical island—and Palawan Beach is there to prove it. The golden stretch of sand is Asia's closest point to the Equator, boasting a boardwalk full of shops and eateries. A quick monorail ride will get you back to the futuristic downtown. For an even more bucolic experience, locals head to Pulau Ubin, a time capsule of Singapore's yesteryears. One of the last of the kampong, or villages, features charming wooden shop houses run by the rural island's 100-odd inhabitants.

A quick ferry ride from the skyscraper jungle of mainland Singapore is a landfill that welcomes visitors. The 865-acre (350 ha) Pulau Semakau, created almost entirely with ash from Singapore's garbage incinerators, has enough capacity to serve as a functioning garbage dump at least until 2045. But don't expect smelly piles of trash. Like the rest of the country, Semakau is immaculate. Locals come for intertidal hikes, bird-watching, and even sportfishing. ∎

Palawan Beach is just a monorail ride away from the bustling downtown.

THE BEST
Happiest Cities

Close-knit communities and spectacular surroundings raise the bliss in these urban oases.

Queensland hosts various lifesaving competitions.

Gold Coast, Australia

Marked by miles of seaside resorts, this coastal city in Queensland is on perpetual holiday, constantly hosting crowds of surfers drawn to the golden beaches and world-class waves breaking off such famed spots as the Spit and Rainbow Bay.

Åarhus

Monterrey, Mexico

The capital of Nuevo Léon, Monterrey was founded in 1579 as a Spanish settlement. Although there are booming industries, residents point to their emphasis on their social lives over their professional lives as the basis for the city's strong community bonds.

Åarhus, Denmark

Coastal Åarhus, one of Scandinavia's oldest cities, blends a medieval Old Town with modern living around its large natural harbor. Local residents celebrate their city's income equality, free health care and day care, and excellent education from the many local colleges and universities.

Ko Samui, Thailand

One of Thailand's largest islands after Phuket, Ko Samui has steadily become more prosperous with the recent influx of visitors drawn to its intoxicating blend of street food stalls, hidden Buddhist temples, jungle waterfalls, and palm-fringed beaches.

Secret Buddha Garden, Ko Samui

Madison, Wisconsin

Locals stay active all year-round in the Wisconsin capital, kayaking, cross-country skiing, and jogging along landscaped lakeshores. The University of Wisconsin–Madison Arboretum boasts prairies, savannas, and 20 miles (32 km) of hiking trails.

San Jose, California

Organic produce flourishes in this sunny California city southeast of San Francisco Bay. Residents get their hands dirty in over two dozen community gardens, as the warm climate is ideal for farming.

San Sebastián, Spain

Lovely San Sebastián, Spain

Featuring Michelin-rated restaurants, three picturesque beaches, and the Monte Igueldo amusement park that promises the best views of the city, San Sebastián charms locals and tourists alike. The city also boasts a state-of-the-art culinary school and was recently deemed a 2016 European Capital of Culture.

Dubai, United Arab Emirates

Renowned for its gleaming new everything, from roads to rails, the city in the sand boasts the world's only "seven-star" hotel, free education and housing for Emiratis, and the world's tallest building at 2,717 feet (828 m) high, the Burj Khalifa. The city also boasts white, sandy beaches, and an indoor ski slope.

Kuala Lumpur, Malaysia

Kuala Lumpur may mean "muddy estuary" in Malay—it's located where the Klang and Gombak Rivers meet—but development has transformed the former colonial capital into a thriving, multicultural, cosmopolitan center with top-notch restaurants and services, dominated by the landmark Petronas Twin Towers skyscrapers.

Auckland, New Zealand

From world-class dining and a vibrant nightlife in the bustling city to serene escapes on its tranquil black-sand seashores, lush forests, and 48 volcanic cones, Auckland's appeal isn't lost on its 1.5 million residents. The locals enjoy a thriving economy, impressive education system, spacious green parks, along with New Zealand's universal public health care.

Another carefree day in Auckland, New Zealand

Pennsylvania
PHILADELPHIA

A thoroughly 21st-century colonial city with a keen eye on the future

The mid-Atlantic cityscape blends charming row houses and simple sky-rises.

Philadelphia's neighborhoods reflect its many personalities. Explore the galleries of Old City, the vibrant history of Independence Mall, the restaurants of East Passyunk, and the city's intense sports fandom (and love of craft beer) at a bar in any 'hood.

SHOPPING CART

LOVE and Prosciutto

From Philadelphia, with LOVE The "LOVE" statue is just one of Philadelphia's memorable landmarks; find it and other city architecture at the *AIA Bookstore* (1218 Arch St.). The *Mural Arts at the Gallery* (901 Market St.) renders the city's majestic murals in porcelain, on note cards, and limited-edition mugs. **A Taste of Philly** Take a bit of the city's vibrant food scene home with you. Historic *Reading Terminal Market* (51 N. 12th St.) offers tasty reminders of the city like local honey, jams, and jerky from the *Fair Food Farmstand*. The *Italian Market* (9th St. between Christian Street and Washington Avenue) is heaven for home cooks: cheese from *Di Bruno Bros.* and *Claudio's*, charcuterie from *D'Angelo Bros.*, and kitchen wares from *Fante's*. In East Passyunk, *Green Aisle Grocery* (1618 E. Passyunk Ave.) stocks your favorites from the city's top restaurants like Zahav. ■

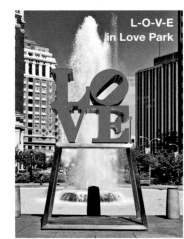

L-O-V-E in Love Park

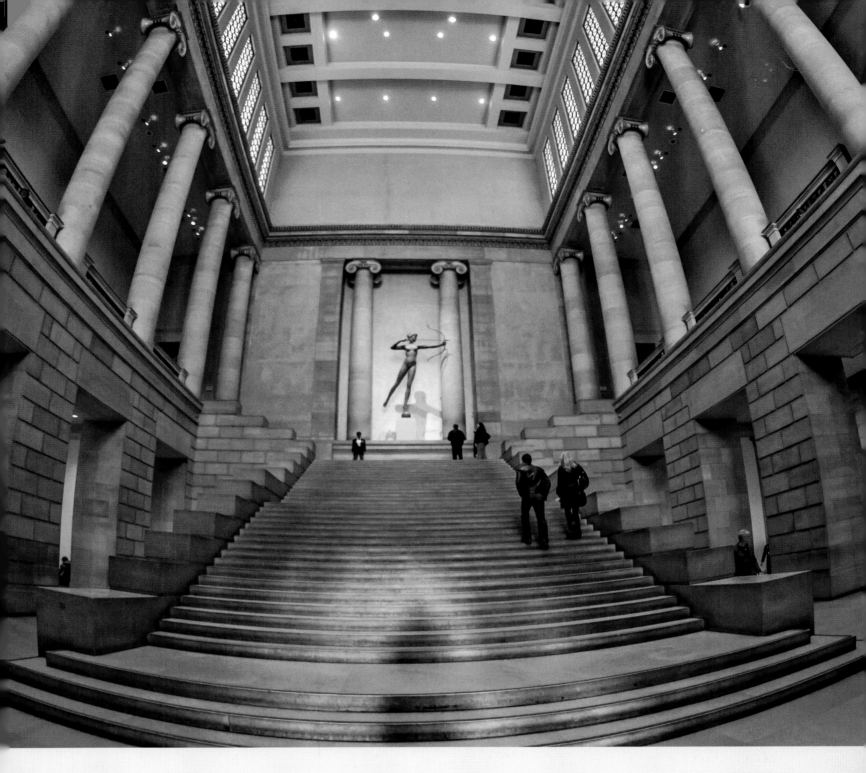

Philadelphia Museum of Art

More than a gallery, the Greek-inspired Philadelphia Museum of Art is the city's front porch, where Rocky strutted and residents come out for city festivals and Fourth of July fireworks. The country's third largest art museum is home to Vincent van Gogh's sunflowers, Cézanne's bathers—and a Rocky statue. Honor the fictional boxer by running up the 72 front steps and throwing your arms into the air like a true champion for a classic Philly selfie. • This bronze likeness of Sylvester Stallone's iconic character Rocky Balboa was created for the 1982 film *Rocky III.* • The museum collection numbers over 227,000 pieces. • One of the best city panoramas can be had at the top of the stairs, where you are also treated to a view down the museum-filled Benjamin Franklin Parkway toward Alexander Calder's Swann Memorial Fountain and Robert Indiana's "LOVE" statue. • On Wednesdays after 5 p.m. and the first Sunday of the month, the admission is a pay-what-you-want fee. ■

The Italian Market

The Italian Market is a taste of Philadelphia's history—and its future. This collection of shops and street vendors, stretching along 9th Street from Fitzwater to Wharton, got its start in the mid-to-late 1880s, when an Italian immigrant opened a boardinghouse nearby. By the 1930s, the street was a shopping destination for the city's growing Italian population. You could buy anything—from ricotta and salami to shoes and fabric—along this half-mile (0.8 km) corridor through South Philadelphia.

Today, the mix of hardworking proprietors and daily shoppers still creates a constant buzz—but with some new flavors. Alongside Italian classics like Ralph's Italian Restaurant (in its current location since 1915), Di Bruno Bros. provisions (which opened in 1939), and 9th Street's iconic produce vendors, you'll find a colorful assortment of relative newcomers: Mexican, Vietnamese, Korean, and Thai restaurants and shops. ∎

Philly Faves—From Cheesesteak to Chilly Sweets

High-brow cheesesteaks

• Cheesesteak is the city's best known culinary export. Neon lights shine 24 hours a day at South Philly's Geno's Steaks (1219 S. 9th St.) and—right across the street—its longtime competitor Pat's King of Steaks (1237 E. Passyunk Ave.). Just as storied is art deco Jim's Steaks (400 South St.).

• Locals may love *roast pork*—with sharp provolone and broccoli rabe—even more than the cheesesteak. You'll understand after a bite at Tommy DiNic's (Reading Terminal Market, 1136 Arch St.) or John's Roast Pork (14 E. Snyder Ave.).

• Pretzels are a Philadelphia staple; Philadelphians even eat them for breakfast. Know your twists: There's the loopy Amish soft pretzel, brushed with butter (try them at Miller's Twist in the Reading Terminal Market, 1136 Arch St.) and the smaller, mustard-slathered street vendor-style pretzel (get them from Philly Soft Pretzel Factory, multiple locations).

• Every city has its own icy treat. In Philly, it's the backward-sounding *"water ice."* It's actually a very descriptive name for the slushy summertime dessert, sometimes served with both a straw and a spoon. Rita's Water Ice (multiple locations) is a favorite local franchise, while John's Water Ice in South Philly is a classic (701 Christian St.). ■

Geno's, the 24-hour cheesesteak mecca

ODDITIES

"Dem Golden Slippers"

On New Year's Day, the mummers—men and women dressed in sequins and feathers, showing off elaborate routines—reign over Philadelphia's Mummers Parade. "Oh, Dem Golden Slippers" is the unofficial theme song for the mummers' strut.

The Curse of Billy Penn

In March 1987, One Liberty Place exceeded the height of the William Penn statue on top of City Hall. For the next 30 years, no major Philly professional sports team won a championship. In June 2007, a small figurine of Penn was affixed to the top of the Comcast Center, the tallest structure in the city. In the fall of 2008, the Philadelphia Phillies won the World Series.

Body Parts

The Mütter Museum houses more than 20,000 anatomical anomalies, historical medical tools, and other odd exhibits, including a seven-foot-six-inch (2.3 m) human skeleton, a jar of pickled human skin, and 139 human skulls from the collection of a 19th-century anatomist. ■

ST. PETERSBURG

An imperial city that glitters day and night, strutting its opulent past and modern inclinations

This canal-entwined "Venice of the North" shimmers along the Neva River.

VITAL STATS

- **Latitude** 59° N, the northernmost city in the world with a population over a million

- **Number of waterways** 93 rivers and channels spanning 186 miles (300 km)

- **Objects in the State Hermitage Museum** More than 3 million, one of the largest collections in the world

My City: Candice Pareshnev

St. Petersburg, or "Piter" as it is lovingly nicknamed by its inhabitants, found its way into my soul and has not let go.

Piter is made for walking—there is too much beauty packed into each foot of the city to absorb at any pace faster than a saunter. The famous Nevsky Prospekt is great for people watching, but a stroll along the canals and bridges at dusk is a nearly hedonistic pleasure. The pastel neoclassical and baroque facades that line the Moika River take on a surreal hazy glow that make me feel that I am actually wandering into a different era altogether.

My favorite eateries are just a few steps off the beaten path and usually halfway underground. A café called Zoom on Gorokhovaya Street has a mean cream soup and a hip crowd. You will never find a more succulent bang for your buck than at the little Soviet-style Pyshki (donut) shop on Bolshaya Konyshenaya. Grot, which offers a very tasty Uzbek *plov* (a rice and meat dish), is tucked downstairs and nearly hidden along the Fontanka Canal. For a special treat, traditional Georgian musicians entertain diners at Suliko on Kazanskaya Ulitsa (just a few blocks beyond the Kazan Cathedral).

A nice place to escape the traffic is Yelagin Island, where motor vehicles are not allowed. I enjoy picnicking in the quiet little corners tucked among the trees, watching children feeding ducks, and lovers renting rowboats. The island is also a popular spot for young locals to congregate for pickup ultimate Frisbee.

A great hangout for live jazz is the JFC Club, although it is easy to miss—the entrance is inside the courtyard of a rather unassuming building on Shpalernaya Ulitsa. It must not be too hard to find, however—it is usually packed.

The shops along Nevsky Prospekt offer some of the city's best clothes shopping, but I'd rather buy books, and Dom Knigi, housed in the historic Singer Building opposite the Kazan Cathedral, offers a beautiful selection of both books and maps. Another fascinating bookstore is Staraya Kniga, on Vasilyevsky Island, that sells used books; I picked up my beloved ten-volume set of Dostoevsky's works here at a very reasonable price.

Visitors to St. Petersburg can stay up until the early morning hours and watch as the many long bridges that span the Neva River are drawn up to allow the crowds of waiting ships to pass. This is especially enjoyable during the White Nights, an enchanting couple of weeks every summer when dusk skips night and spills directly into dawn. It is a magical time to visit the Church of Our Savior on Spilled Blood with its sparkling cupolas.

Piter's uniqueness lies partly in its cohesiveness; it is not merely a collection of disparate sites, but a harmonious whole with a rich history—a history in which it is a privilege to take a tiny part.

Russian linguist Candice Pareshnev studied and volunteered in St. Petersburg before a job at the U.S.-Russia Business Council brought her to Washington, D.C. She returns to the Russian capital regularly with her St. Petersburg–born husband. ∎

The Church of the Savior on Spilled Blood

"The most abstract and intentional city on the entire globe."
—Fyodor Dostoyevsky, *Notes from the Underground* (1864)

ICON

The Winter Palace

A symbol of Russia's imperial past as well as the revolution that dismantled it, the Winter Palace embodies the extremities of Russian history. The former royal residence turned Hermitage Museum now houses millions of works of art in a restored palace setting that is an architectural work of art in and of itself. •

The museum-esque nature of the Winter Palace began with Catherine the Great, who used the palace as a repository for her massive art collections. • The palace holds more than three million works of art and artifacts, including paintings by Rembrandt and Monet and ancient Egyptian sculptures. • More than 350

rooms are open to the public, through which more than 2.5 million visitors walk each year. • During World War I and into the first months of the 1917 revolution, the palace partially functioned as a hospital. • During the Bolshevik Revolution, the palace was ransacked, including its priceless wine cellar. ■

St. Pete Plush—From Fancy Shops to Tsarist Tableware

Imperial Browsing Shopping in St. Petersburg bridges extremes, from high-end international products to handmade textiles. Browse in lavish luxury on *Nevsky Prospekt*, St. Petersburg's main road and shopping hub. *Great Gostiny Dvor* (35 Nevsky Prospekt), one of the world's first shopping malls with its colonnaded, neoclassical facade, stretches across a city block and designer shops. Farther down the boulevard is *The Passage* (48 Nevsky Prospekt), another luxury mall dating to the 1850s. For Russian-made souvenirs, including the ubiquitous nesting dolls, check out *Babushka* (33 Naberezhnaya Leitenanta Shm.) or *Pryalka,* or Spinning Wheel (10 Push-kinskaya Ulitsa), for handmade scarves and blouses.

Porcelain egg

Tableware to the Tsars *Imperial Porcelain Factory* (151 Obukhov Defense) continues the craft that originated in St. Petersburg in 1744, when the handmade porcelain was manufactured to produce porcelain for the Romanov family. Check out tableware with the traditional cobalt-blue net patterns, a design inspired by Catherine the Great's style. Native to the Baltic coast, amber is another popular gift steeped in royal history—literally tons of the red-orange gemstone once covered the walls of the infamous Amber Room of the Catherine Palace. Check out amber bracelets, pendants, and earrings at *Babushka* (33 Naberezhnaya Leytenanta Shm.). ∎

NOVEL INTRODUCTIONS

The Nose
Nikolay Gogol (1836) In this short story, the king of satire and social commentary explores the divide between rich and poor—and between the bureaucracy and everyday life—in 19th-century Russia that eventually led to revolution.

Crime and Punishment
Fyodor Dostoyevsky (1866) Running through Dostoyevsky's famously dark book like a refrain, the grim and dusty alleys of 19th-century St. Petersburg form the ring in which main character Raskolnikov fights his demons.

The Master of Petersburg: A Novel
J. M. Coetzee (1994) A fictionalized Dostoyevsky returns from his home in Germany to St. Petersburg to investigate his stepson's death, crossing the line between imagination and reality against the backdrop of 19th-century St. Petersburg society and politics. ∎

The Dom Knigi bookshop and café are housed in the former Singer Company Building, a colossal art nouveau achievement on Nevsky Prospekt.

Royal Digs and Sandy Shores

Historic reenactors at Yelagin Palace, a royal summer retreat

It's no secret that St. Petersburg is entrenched in a tsarist-era Russian aesthetic. Palace Square oozes with opulence. Lesser known, however, are the royal retreats—palaces on St. Petersburg's islands where the nobility retired from public view. Wander the grounds of Yelagin Palace (4 Yelagin Ostrov), a royal summer estate, or explore the mansion-lined streets of Kamenny Island, where many noble families built early 20th-century mansions.

In a city far enough north to catch a glimpse of the northern lights, a bathing suit is the last item you might expect to pack. Locals know otherwise. The stretch of riverside sand outside the Peter and Paul Fortress (3 Petropavlovskaya Krepost) is a popular spot for sunbathing in the summer and polar bear diving in the winter.

Cruise the 'Burbs: Think beyond the heavily trafficked canals with an overnight cruise, whose path will follow the Neva beyond the city center as it weaves through wooden church-lined banks of St. Petersburg's outskirts and into Lake Ladoga, one of Europe's largest. ■

Drawbridges along the Neva allow ships to pass, a shimmering sight in the peak of summer when the sun never sets.

A day trip from St. Petersburg, Peter-hof Palace wows visitors with its exquisite vistas and sheer opulence.

Australia
SYDNEY

Where sophisticated and sassy meet vibrant and multicultural

The steel Harbour Bridge contrasts dramatically with the billowing sail-like rooftop of Sydney's Opera House.

VITAL STATS

- **Size** 4,774 square miles (12,365 sq km), one of the world's largest metro areas

- **Ferry passengers** 14.8 million passengers a year

- **Number of years Aboriginal peoples lived in the Sydney area** At least 30,000

- **Height of Sydney Harbour Bridge** 440 feet (134 m), one of the highest bridges in the world

My City: Mary O'Malley

At 6:30 every morning, I'm woken by the shrill song of lorikeets in the melaleuca trees that line my inner Sydney street. Those birds pretty much exemplify my Sydney. Flashy, loud, attention seeking, and yet somehow lovable for their sass, their color, and their cheeky Southern Hemisphere style.

They herald mornings that make coastal Sydney a glorious place to live. At Bronte Beach sea pool on Nelson Bay, I join the early risers doing their laps under brilliant blue skies—the older Europeans, the younger Asian families, the immigrants who've made our Sydney the patchwork quilt of cultures that it is, splashing about in the Pacific Ocean before our day's work.

In the afternoons, birdsong welcomes me home, too. Up to 124 native species live in Centennial Parklands, the "Central Park of Sydney," where we bike ride and walk our dog every day.

Just three miles southeast of the central business district is this gentle world of lakes and trees, horse riders and bikers, joggers and dog walkers, toddlers feeding ducks, and families picnicking in the dwindling daylight.

Our Sydney is very much about the coast and its surrounding suburbs. We head to Bondi Beach to snorkel off the rocks and let our dog await his admirers; Bronte for the pool and parklands that run right up to the boardwalk. The coastal walk from Bondi to Bronte must be one of the world's most stunning promenades.

When we eat out, it's in a handful of local family-run restaurants where we're on first-name terms with the owners. Our favorites: Pompei's in Bondi, for George and Adisa's artisan pizza and gelato; Java, an Indonesian restaurant in Randwick, for Joe's mum's fried squid and eggplant in honey soy; and Uyen Vietnamese in Waverley for Richard's soft-shell crab, chili garlic squid, and fish in earthenware pot.

If we catch a movie, it's in Bondi Junction where the Westfield shopping center cinema bar provides one of the best views of Sydney Harbour and its famous bridge. We sip wine and watch yachts glide over the snaking waterways that lap the walled homes of the millionaires and billionaires edging the harbor.

Shopping for me is best done in the artisan markets of Paddington, Rozelle, and The Rocks, a central city market stretching through the convict-built laneways that mark Sydney's colonial history. Paddington has its big-name designer boutiques, but for me it's the quirkier finds of the clothing and jewelry stalls that capture my imagination.

I sometimes joke that we've shrunk our world to a six-mile radius. But when you live in a parkland surrounded by beaches, where the weather is invariably kind for outdoor-loving people, where we can eat, play, and sing with our friends gathered from local choir and pub gigs, why wouldn't we be grateful that a large city like Sydney can be so benign?

Residents of Sydney for more than 20 years, Mary O'Malley and her husband Larry Gray run the documentary film production company Primal Vision and lead tribal cultural tours to Vanuatu Islands. ■

Sydney locals include rainbow lorikeets.

ODDITIES

From Death to Marriage

A hotel and conference center in Sydney Harbour National Park is the site of the Old Quarantine Station once rife with smallpox, cholera, and even bubonic plague. It was open for the infectious until as recently as 1984. These days, you can the tour the old hospital, disinfecting showers, and mortuary where some immigrants ended their long journey to down under—and even get married there.

Little Bugger

Down under's most dangerous animal isn't the saltwater croc or great white shark, but the Sydney funnelweb spider *(Atrax robustus)*. Found only within a 62-mile (100 km) radius of Sydney, the spider's bite can be fatal if left untreated. Highly aggressive, it bites victims repeatedly with fangs that can slash through gloves or clothing. ■

"One of the great things about Sydney is that it has a great acceptance of everyone and everything. It's an incredibly tolerant city, a city with a huge multicultural basis."

—Sydney-born film director Baz Luhrmann

The Royal Botanic Garden offers a quiet repose from the city's hubbub.

ICON

Sydney Opera House

The billowing Opera House was a gamble when it started. Literally. Most of the funds for construction came from the New South Wales State Lottery. Today, millions of tourists flock to the Opera House annually, photographing its gleaming roof. • The Opera House hosts 1,800 performances a year at seven venues. • Danish architect Jørn Utzon won the design competition to create the building in 1957. • It took 14 years (1959 to 1973) to erect the revolutionary edifice. • During construction the cost soared from $7 million to a final price tag of $102 million • The roof is covered in 1,056,006 white ceramic tiles. • Queen Elizabeth dedicated the building on October 20, 1973 and has visited four times. • In 1980 Arnold Schwarzenegger won the "Mr. Olympia" bodybuilding contest held in the Concert Hall. • Opera singer Paul Robeson performed for construction workers on the building site in 1960. ■

All Things Sydney—From Bushman Chic to Local Opals

Dundee Duds Outback Aussies have pioneered a rustic savoir faire when it comes to fashion. Get fitted for an authentic Akubra hat at *Strand Hatters* (Strand Arcade, 412 George St.), which carries both men's and ladies' versions. And then waltz down the street to *R.M. Williams* (389 George St.) for the rest of your bushman wear—bespoke riding boots, Calder jackets, Mulyungarie pullovers, and perhaps even a handmade saddle if you're so inclined.

"Crocodile" Dundee style

All that Glitters Australia's national stone is the venerable opal, a gem of many colors once favored by European royalty. Roughly 97 percent of the world's opals are mined in Australia, many of them in the legendary town of Coober Pedy. The Rocks neighborhood boasts several tourist-oriented rock shops including *Opal Minded* (55 George St.), which still operates its own outback opal mine. Avoid the crowds and check out *Giulians* in the Four Seasons Hotel (199 George St.), which features earrings, necklaces, rings, cuff links, and other jewelry made from black and boulder opals.

Retro Refreshments True to its mission of protecting Australia's heritage, the *National Trust Centre* on Observatory Hill (Watson Rd.) sells gift-packaged food items popular in Sydney's bygone days including grapefruit and wild hibiscus cordial, mango and vanilla bean jam, Anzac biscuits, plum pudding, and handmade rock candy. ∎

Anzac (Australian and New Zealand Army Corps) biscuits, named for the soldiers who ate them

Irresistible Aussie Eats: Meat Pies to Minties

Dinghies pull right up to Doyles on Watsons Bay.

• Exalted by some as Australia's national dish, meat pies are a legacy of British colonial rule that Aussies have transformed into a culinary obsession. The selection at Pie Tin in Newtown (1 Brown St.) runs a savory gamut from old-school steak and kidney to chicken carbonara and spicy Cajun pork pies. A Sydney landmark since 1938, Harry's Café de Wheels (Cowper Wharf Rd. at Brougham Rd., Woolloomooloo) is renowned for its Tiger Pies—beef topped with mashed potato, mashed peas, and gravy.

• Given its long seafront and huge harbor, it's no surprise that Sydney seafood is a standout. Doyles on the Beach (11 Marine Parade, Watsons Bay), around since the 1880s, serves up copious portions of rock oysters, scallops, lobster bug tails, king prawns, mud crab, Barramundi, and snapper.

• Sydneysiders love their sweets—Tim Tams, Lolly Gobble Bliss Bombs, Freddo Frogs, and beloved Minties. Parry's Milkbar (347 Kingsway, Caringbah) carries many local candy favorites. Sticky (12–24 Playfair St., The Rocks) makes the city's best rock candy. Or buy in bulk at the Candy Bar Sydney Warehouse (5/9 Stanley St., Peakhurst). ■

Sydney's Urban Outback

The Aussie outback comes to the big city at Garigal National Park, a giant green space that hugs the inner reaches of Middle Harbour. This patch of pristine bushland preserves native flora and fauna, as well as waterfalls, secluded beaches, and Aboriginal sites.

One of the more unusual ways to while away a Sydney night is the "Roar and Snore" program at Taronga Zoo (Bradley's Head Rd., Mosman). Sleep in tents on the grassy courtyard and hear zookeepers spin tales of Australia's weird and wonderful wildlife. The experience includes hands-on encounters with koalas and other animals.

Sydney sports a number saltwater swimming pools, built to protect swimmers from the churning seas, right on the shore. All are open to the public. The Bondi Icebergs Baths with its Olympic and children's pools is one of the oldest and most renowned. Others: the women-only McIvers Baths at Coogee, the rocky Mahon Pool in Maroubra, and the Ocean Pool next to the golf course in Malabar. ■

The Icebergs Pool at Bondi Beach

Restaurants sprinkled along Sydney Harbour excel at alfresco nightlife.

Florida
MIAMI

A sultry, sophisticated coastal city of earthly pleasures and high culture

Art deco neons epitomize Miami glamour.

VITAL STATS

- **Year founded** 1896

- **Average daily temperature** 76°F (24°C)

- **Cruise passengers visiting Port of Miami** 3.5 million a year

- **Art deco buildings in the Art Deco District** 800

- **Miles of beaches** More than 15 (24 km)

- **Diveable wreck sites** More than 50

- **Percentage of residents who speak Spanish at home** 62 percent

In little over a century, Miami morphed from being a mosquito-laden swamp to a multicultural metropolis with soaring skyscrapers and art deco monuments. This just shows how fast things move in Miami: Famous for its steamy nightlife, voluptuous vibe, and fashionable denizens, the main risk is overstimulation, but that's what the beach is for.

À LA CARTE

Cuban Cuisine and Seafood Trucks

• Head to 8th Street, or Calle Ocho, in Little Havana, for authentic Latin American fare. At Exquisito (1510 SW 8th St.) , order the *vaca frita*, or shredded beef. For lunch at Versailles (3555 SW 8th St.), go for the traditional *Cuban sandwich*, which has sweet ham, roast pork, and Swiss cheese. If you need a pick-me-up, get a *Cuban coffee*, espresso with tons of sugar. Be warned: It's very strong.

• Miami honors its prime coastal location with a delicious array of fish and shellfish. For some of the best, get *stone crabs* at the aptly named Joe's Stone Crab (11 Washington Ave., Miami Beach), the *fried fish* sandwich at La Camaronera (1952 W. Flagler St.), and seafood of all stripes at Area 31 (270 Biscayne Blvd. Way). ■

Miami Finds: Sublime Stogies and Deco-to-Go

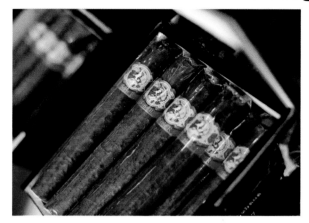

Hand-rolled smokes in Little Havana

Cigar Heaven If you're a cigar aficionado, you've come to the right place. Once you've had your fill of Cuban food on Calle Ocho, head to *El Credito Cigar Factory* (1106 SW 8th St.), where you can take a tour of one of the oldest cigar factories in the country. Also along Little Havana's main drag are *El Titan de Bronze* (1071 SW 8th St.), a small establishment that rolls cigars in situ, and *Sosa Family Cigars* (3475 SW 8th St.), replete with a smoking lounge and a dominoes table.

Loco for Deco The Miami Beach Architectural District, listed on the National Register of Historic Places, is famous for its whimsical art deco architecture, and you can take a piece of Miami Beach home by stopping at *Artisan Antiques Art Deco Gallery* (110 NE 40th St), which stocks an impressive collection of lighting fixtures, furniture, and accessories. Or get a quick fix at the *Official Art Deco Gift Shop* (1001 Ocean Dr.) where you'll find deco-inspired memorabilia and posters. ∎

NOVEL INTRODUCTIONS

Street 8
Douglas Fairbairn (1976)
Fairbairn's underrecognized noir novel, set in Miami's Little Havana, masterfully portrays the collision of old Miami with the influx of Cuban exiles.

Lost Memory of Skin
Russell Banks (2011)
The Kid, a 22-year-old sex offender, lives in a tent underneath a causeway in a Floridian coastal city, the only place he could legally live.

Back to Blood
Tom Wolfe (2012)
In this 700-page novel, Wolfe presents an epic, wide-ranging cross section of Miami life. The result is a rowdy rendering of a racial, ethnic, and experiential melting pot. ∎

Strolling Lincoln Road, part of the Miami Beach Architectural District

THE BEST
All-American Cities

Discover authentic America in unique cities and sites across the country.

The Mule Mountains of Bisbee, Arizona

Bisbee, Arizona

Once a rough-and-tumble mining town, Bisbee found new life in the 1970s as it began to attract artists and musicians to the Mule Mountains. Now Bisbee supports a thriving arts scene with galleries, shops, and museums.

Dinosaur Park, Rapid City

Birmingham, Alabama

Instead of hiding from its race-torn history, the city has embraced it with the stirring Civil Rights Institute, commemorating the pivotal 1960s protests, and Kelly Ingram Park with statues of water cannons and police dogs.

Rapid City, South Dakota

Most know this rugged town for its proximity to Mount Rushmore. But it's also home to Dinosaur Park, a Depression-era public works project with towering statues of far older luminaries including *Tyrannosaurus rex,* triceratops, and stegosaurus.

1960 Chevrolet Corvette

Bowling Green, Kentucky

What could be more American than the Corvette? Not only is this western Kentucky town home to the only factory producing the classic American sportster, but it also houses the National Corvette Museum and a new motor sports park.

Buffalo, New York

America's most beloved architect, Frank Lloyd Wright, spent plenty of time in Buffalo. Visitors can see a half dozen homes, including the Graycliff mansion, plus a mausoleum and boathouse, both recently built from Wright plans.

Cedar Rapids, Iowa

The home to "American Gothic" painter Grant Wood also has a deep Muslim heritage as the site of the Mother Mosque of America, the nation's longest-standing Islamic house of worship.

Toledo baseball

Toledo, Ohio

It's hard to resist a baseball team named the Mud Hens. The Detroit Tigers' minor league affiliate attracts crowds with wacky promotions and a memorable mascot. Throughout the year, diners pack Tony Packo's for fried pickles and to see hot dog buns signed by visiting celebrities.

Roanoke, Virginia

Steam trains once tied together the rapidly expanding country. As the era was ending, photographer O. Winston Link captured unforgettable images of mighty locomotives, now displayed in his namesake gallery in the city's historic rail district.

Marshall, Texas

This Lone Star town loves to celebrate—anything. Fire ant festivities take center stage every October with street concerts, bike rides, and a colorful parade of larger-than-life insects. A few months later, the historic town square glows with millions of bulbs during its monthlong Wonderland of Lights.

Santa Cruz, California

Beach boys (and girls) love this classic oceanfront town, home to a century-old amusement park pier. Two rides at the Beach Boardwalk are national historic landmarks: the Giant Dipper roller coaster and the Looff Carousel.

The all-American view: Santa Cruz's red-and-white "Giant Dipper" under a California sky

Australia
MELBOURNE
A world-class 21st-century metropolis with its own modern pulse

The eclectic Webb Bridge allows pedestrian and cycle traffic to cross the Yarra River in style.

VITAL STATS

- **Size of the city** 4,971 square miles (12,875 sq km), about seven times bigger than New York City

- **Size of the stained glass ceiling at the National Gallery of Victoria** 167.3 feet (51 m) long by 49.2 feet (15 m) wide, the world's largest

- **Cricket fans** 91,092 spectators, who watched the annual Boxing Day match on December 26, 2013, at Melbourne Cricket Ground, a record for the sport

- **Miles of tram** 155 miles (250 km) of double track and 1,763 stops, the world's largest operating tram network

- **Percentage of residents born overseas** 48 percent

Named the world's "most livable city" three years in a row, with its exploding music scene pushing it to its top perch, Melbourne no longer plays second fiddle to longtime rival Sydney. In recent decades the city's urban fabric has been indelibly altered by thousands of immigrants, entrepreneurs, and astonishing modern architecture.

SHOPPING CART

From Arcades to Australian Rules

Destination Shopping A warren of shop-filled Victorian arcades dating back to the 1890s fills a three-block space. The *Block Arcade* (282 Collins St.), with its rich decoration and glass canopy, is the most photogenic, and the mall's vintage Hopetoun Tea Rooms is a trip back in time. Even older is the 1869 *Royal Arcade* (335 Bourke St.), where boutiques dispense designer jewelry, gourmet chocolates, and specialty toys beneath a historic clock that chimes every hour.

Footy Finds Join the Melbourne frenzy and stock up on official guernseys, scarves, trading cards, footballs, and other Aussie Rules Football merchandise at *AFL Stores* scattered around the metro area, including Chadstone Shopping Centre (1341 Dandenong Rd.). Similar gear is available at *Rebel Centrepoint* (283–297 Bourke St.) in downtown Melbourne. ∎

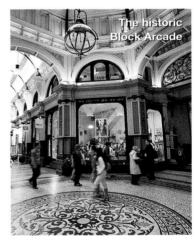

The historic Block Arcade

Flinders Street Station

Opened in 1910, Flinders Street Station in downtown Melbourne was both an architectural and transportation wonder. Crowned by a copper dome at one end and a clock tower at the other, the sprawling station mixed Edwardian baroque, French Renaissance, and art nouveau design elements into a streamlined structure that was both eye-catching and extremely functional. By the 1920s, it was the world's single busiest train station, reflecting the tremendous population growth of Melbourne at the time.

More than a century after its birth, Flinders Street Station remains a Melbourne landmark and meeting place, as well as a functioning station for both daily commuters and long-distance rail travelers. More than 150,000 passengers a day pass through the station. The station's noble stone architecture continues to stand proud. ■

Melburnians' beloved Yarra River, city center of promenading, relaxing, and taking in the sun

Funky Pubs, Grand Cafés, and Some Barbie

Pellegrini's Espresso Bar

• The old amber nectar flows as freely in Melbourne as anywhere else down under. The funky Fitzroy neighborhood hosts some of the best "hotels" (*pubs*). Pop into the Napier Hotel (210 Napier St.) for its selection of Australian artisan beers, the ancient Standard Hotel (293 Fitzroy St.) for its leafy beer garden and bygone ambience, and the Fitzroy Pinnacle (251 St. Georges Rd.) for its "pointy pub" architecture and large beer garden.

• Melbourne's rich *coffee* culture dates back to the 1830s, when grand coffeehouses sprung up as alternatives to bars during the temperance movement. Today, the city is Australia's java capital. Among the oldest and most authentic coffee drinking experiences is Pellegrini's Espresso Bar (66 Bourke St.), while Brother Baba Budan (359 Little Bourke St.) represents the hip.

• Immigrants have transformed Melbourne into an international food fest, including barbecue from a dozen different nations. Grill your own tandoori dinner at BBQ Nation (16/111 Market St., South Melbourne), savor *parrilla*-style Argentine steaks at San Telmo (14 Meyers Place), or toss a shrimp on the barbie at Big Boy BBQ (764 Glenhuntly Rd.), an Aussie-style barbecue joint in Caulfield South. ■

The tried-and-true Napier Hotel brims with pints and footy memorabilia.

ODDITIES

Antipodean Athens
Melbourne has the world's largest ethnic Greek population outside of Greece (about 300,000). Greek is the city's second most spoken language.

Fan Nation
Sports of all sorts rule here. Birthplace of Australian Rules Football, Melbourne is also home to the prestigious Melbourne Cup horse race, and the only city that boasts both a grand slam tennis event and Formula One grand prix. Not to mention the birthplace of cricket.

Hollywood Down Under
With year-round inviting weather and a cadre of cutting-edge filmmakers, Melbourne was one of the cradles of modern cinema. Produced by the local branch of the Salvation Army, *Soldiers of the Cross* (1900) was one of the world's first dramatic movies, while its *The Story of the Kelly Gang* (1906) is even recognized by the UNESCO Memory of the World Register as the world's earliest full-length feature film. ■

MONTREAL

The cosmopolitan, cultural heart of Canada's Euro-influenced corner

The Gothic Revival Notre-Dame Basilica stands out in a city of churches.

VITAL STATS

- Catholic churches 194

- Bridges to Island of Montreal 28

- National Hockey League championships won by the Montreal Canadiens 24, more than any other team

- Miles of pedestrian pathways in the "Underground City" 20.5 (33 km)

My City: Joel Giberovitch

Montreal is where my home, my heart, and my family (my wife, Emilie, and our two young children, Noah and Ella) are. It is a city with a strong sense of identity and a vibrant emphasis on culture and the arts, both so important to me.

Many chefs have decided to call Montreal their home, and the city has so many excellent restaurants. Garde Manger in Old Montreal has two intimate rooms. The last time Emilie and I went, we sat at the seafood bar, and watched the barman shuck oysters. He made me the best Bloody Caesar, Canada's version of a Bloody Mary and made with Clamato juice, I have ever had. The fresh gnocchi with scallops was a savory blend of taste and perfection. Our very favorite restaurant is Faros, a Greek seafood restaurant in the Mile End. Whether we go with our family or friends, chef and owner Benny always makes us feel welcome.

We love the freshness of the food. We order the fried zucchini and eggplant with homemade *tzatziki,* and grilled octopus, which our six-year-old son loves. Their Greek salad is a work of art.

Emilie and I used to live in the quiet Saint-Henri neighborhood, next to the Atwater Market, where I would go Rollerblading and biking on the path next to the Lachine Canal down to the docks in Lachine or to Old Montreal. During the summer, we go for walks at Beaver Lake, a beautiful green space in the middle of the city and a landmark in Montreal. In the fall, we love to go to the Botanical Garden with our family to see the Chinese lanterns garden. They are especially stunning at night as they glow in the dark.

Montreal has no lack of places to shop. Downtown has every store you could possibly wish for, much of it connected by the "Underground City." St. Denis Street is lined with trendy shops, cafés, and excellent restaurants such as L'Express, one of the best and oldest bistros in Montreal. I love their *bavette* (steak) and fries. Classy Laurier Avenue, bordering Outremont and the Plateau, is another delightful street for browsing, with lots of charming boutiques. Monkland Avenue a commercial strip in the middle of Notre Dame de Grâce (N.D.G.), the family-friendly neighborhood where we used to live about a 25-minute metro ride from downtown, is another favorite shopping spot, with toy stores, cafés, and a great butcher, Maître Boucher. We also still spend a lot of time at N.D.G. Park, a year-round destination with two skating rinks and a water park in the summer.

Montreal beats to its own drum thanks to the diverse and unique people that choose to live here. It is for that reason that I am especially proud to say that I am a Montrealer.

Joel Giberovitch is the owner and artistic director of Montreal's Upstairs Jazz Bar & Grill. ∎

Montreal's trendy St. Denis Street

ODDITIES

Heart of a Saint
Saint Brother André, founder of Montreal's Saint Joseph's Oratory of Mount Royal (3800 Chemin Queen Mary), the largest church in Canada, gave his heart and soul to the church— literally, in the case of his heart. Church visitors can view remnants of it inside a glass vial.

Prohibit This
During Prohibition in the United States, Americans often traveled to Montreal to gamble, drink, and party. Red lights shining on the streets of downtown's Quartier des Spectacles are a nod to the neighborhood's past as a red light district.

"Revenge of the Cradle"
Early French and English settlers fought for control of the prized Quebec region. One reason why Francophone language and culture came to dominate this corner of Canada is that the Catholic Church encouraged (some say pressured) French families to have lots of children. Couples had as many as 20 offspring. The tactic was known as "the revenge of the cradle." ∎

"In Montreal, spring is like an autopsy. Everyone wants to see the inside of the frozen mammoth. Girls rip off their sleeves and the flesh is sweet and white, like wood under green bark. From the streets a sexual manifesto rises like an inflating tire, 'the winter has not killed us again!' "
—Canadian singer-songwriter Leonard Cohen

Mount Royal Park, a refuge in
the middle of Montreal

The interior of Notre-Dame Basilica

Indulgences: From Furs to Maple Anything

Street art alongside Old Montreal

New Soft Touch French fur traders developed this region centuries ago, and their legacy lives on in ample (and relatively inexpensive) supplies of mink, sable, lynx, and other furs. Prices can run thousands less than in the United States, and the quality is often higher. Leading retailers include *McComber Furs* (440 Boulevard de Maisonneuve W.) and neighboring *Grosvenor Furs* (400 Boulevard de Maisonneuve W.). Vintage stores like *Folles Alliées* (365 Du Mont Royal Ave. E.) also often stock furs at substantial savings. Or pick up a recycled fur transformed into a new design by *Harricana par Mariouche* (3000 Saint-Antoine W.).

Made in Montreal Stroll the cobbled streets of Old Montreal, especially the city's first main street, Rue Saint-Paul, for all things local. *Canadian Maple Delights* (84 Rue Saint-Paul St. E.) plies customers with plenty of free samples and in-house specialties like maple gelato and coffee. *Bonsecours Market* (350 Rue Saint-Paul E.) is one of several top spots for picking up First Nation and Inuit art. The small *Zone Orange gallery* (410 Rue Saint Pierre) has rejuvenating espresso, as well as jewelry, ceramics, and art pieces by local designers. Previously Web-only Montreal brand *Frank & Oak* (160 Rue Saint-Viateur E.) decks out its clients with custom-fitted clothing at its atelier in the hip Mile End district. ∎

Cobbled-street charm in Old Montreal

Amazing Bagels, Ethnic Treats—and Elvis Poutine

Poutine, the ultimate Québécois indulgence

• Montrealers will tell you their bagels beat even Gotham's best. They're thinner, with the dough boiled in honey water to give a sweet taste and appetizing shine. St-Viateur (263 St Viateur W.) and Fairmont (74 Avenue Fairmount W.) are Montreal institutions, baking and serving bagels around the clock.

• Montreal is famous for its smoked meat. Nearly a century old, Schwartz's (900 Saint Laurent Blvd.) is the place to tuck into a classic smoked meat sandwich made from founder Reuben Schwartz's original herby-spicy recipe.

• Montrealers won't let you leave without sampling the famous *poutine,* a calorie-bursting mound of fried potatoes with cheese curd and brown gravy. La Banquise (994 Rue Rachel E.) serves not only the standard variety, but also twists on the classic, including La Kamikaze, La T-Rex, and the king of poutines, La Elvis, with added ground beef, mushrooms, and green peppers.

• Montreal benefits in every way possible from being a city of immigrants. Korean, Portuguese, Vietnamese, German, and Chinese cuisines are all represented alongside a clear French influence in its bistros, *boulangeries,* and restaurants, such as "godfather of Quebec cuisine" Normand Laprise's innovative Toqué! (900 Place Jean-Paul-Riopelle). Sample exquisite French pastries at Maison Christian Faure (355 Place Royale). ■

Of Wine and Music

With wide green spaces and great hilltop views, Montreal's centerpiece, Mount Royal Park, makes it easy to escape the noise of the city. But sometimes those sounds are a good thing. Every Sunday throughout the summer (early May to late September), crowds of musicians gather at the Sir George-Étienne Cartier Monument at the bottom of Mount Royal, armed with drums, bongos, and djembes for Tam Tam Jams. There's no structure or official timing for the event, but the tradition's now more than 30 years old and shows no signs of losing its rhythm.

The dramatic Notre-Dame Basilica in Old Montreal's historic district is one of the most striking sights in the city. Visitors have to pay to enter most of the time, but attending mass is free and a good opportunity to see the basilica in all its splendor.

There's no corkage fee in Montreal, so enjoying a good bottle of wine with your meal at restaurants is easy and relatively cheap. The city has 368 BYOBs, including O-Thym (1112 Boulevard de Maisonneuve E.) and Le Quartier Général (1251 Rue Gilford). ■

Summertime drum circles crop up in Mount Royal Park.

The Port of Montreal

The St. Lawrence River played a crucial role in the history of North America, opening up the land to new arrivals from Europe.

The first colonists, led in 1641 by Paul de Chomedey de Maison-neuve, arrived on the river's shores. Prevented from venturing farther by the treacherous Lachine Rapids, they established Ville-Marie, which grew to become Montreal. The port and trading post were critical to the fur and lumber trades and other industries. The later opening of the Lachine Canal made it possible to sail up the St. Lawrence to the Great Lakes. The railways also grew out of the Old Port, making Montreal Canada's primary transport hub.

Today, Montreal remains a major port for cargo ships. But it's also a hub for cruise ships, pleasure boats, and over eight million visitors a year, drawn to its Science Centre, restaurants, skating rink, and even a beach. ■

Massachusetts
BOSTON

Tradition meets innovation in this New England capital, with new finds popping up daily on its historic streets

Revolutionary history and modern industry intersect in Boston.

VITAL STATS

- **Size of the famous CITGO sign** 3,600 square feet (335 sq m)

- **Height of the Prudential Tower** 750 feet (229 m)

- **Depth of Ted Williams Tunnel** 90 feet (27 m) in some parts, the deepest in North America

- **Area of Boston Common, the first public park in America** 50 acres (20 ha)

- **Cost of 1990 Isabella Stewart Gardner Museum theft** 13 paintings worth some $300 million, the largest art heist in U.S. history

- **Length of Freedom Trail** 2.5 miles (4 km), with 16 significant historic sites

Cradle of America's past and laboratory for its future, Boston is above all a city of neighborhoods and one of the most walkable in the world, from patrician Back Bay and quirky Jamaica Plain to newly hip "old Southie."

À LA CARTE

Beantown Bites: From "Chowdah" to Ice Cream

• Boston *clam chowder* is thick and creamy—not tomato-based like that Manhattan version—rich with potatoes and plump clams. The city's restaurants compete for bragging rights: Summer Shack (50 Dalton St.) and Barking Crab (88 Sleeper St.) are two local favorites. But it's hard to believe anyone serves more than Legal Sea Foods's flagship location (26 Park Plaza).

• Frozen must-haves: Maybe it's the Boston winters that have given locals a taste for cold treats. All year-round, *ice cream* is on the menu. For inventive flavors like Earl Grey or bourbon-black pepper, it's Toscanini's (899 Main St., Cambridge) or J.P. Licks (multiple locations). But for a classic sundae with sprinkles or a frappe—that's Bostonian for a thick milk shake—it's Lizzy's Homemade (multiple locations). ∎

Scoops of gelato, a nod to Italy

While the Public Garden may be gorgeous in winter white, spring blossoms, and summer greens, it's at its best in autumn.

ICON

Fenway Park

For more than 100 years, Fenway Park has been home to Boston's beloved Red Sox. Bostonians cherish their urban temple of baseball. Despite updates (the last of its wooden seats were finally replaced in 2010), the ballpark seems frozen in time, brimming with memories both painful (the Red Sox's 86-year-long "Curse of the Bambino" World Series drought) and ecstatic (becoming World Series champions after the marathon bombing in 2013) • The Green Monster, the park's outfield wall, is 37 feet, two inches (11 m) tall (Major League Baseball's second highest). • Fenway holds just over 37,000 seats, making it one of the smallest parks in baseball. • The sole red-backed chair (Section 42, Row 37, Seat 21) marks the longest home run ever hit here: Ted Williams's 502-foot (153 m) blast in 1946 • Red Sox fans sing Neil Diamond's "Sweet Caroline" in the 8th inning. And, if the Red Sox win, "Dirty Water," a 1966 song inspired by Boston Harbor, plays on the sound system with the lyrics, "Well, I love that dirty water; Oh, Boston, you're my home." • An estimated 1.5 million Fenway Franks (hot dogs) are sold each season. ∎

Boston Bling: From Ivy League to Underwater

The Sam Adams brewery

Dressing Without the Degree There are two ways to get a Harvard sweatshirt. Be a student or hop across the Charles River to the *Harvard Coop* (1400 Mass. Ave., Cambridge), a mammoth bookstore brimming with Harvard and MIT gear, from lamb's wool sweater vests to boxer shorts. The store has been serving (and dressing) the city's intellectual community since 1882. But if your allegiance lies elsewhere, you can get spirit wear from the Boston area's 50-plus other institutions of higher education, from the *Berklee College of Music* shop (1090 Boylston St.) to the *New England College of Optometry* store (424 Beacon St.).

For the Love of Beer Who says beer is just for drinking? Bostonians love their Sam Adams so much, it's even made into soap so you can lather up with lager. But don't try to order *Fenway Beer Soap* at a bar. Instead visit *Sault New England* (577 Tremont St.), a men's store that carries quirky and regional gifts, plus fittingly natty duds. (For other Sam Adams paraphernalia, head to the source. The brewery's gift shop at 30 Germania Street stocks a store full of the stuff.)

Ocean Bling Waterfront Boston started as a port city, and despite its urban trappings, retains its ties to the sea. Choose a one-of-a-kind piece of *sea glass jewelry* at *Noa Jewelry* (88 Charles St.). And if you want to search for the treasure yourself, take a ferry to *Spectacle Island* in Boston Harbor. The recreation area is considered one of the world's top spots for sea glass. ∎

The Harvard Coop, catering to the Harvard and MIT communities since 1882

NOVEL INTRODUCTIONS

The Scarlet Letter
Nathaniel Hawthorne (1850) The classic is a scandalous tale of adultery, revealing the mores of 17th-century Boston. Though more than 250 years have passed and crime is not punished in the city square, many Bostonians still cherish the city's Puritan roots.

Make Way for Ducklings
Robert McCloskey (1941) This Caldecott Medal–winning illustrated children's book follows a mallard family with eight ducklings through the iconic sites of Boston. Today, a well-loved bronze statue of the quackers stands in Boston Public Garden.

Mystic River
Dennis Lehane (2001) Dorchester-native Lehane has set many of his mystery novels on the streets of his hometown. "East Buckingham," where the lives of three Boston Irish boys meet tragedy, is a fictionalization of blue-collar Boston neighborhoods such as Dorchester and Roxbury. ∎

District of Columbia
WASHINGTON

A nation's capital animated by history, art, and a growing, youth-infused scene

The Gothic majesty of Georgetown University rises above the Potomac River.

Beyond the headlines and the political Washington that Americans love to hate lies a vibrant, evolving city: opulent, beautiful, and made for fun, brimming with both historic treasures and new neighborhood hot spots.

LOCAL SECRETS

The Capital's Wild Side

A big part of Washington's attraction these days is its older neighborhoods, now preserves of the young and hip. Current up-and-coming areas include the Atlas District, along H Street NE, and Southwest Washington around the Anacostia waterfront.

One of Washington's graces is that nature is never far away. On the Mall, seek out the Smithsonian's charming Butterfly Habitat Garden, or join Washingtonians for a walk along the scenic towpath of the Chesapeake & Ohio Canal in Georgetown. The Hillwood Museum and Gardens (4155 Linnean Ave., NW), an estate of retro splendor near Rock Creek Park, houses an astounding quantity of classic decorative arts in a setting of lush formal gardens. ∎

D.C. Eats: Crab Cakes to Power Chili

Hands-on Ethiopian dining

• The city's shrine to food is Eastern Market (225 7th Street, SE). Even if you don't have a kitchen, come for the boisterous atmosphere, the arts and craft vendors, the weekend flea market, and famous blueberry buckwheat pancakes or Chesapeake Bay crab cakes at Market Lunch.

• Long before U Street became cool, Ben's Chili Bowl (1213 U St., NW) and its trademark half smokes with chili was a local institution. Today celebrities from Bill Cosby and Anthony Bourdain to Barack Obama have been known to walk through the door. There's plenty of more upscale competition around the neighborhood, such as Marvin (2007 14th St. NW), featuring southern and Belgian cooking and drinks on a rooftop deck.

• D.C. has gone wild for food trucks and boasts some of the nation's best. Catch them around the Mall (near the Smithsonian), on Farragut Square, or along H Street NW, in the Foggy Bottom neighborhood.

• Spicy stews and *injera* bread make Ethiopian restaurants a popular and unusual part of D.C.'s dining scene. Two excellent ones are Dukem (1114 U St., NW) and Meskerem (2434 18th St., NW). ■

Food trucks and cupcakes: That's what District foodies do best!

ODDITIES

Washington's (Other) Monuments
The capital city is littered with monuments, memorials, and outdoor sculpture, and not just to presidents. One of the area's favorite pieces depicts a giant bearded man struggling to free himself from the ground. "The Awakening," by J. Seward Johnson, Jr., is found at National Harbor in nearby Prince George's County, Maryland. Other surprising pieces include a statue of John Ericsson, inventor of the screw propeller (in West Potomac Park, near the convergence of Independence Avenue, 23rd Street, and Ohio Drive, SW), and a *Titanic* memorial at Washington Channel Park near Fort McNair.

Capital Wonders
The city has been influenced by Freemasonry since the days of Master Mason George Washington—the brothers have replicated two of the Wonders of the Ancient World here: the Mausoleum of Halicarnassus (House of the Temple, 1733 16th St., NW) and the Pharos Lighthouse (George Washington Masonic National Memorial, in suburban Alexandria, Virginia). Both welcome visitors. ■

The majestic Jefferson Memorial
dominates the cherry tree–fringed Tidal Basin.

South Africa
CAPE TOWN

A cosmopolitan metropolis at the bottom of the African continent

The well-to-do Camps Bay beach town along the Western Cape

VITAL STATS

- **Year founded** 1652, by the Dutch East India Company as a resupply stop

- **Latitude** 33.55° S, roughly the same distance south of the Equator as Los Angeles is north

- **Coastline** 183 miles (295 km) within the city limits

- **Languages** 3 main languages, Afrikaans (spoken by 50 percent), isiXhosa (25 percent), and English (20 percent)

My City: Rashiq Fataar

I live in a city known for its majestic beauty. But Cape Town is infinitely more layered and textured than the iconic images of Table Mountain, Robben Island, and our many white-sand beaches.

Cape Town is a city that, while being the oldest in South Africa, is still writing and building its story of possibility just two decades after the dawn of democracy. The beauty of our people, their stories, aspirations, and dreams, is why my city is special to me. My passion and career is this city.

When I'm downtown, walking, cycling, or busing between meetings and events, I usually need a peaceful break. I love places like the Company's Gardens, which are such dignified, beautiful, generous spaces that, when I see Capetonians walking and reading and lying on the grass there, I cannot help but feel that the kind of city we're working toward is actually on its way. My favorite hangouts downtown are usually Clarke's Bar and Dining Room, the Truth Coffee shops, Loading Bay, a café and clothes shop, surf-inspired Latitude 33, and airy Hemel-huijs restaurant. Each has very different crowds, so it depends on how I'm feeling.

I recently moved from downtown to a little studio in Three Anchor Bay, which I love. It's closer to the Sea Point Promenade and Atlantic Ocean—perfect for a long walk or leisurely cycle to catch up with a friend and clear the mind after a frantic day.

But the urbanite in me is still drawn to downtown and the energy of Bree or Adderley Streets. The first Thursday of every month, it all comes alive with people, art, and food when the galleries—and now restaurants, too—stay open late. My personal favorites are the Stable on Loop Street, the Beautifull Life building, Chandler House, and the AVA Gallery. I must admit, though, that I love the architecture and bumping into friends more than the art.

Although I am not much of a shopper, the V&A Waterfront is a pleasant mall perched along the edge of the ocean in a working harbor and filled with locals and tourists. With some great ice cream in hand from The Creamery, I enjoy visiting the Zeitz Museum of Contemporary Art Africa there, or watching the world go by. Just a bus or cycle from downtown, the Woodstock Exchange always has a new design store or interesting small business opening. The area has gone through a massive renewal, and its great street art, which covers the walls of some homes, has attracted global attention.

I've decided not to own a car this year, so that means walking and using public transport to get around. MyCiTi bus routes are still rolling out, and different parts of the city are becoming more accessible. Our city is still unfolding, and revealing itself to all the people who love it.

Capetonian Rashiq Fataar is the founding director of Future Cape Town, and an urban consultant, speaker, and writer. ∎

Contemporary South African art on display at AVA Gallery

"This is a pretty and singular town; it lies at the foot of an enormous wall (the Table Mountain), which reaches to the clouds, and makes a most imposing barrier.
Cape Town is a great inn, on the great highway to the east."
—British naturalist Charles Darwin, who visited Cape Town in 1836

THEN & NOW

Table Mountain

So perfectly paired are these twin scenes of Table Mountain that it's as if an artist had dropped a computer-enhanced urban scene into an empty landscape. In 1917, when this black-and-white image was shot, Cape Town was home to South Africa's recently formed parliament—which would draft the apartheid laws that for decades banished the "Coloureds" to townships on the city's sandy plains while whites enjoyed its salubrious mountain slopes.

Today, with apartheid gone, Cape Town is an urban behemoth of over 3.4 million inhabitants—and South Africa's second largest city. "The place is a little gem, perfectly formed," says photographer Bob Krist, who took this modern picture of Cape Town from a hotel roof. "The South African custom of drinking sundowners, on Table Mountain overlooking the city, is my favorite thing to do there. The views of the city and down to the cape are amazing." ■

Cape Town Creations: Jewelry and Beyond

Waterfront Music Store

All That Glitters Jewelry made with South African diamonds and gold is readily available in Cape Town. *Amulet Goldsmiths* in Tamboerskloof (14 Kloof Nek Rd.) features modern, one-off gold pieces. If diamonds are more your thing, browse the gorgeous necklaces, rings, and broaches at *Peter Gilder's* boutique in Constantia Village. Gilder also takes bespoke commissions for diamond and gold jewelry.

Art & Soul Cape Town's unique "township crafts" comprise decorative items—animals, flowers, automobiles, bags—made from recycled wire, tin, plastic, bottle tops, and other materials. The *Blue Shed* craft market at V&A Waterfront is a great place to hunt for township treasures. *Waterfront Music Store* specializes in electric guitars fashioned from discarded oilcans. The nonprofit *heART at Work* sells mobiles, mosaics, and other crafts made in disadvantaged communities around Cape Town.

Home Improvement Cape Town has emerged as a hub of cutting-edge interior design and home décor. *Skinny laMinx* (201 Bree St.) features local artist Heather Moore's distinctive kitchen and house creations—aprons, towels, table runners, napkins, and pillows. Capetonian innovation is also the vibe at *Gregor Jenkin Studio* (1 Argyle St.), where the unique handmade tables, chairs, and lighting double as artwork. ∎

Support the local economy at Skinny laMinx, where everything is "made in South Africa."

"Rainbow" Eats and Local Gourmet Treats

Bobotie, a dish of curried mincemeat

• Pioneered by innovative young chefs, Cape Town's "rainbow cuisine" reflects myriad cultural and culinary influences. Planet Restaurant (76 Orange St.), an eco-friendly eatery in the posh Mount Nelson Hotel, features an ethereal mix of Victorian architecture and outer space–themed décor, and a menu that includes monkfish, biltong-dusted springbok, and fynbos salads. Test Kitchen (375 Albert Rd.), the latest offering from award-winning Capetonian chef Luke Dale-Roberts, presents dishes like South African ceviche and tofu miso soup.

• Indigenous African edibles are just coming into their own as a gourmet cuisine, in particular *braai*—the South African version of barbecue. Cape Town's booming braai scene ranges from simple affairs like the Backyard Grill Lounge in Sea Point (72 Regent Rd.) to the over-the-top Galbi Restaurant (210 Long St.), where the waiters make a show of serving African game on spits.

• Descended from Asian slaves brought to the Cape centuries ago, the Cape Malays are one of the city's most distinct ethnic groups. Their unique food is the forte at Biesmiellah Restaurant (2 Wale St., Bo-Kaap), where dishes like *bobotie* (curried mincemeat) and *denning vleis* (lamb stew) blend Asia and Africa. ■

From Seaside Splendor to Hikes on High

Avoid the crowds at strands farther south along the peninsula. Noordhoek Beach stretches 5 miles (8 km) along the Atlantic seaboard, a white-sand wonder backed by unspoiled wetlands. Scarborough village offers a small, sandy cove near the Misty Cliffs. Around the False Bay side is dramatic Boulders Beach, where humans share the sand with African penguins.

The Kirstenbosch National Botanical Garden (Rhodes Drive) hosts the Kirstenbosch Summer Sunset Concerts between November and April with Table Mountain as a backdrop. Artists range from the Cape Philharmonic Orchestra to jazz legend Hugh Masekela. Guests can bring their own wine and picnic dinner or order takeout from the garden's Silvertree Restaurant.

Everyone knows the Table Mountain Aerial Cableway, opened in 1929. Far less famous is the extensive trail network atop the iconic mesa, including the 55-mile (88 km) Hoerikwaggo Trail, which takes five days to complete with overnights at four tented camps. Among other places to sleep in the national park are the self-catering Olifantsbos Guest House and Eland and Duiker Cottages. ■

Penguins take a waddle by the water at Boulders Beach.

Cape Town Carnival heats up annually in March.

BERLIN

A famed haven for artists and immigrants sporting a sleek high-tech vibe

Berlin: The capital of cool along the Spree River

VITAL STATS

- **Museums** 175 (more than the Berlin average for rainy days)

- **Restaurants** 4,650

- **Bars and clubs** 1,090

- **Height of the Fern-sehturm tower** 1,207 feet (368 m). The television tower is the tallest structure in Germany.

- **Bunkers** More than 300, and hundreds of miles of tunnels, from the Nazi era

My City: Joe Jackson

In 1910, writer Karl Scheffler called Berlin "a city condemned forever to becoming and never being." A hundred years later, a Berliner friend of mine described it as *"gebrochen:* broken—so badly, and so many times, it can never really be fixed." Either way, it has an anarchic quality that still attracts artists, hedonists, and bohemians. Many cities are more beautiful, but Berlin makes them seem a bit too neat, too comfortable, too *finished.*

Such messiness strikes some people as un-German. But Berlin *is* German, and so manages to be both edgy and safe, and to have both anything-goes nightlife and good public transport. Tolerance is deeply ingrained: In the 1920s, there were more than 50 gay bars in the district of Schöneberg alone, at a time when even *one* would have been unthinkable in, say, England. The city is also a boozer's paradise, with everything from 24-hour dives to posh cocktail lounges—though the latter (for instance, the Green Door in Schöneberg or Würgeengel in Kreuzberg) are much less snooty than their counterparts in other cities. Café Einstein, with a gem of a cocktail bar in the old West Berlin, was once a silent film star's villa and Nazi hangout. Personally, though, I love *Eck-Kneipen*, traditional working-class corner pubs with cheap beer and terrible jukeboxes, which still abound in the "uncool" areas I like, such as southern Neukölln.

But if Berlin is decadent, it's also cultured, with plenty of theater, opera, galleries, and bookshops, and the world's greatest orchestra (whose home, the Philharmonie, sounds fantastic and feels much smaller than it is). And if you find some of the eastern neighborhoods too gritty or too trendy, Charlottenburg, in the west, maintains its historic elegance, around Savignyplatz or the tree-lined streets named after Goethe, Schiller, and Pestalozzi. On Friedrichstrasse in the central district of Mitte, there's Dussmann: five floors of CDs, vinyl, books, DVDs, sheet music, stationery . . . it sucks me in for hours at a time, while sucking hundreds of euros from my wallet.

Above all, what draws me to Berlin is a sense of freedom. Life is still cheaper and less stressful here than in New York or London, and the sprawling scale of the place makes other cities seem claustrophobic. The parks are unmanicured; the Tiergarten feels more like a forest, albeit one with a nice beer garden (Café am Neuen See) while Treptower Park, in former East Berlin, has an astonishing Stalinist memorial to the invading Soviet Army. Berlin is amazingly green, and its summers can be glorious, with everyone and everything spilling out onto sidewalks wide enough to accommodate everyone and everything. There's also much more water than you'd expect: Take a boat trip around the rivers and canals or out to one of the surrounding lakes. You feel a million miles from urban life, but you're still in Berlin.

Joe Jackson is a Grammy-winning musician and recording artist, and the author of a memoir, A Cure for Gravity. *Raised in England, he lived for many years in New York before moving to Berlin in 2008.* ■

"Berlin," a sculpture symbolizing the old divided city

"All free men, wherever they may live, are citizens of Berlin, and, therefore, as a free man, I take pride in the words: *Ich bin ein Berliner!*"
—John F. Kennedy, speaking in Berlin in 1963

„Three girls and a boy"

The Berlin Cathedral,
the city's largest
Protestant church

The Brandenburg Gate, a symbol of
Berlin for more than 200 years

Only in Berlin: Toys and Fashion Trinkets

Haute hats at Fiona Bennett's studio

Made in Berlin With over 250,000 people attending Berlin's Fashion Week, the city is gaining a reputation as a leading fashion city. Find local designers in trendy Mitte, at places like *Lala Berlin* (Mulackstrasse 7), a honeypot of young Berlin labels. Out in the up-and-coming Wedding district, flashy fashionistas hit *Schuldig groben Unfugs* (Föhrer Strasse 10) for experimental outfits sprouting palm fronds, sensuous swans, and even folded paper boats. With her ethereal plumes of feathers and straw, the showroom of glamorous hatmaker *Fiona Bennett* (Potsdamer Strasse 81) seems more like an art gallery.

Christmas Cornucopias Decked-out Christmas markets are Berlin's seasonal markers. *Gendarmenmarkt Christmas market* (Gendarmenmarkt 1) stocks handmade toys and fine embroidery, not to mention mulled wine to keep you going in this sumptuous plaza surrounded by neoclassical buildings. At the brewery complex turned cultural institution *Kulturbrauerei* (Schönhauser Allee 36), log fires light the courtyards filled with quirky gifts at the annual Lucia Christmas Market. If you're still craving that fairy-tale feeling, head to the cobblestoned *Spandau Christmas Market* (Altstadt Spandau) which boasts up to 250 stands in varying degrees of kitsch. ∎

Berlin's Gendarmenmarkt transforms into a colorful holiday market in the weeks leading up to Christmas.

Scrumptious Sausage and Swabian *Spaetzle*

Veal dumplings in a caper sauce

• Berliner food, characterized by unpretentious heartiness, has stayed true to its working-class roots. Try the homemade meatballs at Gerichtslaube (Poststraße 28) and pickled ham hock at Zum Schusterjungen (Danziger Straße 9). Konnopke's (Schönhauser Allee 44a), sheltered under a U-Bahn viaduct, is one of many street vendors who claim to have invented currywurst, a revered Berlin sausage specialty smothered in ketchup and curry powder.

• What kept Prussia's soldiers going during long winter campaigns? Find out at Marjellchen (Mommsenstrasse 9), specializing in East German fare, with a *Pillekaller,* a potent schnapps topped with a slice of liver sausage, and a hearty serving of *betenbarsch* (a kind of borscht), or steamed pork belly stuffed with prunes. The starlet at celebrated chef Tim Raue's La Soupe Populaire (Prenzlauer Allee 242) is its *Königsberger Klopse*, an East Prussian specialty of veal dumplings in a creamy caper sauce. At Alpenstueck (Gartenstrasse 9), which updates the hearty southern German cuisine, dig into venison ragout or a wafer-thin schnitzel, and admire the witty take on après-ski chalet décor. Schwarzwaldstuben (Tucholskystraße 48) elevates down-to-earth Swabian dishes like square meat dumplings and cheese-topped *spaetzle* noodles. Or get a slice of Bavaria (and its white *wurst* topped with sweet mustard) at Weihenstephaner (Neue Promenade 5). ■

Secret, Sacred, and Soothing

Did you know the Nazis made bombers underground? Find out more at Berliner Unterwelten (Berlin Underworlds, Brunnenstrasse 105), which has fascinating tours of air-raid shelters, tunnels, and vaults going back to the 19th century. Be sure to see the Fuhrerbunker (chauffeurs' bunker); a mural depicting SS soldiers protecting the *Volk* was painted by guards of Hitler's motor pool.

Deep in Treptower Park looms the Sowjetisches Ehrenmal, a four-story-high memorial to the Soviet victory over Germany in 1945. The gigantic statue portrays a Soviet soldier holding a sword and a child, and stomping a broken swastika. Some 5,000 Red Army soldiers are buried on the grounds below.

The niftiest place for a dip is the Badeschiff (Bathing Ship, Eichenstrasse 3), a retired cargo container moored in the Spree River. Saunas and a deejay lounge add to the fun in winter, when a high-tech shell keeps the shimmering blue waters toasty warm. ■

Guided underground tours reveal the city's underbelly.

The Reichstag

The Reichstag, Germany's pre–World War II parliament building, was partly gutted by fire in 1933 (Hitler blamed anti-Nazi Communists), hammered by Allied bombers during the war, and captured by Soviet soldiers in 1945. A year later its burned-out husk grimly overlooks Berliners (above) who till the soil in a desperate attempt to ward off starvation.

After the war, Bonn inherited the seat of government until it returned in 1999 to occupy the rebuilt Reichstag (right), a marvel of modernity. It symbolizes the Neue Berlin that has emerged since the Wall fell on the night of November 9, 1989.

Youth now sets the agenda in Berlin. There's a raffish, bohemian feel. Shops are more adventurous, and the restaurants have moved light years beyond the stodgy fare of old, making it one of Europe's most engaging big cities. ■

THE BEST
Nightlife Cities

The globe's hottest party spots cater to all tastes—glitzy, gritty, seductive, and strange.

Temple Bar district, Dublin

Dublin, Ireland

Wedged between Trinity College and the old city, the Temple Bar area is a decadent neighborhood of watering holes and nightclubs. The beer flows in torrents at the Brazen Head, reputedly Ireland's oldest pub (established 1198) and a fixture in James Joyce's opus *Ulysses*.

Belgrade

San Juan, Puerto Rico

Flirt like the devil in fashionable bars along San Sebastián Street, then twist to sweaty abandon in tropical clubs like Rumba—all with a piña colada in hand, of course.

Belgrade, Serbia

No one would describe Belgrade as beautiful, but its rollicking nightlife is world-class. *Splavovi*—riverboat clubs—boom in the glorious warmth of summer. The dancing shoes come out again in the postindustrial venues of the Savamala district.

La Paz, Bolivia

At 11,800 feet (3,597 m), the Bolivian capital gets a tad chilly after sunset, when residents flock to cozy drinking holes to warm their cockles and trade secrets. Don't be bashful: This sophisticated lady greets visitors with open arms.

São Paulo, Brazil

The choice is overwhelming in Brazil's sensuous megacity and the traffic deadly, so spiffed-up *paulistas* grab a meal or drink, walk to the nearest joint, and shake it, baby, to samba, bossa nova, or (maybe) Brazilian thrash punk.

Goa, India

Whether you're seeking a secluded bolthole or all-night gyration, Goa's beaches are right for your fantasy. Channel Goa's hippie '70s heyday at laid-back locales along the golden south shore. A city ban on all-night fests hasn't stopped the fun.

Flight of beers

Foam party on Ibiza

Ibiza, Spain

If your dial is permanently set to party, Ibiza's club circuit will keep you energized late into the Spanish night. Slide on dance floors covered in soapsuds or join pool revelers under a suspended deejay cabin. Then catch a Discobus to your next adventure.

Houston, Texas

Take a vat of oil money, add pressed jeans and a toothy Texas grin, and you've got some mighty fine entertainment after sunset. Club hopping along Washington Avenue is buzzy, unpretentious fun. The city isn't all Stetson-and-spur cowpoke—there's excellent theater and jazz for the artsy crowd, too.

Thessaloniki, Greece

Remember those playful old Grecian mosaics? The spirit's alive and well in the Syngrou/Valaoritou and Ladadika districts, not to mention all those beaches. Thessaloniki has more cafés and bars per capita than any other European city.

Baku, Azerbaijan

Waves of oil money crashed over rough-edged Baku, and what washed up became the coolest bar scene this side of the Caucasus. At the William Shakespeare, expats and Azeris might jump on the counter and get jiggy together; Konti Pub lets you tap beer from barrels above your table.

Fine dining, the start of a night out in oil money–fueled Baku, Azerbaijan's capital

Greece
ATHENS

An ancient Mediterranean capital abuzz with new energy and optimism

The ancient Monastiraki square, home to Byzantine architecture and a modern flea market

VITAL STATS

- **First human habitation at the Acropolis** As many as 9,000 years ago, in Neolithic times

- **Height of Mount Lycabettus, one of the "seven hills of Athens"** 909 feet (277 m).

- **Year Parthenon competed** 438 B.C.

- **Theatrical stages** 148

- **Hottest temperature on record** 18.4°F (48°C), in 1977

- **Percentage of Greece's residents who live in Athens** 35.45

- **Female athletes at the first modern Olympic Games in 1896** 0 (250 men represented 14 nations)

Once the seat of a glittering empire, Athens no longer needs to rest solely on its ancient laurels. Visitors find inspiration in modern museums, a glittery nightlife, and alfresco dining.

À LA CARTE

Of Sweets and Stuffed Grape Leaves

• The *taverna* plays an essential role in Athenian life. The informal eateries serve up traditional dishes like grilled octopus and stuffed grape leaves, often consumed to the joyous rhythms of the bouzouki, a traditional stringed instrument. Try Klimataria (Platia Theatrou 2), which also offers cooking classes. Sholarhio (Tripodon 14, Plaka) serves free halva for dessert. And if you're craving lamb chops, you cannot do better than To Steki tou Ilia (Eptachalkou 5, Thisio).

• The Greek love for desserts is evident everywhere you turn—Athens is dotted with destinations for the honey-soaked nut pastry baklava, sugar-dusted almond cookies called *amigdalota*, and fruit treats known as spoon sweets. Among the best: Varsos (Kassaveti 5 Kifissia), Fresko Yogurt Bar (Dionysiou Areopagitou 3), which also has spoon sweets, and Takis bakery (Misaraliotou 14) with its buttery *koulourakia* twists. ■

Quintessential Greek dining in a *taverna*

The Parthenon

The symbol of ancient Greece, the Parthenon rests on the highest point of the Acropolis, the rocky plateau at the heart of Athens. Commissioned by Pericles as a tremendous monument to the goddess Athena, the temple was completed in 438 B.C. Its most spectacular friezes, the controversial Elgin Marbles, are housed in London's British Museum—and Greece is fighting to get them back. • An immense statue of Athena some four stories tall and made of gold and ivory once stood inside. A Roman copy from circa A.D. 200 is displayed in Athens's National Archaeological Museum. • The temple's columns are subtly curved to create an optical illusion of perfect form. • In the fifth century the temple became a Christian church, and then a mosque in 1458, when the Turks seized the Acropolis and added a minaret. • In 1687, the center of the Parthenon was destroyed when the Venetians bombarded the Acropolis. ■

Orizontes Café offers one
of the best vantages.

From Ancient Wonders to Watches

Artifacts and travelers share space in metro stations.

Traveling on Athens's modern Metro is actually a trip through ancient Greece. While digging new sections of the subway in the 1990s, excavators unearthed extensive archaeological remains such as an ancient bathhouse, metalworking shops, aqueducts, roads, city walls, and cemeteries. Artifacts are displayed behind glass panels at several stations in the city center, including Syntagma and Monastiraki.

Nestled at the foot of the Acropolis is Anafiotika, a delightful, relatively modern village of whitewashed houses and bright blue doors, with narrow lanes keeping out city traffic. Master stonemasons from the island of Anafi who came to Athens for work built it in the 19th century.

Athens's Roman Forum is usually overshadowed by the flashier nearby Ancient Agora, but it contains one of the city's most distinctive landmarks: the Tower of the Winds, an eight-sided marble edifice built to tell time in the first or second century B.C. Each side faces a main compass point. ■

Whitewashed cottages and bougainvillea add to Anafiotika's village charm.

NOVEL INTRODUCTIONS

The Colossus of Maroussi
Henry Miller (1941)
Considered by some the famed American writer's best work, this engaging narrative follows Miller's prewar travels from Athens to Crete and Corfu.

Apartment in Athens
Glenway Wescott (1945)
A searing story of wartime humanity and evil, this novel tells the story of the relationship between a Greek couple and their German soldier neighbor during the city's World War II occupation.

Les Liaisons Culinaires
Andreas Staikos (2000)
Cookbook meets novel in this contemporary Athenian love triangle. Two men compete for love while introducing readers to divine gastronomy in Athens. ■

Kenya
NAIROBI

Kenya's highlands capital of modern metro life and unexpected wildlife

Impressive modernity characterizes Nairobi's skyline.

VITAL STATS

- **Year founded** 1899, as a railway depot

- **Distance from the Equator** 87 miles (140 km)

- **Capacity of a *matatu,* or public taxi/mini-bus** 14 to 24

- **Bird species in Nairobi National Park** Approximately 400

- **Size of the Solar Ice Rink** 15,000 square feet (1,394 sq m), likely the largest rink in Africa

Even before your safari adventure, discover plenty of wildlife and natural beauty amid glass skyscrapers, a colorful shopping scene, and a thriving nightlife.

À LA CARTE

Exotic Barbecue and Nairobi Noshes

• Kenya is known for its *nyama choma*—char-grilled meat, aka Kenyan barbecue. Vegetarians, avert your eyes: The offerings at the renowned The Carnivore Restaurant (Langata Road) include ostrich, crocodile, and camel, which are roasted and carved tableside by servers wearing zebra stripes.

• Not a dish on its own, *ugali* provides a solid accompaniment to flavorful soups and stews. It's made of maize or cassava flour, which is mixed in hot water until it attains a breadlike consistency. (Similar dishes make appearances across the continent, under various names.) Traditionally, it's eaten by hand: You form it into a ball, press a little divot into one side, and scoop up the meat or veggies. ∎

Havens and Cheesemaking

Interspecies bonding at the Giraffe Center

Beyond the famed Nairobi National Park, take a nature walk and feed the giraffes at the lesser known African Fund for Endangered Wildlife Giraffe Center (Duma Road). At nearby David Sheldrick Wildlife Trust (Bogan Gate, Magadi Road), see rescued baby elephants and rhinos from 11 a.m. to noon each day, when they get their daily mud bath.

Located on part of the old Karen Blixen estate, Kazuri Bead Factory (Mbagathi Ridge) manufactures more than five million beads a year, which it exports to more than 30 countries. Visitors can tour the workshop where more than 400 women, most of them single mothers, create handmade necklaces, bracelets, and single beads.

Gouda, cheddar, feta, and Brie are just a few of the aromatic concoctions created at Brown's Cheese Farm on the western outskirts of Nairobi (St. George's Rd., Tigoni). Cows owned by more than 3,000 smallholding farmers in the area produce the milk that goes into 17 kinds of cheese produced at Brown's. Visitors can tour the factory, sample cheese, and literally try their hand at milking or mozzarella making. ∎

The train trip from Nairobi to Mombasa is a safari in itself.

ROME

An ancient city rich with high style and indelible pleasures

The ruins of the Roman Forum, a constant reminder of the empire's former glory

VITAL STATS

- **Coins tossed into the Trevi Fountain** An estimated 1.4 million dollars' worth a year

- **Capacity of the Colosseum** An estimated 50,000

- **Fountains** More than 2,000

- **Churches** More than 900

- **Obelisks** 13, more than any city in the world

My City: Ignazio Marino

There is no shortage of places to love in my city, Rome. It is a place to savor and explore. Of course our museums and archaeological sites are unique worldwide, but simply walking around is an amazing experience in Rome. We are now in the process of making some of the most central streets accessible only to pedestrians, with no cars and no mopeds, including historic, shop-lined Via del Babuino.

Since forever, my favorite place to relax in Rome is one of its parks. I love to take walks at the Villa Borghese in the Pinciano neighborhood, or ride my bicycle. I ride my bicycle daily, almost everywhere. The city is becoming more and more bike-friendly, and lots of new lanes are being built. I also often walk along the magnificent ruins of the ancient Roman aqueducts in Parco degli Acquedotti, off the Via Appia Nuova that runs parallel to the Appian Way.

I prefer tea to coffee, and my preferred spot for a nice blend is Babington's, the renowned British tearoom in Piazza di Spagna. For a glass of wine I usually stop by Spirit, in Piazza della Cancelleria, a tiny but charming place between the Pantheon and Piazza Navona in the Campo de' Fiori. I also frequent nearby Etabli, a rustic chic bar that is always lively. In both places, you can just have a glass of wine or enjoy a meal in a relaxed ambience.

My wife is a great cook and the best place to have a great meal is at home. Still, I have several restaurants I love in Rome. For fresh seafood, I go to Sapore di Mare, near the Pantheon. For big family reunions that include my mother and sisters, we usually gather at Al Vero Girarrosto Toscano, behind Via Veneto near Piazza Federico Fellini outside of Villa Borghese—a favorite of the great Fellini himself, with wonderful traditional Tuscan food that is off the tourist track. Some of the best meals I have ever had in Rome happened in tiny *trattoria* that do not even bear a sign on the entrance door!

Sometimes, for a change, we eat sushi. When it comes to food, even we Romans like to mix it up! My wife and daughter love Zen in the Prati neighborhood, and lately, I've been ordering takeout from one of the Daruma Sushi restaurants that seem to be popping up all over town.

I am not a shopper but I do love books, pens, antiquities, and art. The Via Alibert, leading off of Piazza del Popolo, has one of Rome's best art galleries, Galleria Russo. Nearby, on Via Margutta, I visit Marcello Rocchi, who is a friend and a gifted jewel craftsman. Or, I head to Librerie Arion on the Via Veneto, where I buy most of my books or simply browse the shelves, stacked high to the ceiling.

Ignazio Marino was elected mayor of Rome in 2013. ∎

Fried artichoke hearts are a Jewish Ghetto delicacy

"The traveller, who has contemplated the ruins of ancient Rome, may conceive some imperfect idea of the sentiments which they must have inspired when they reared their heads in the splendor of unsullied beauty."
—Historian Edward Gibbon, in *The History of the Decline and Fall of the Roman Empire* (1776)

Castel Sant'Angelo,
onetime mausoleum, fortress,
and castle, today a museum

Fabulous and (Somewhat) Affordable

Handcrafted gloves at Sermoneta

High Fashion Italian designer shopping is a must in Rome, with every major name having an outpost, if not several, often with better pricing than you'll find at home. Some of the most important shopping streets in central Rome are the *Via Vittorio Veneto, Via del Corso, Via Condotti,* and for offbeat, small-designer goods, the *Via del Boschetto.* Specific shops of note include *Brighenti* (Via Frattina 7–10), a baroque boutique filled with sensual fineries and swimsuits; and gallery cum shop *Spazio IF* (Via dei Coronari 44a), which stocks handmade women's couture. For the gents, *Brioni* (Via Barberini 79) has clothed the likes of James Bond (in the movies) and Clark Gable, and the artisan milliners at *Fratelli Viganò* (Via Marco Minghetti 7) continue to put the finishing touch on classically dressed men.

Must-Haves No one crafts leather goods as well as Italians. Find handmade leather gloves at *Sermoneta,* just off the *Spanish Steps* (Piazza di Spagna, 61). At *Braccialini* (Via Mario Dè Fiori 73), score bright and quirky bags (shaped like a Vespa or a lizard, anyone?). For something sexy and strappy to show off at home, Tuscan designer *Salvatore Ferragamo* has a major shop in Rome, also near the Spanish Steps (Via dei Condotti, 65). Good enough for Fred Astaire's dancing feet, surely the footwear by *A. Testoni* (Via Condotti 80) should give men and women an extra lift in their step, as do high-end classic numbers by *Bruno Magli* (Via Condotti 6). Check out seasonal sales in July and January for the best pricing. ∎

Windows at Salvatore Ferragamo reflect its prime location near the Spanish Steps.

When in Rome: Crispy Artichokes, Pizza, and Gelato

Classic brick oven pizza

• **Artichokes**, or *carciofi*, a delight of Roman cuisine since ancient times, are served fried in olive oil—*Carciofi alla Giudia*, meaning "Jewish-style artichokes"—in the Jewish ghetto or in Trastevere, adjacent neighborhoods across the Tiber River. Served year-round and best in early spring, try them at their crispy finest at Ristorante Piperno (Monte dè Cenci, 9). La Campana (Vicolo della Campana, 18) meanwhile celebrates *Carciofi alla romana* ("Roman style artichokes"), braised in extra-virgin olive oil, garlic, and herbs. Nonna Betta (Via del Portico d'Ottavia, 16) and La Matricianella (Via del Leone, 4) are two other notables.

• What is a trip to Italy without pizza? Though it's a staple originating from Naples and other regions in the southern part of the country, the city excels in *pizza al taglio*, Rome's signature oblong take on the dish, oven-baked in an iron pan. There are too many places to list, but for sure try the crispy, thin-crusted pies at Pinsere Roma (Via Flavia, 98), La Pratolina (Via degli Scipioni, 248), and Forno Campo de' Fiori (Piazza Campo de' Fiori), which specialize in it.

• Creamy, thick gelato cannot simply be called the Italian version of ice cream. One of the best, favored by locals and recently discovered by visitors, is I Caruso (Via Collina, 13–15), with a few branches, including one not far from Termini Station. Il Palazzo del Freddo di Giovanni Fassi (Via Principe Eugenio, 65) is a local classic (with its own Wikipedia entry) with 30 flavors, including unusual selections like rice. ∎

Throwback and 360° Roma

The Vittorio Emanuele II Monument or Altar of the Fatherland (Piazza Venezia) is more than just a pretty photo opp. Venture inside to the Museo Nazionale del Risorgimento Italiano to learn about the city's "modern" history since the 1861 unification period. Check out the rooftop, too, for a spectacular 360-degree view of Rome.

The largest collection of Christmas nativity sets under one roof in the world is in Rome. There are more than 3,000 from dozens of countries in the Museo Tipologico Internazionale Del Presepio (Via Tor Dè Conti, 31), a hard-to-find museum on a tiny street close to the Via Del Imperio.

To see Rome as it might have once looked, head to Museo della Civiltà Romana (Museum of Roman Civilization), at Piazza Agnelli 10 in Esposizione Universale di Roma (EUR), a satellite city built by Mussolini accessible by Metro line B. The museum houses an often-photographed reconstruction of ancient Rome in miniature that dates to the late 1930s and early 1940s. Images of the model are still often used in history books. ∎

Molds and miniature models showcase ancient life at the Museum of Roman Civilization.

The Spanish Steps

All roads may lead to Rome, but for travelers, all routes in Rome lead to the Spanish Steps. This all-eyes-on-the-girl shot was taken in 1971 by someone better known for her work in front of the camera than behind the lens: a disguised Gina Lollobrigida, who was working on *Italia Mia,* one of several photo books she'd publish. "Only after we carefully look at others, which photographs help us to do,

can we truly discover ourselves," said the famed Italian actress.

A man lost in his map at the Spanish Steps completely misses out on the moment. It's classic Martin Parr, the British photographer who traveled the world capturing travelers in the act of traveling. "My photographs have a critical bite to them," said Parr, whose pictures of travelers fill the books *Small World* and *The Last Resort.* ■

California
SAN FRANCISCO

Laid-back yet ambitious, a perennial boomtown bent on reinvention

Eye-popping "painted ladies" and a skyscraping skyline embody San Francisco's diversity.

VITAL STATS

- **Average apartment rental** $2,898 a month for a one-bedroom, the most expensive in the United States

- **Highest point in the city** Mount Davidson at 938 feet (286 m)

- **Number of cable cars in service** 40, operating on 8.8 miles (14 km) of track

- **Fog signals around San Francisco Bay** 32

- **Steepest hill** Filbert Street between Leavenworth and Hyde streets (31.5 percent grade)

Condense time-honored Victorian homes, approximately 400 food trucks, hundreds of multistarred restaurants on Yelp, ambitious Internet entrepreneurs, and old-time hippies onto a 49-square-mile (127 sq km) peninsula. You have San Francisco, an inimitable hub of creativity blessed with a breathtaking bay, towering woods, and atmospheric fog.

SHOPPING CART

The Best Beat Books

Book Smart Honor San Francisco's proud literary heritage. Pick up volumes of poetry **and** "HOWL if you love City Lights" bumper stickers at *City Lights Bookstore* (261 Columbus Ave.), the symbol of the beat movement, founded in 1953 by Lawrence Ferlinghetti, that continues to publish its own imprint. Campy, vintage pulp fiction fills *KAYO Books* (814 Post St.); *Omnivore Books on Food* (3885 Cesar Chavez St) has comprehensive food and wine books signed by the area's chefs—appropriate for a city that revolutionized American cuisine. In the countercultural hotbed of the Haight, *Booksmith* (1644 Haight St.) champions local authors with frequent readings. ■

Treats From the Market to the Mission

Veggie wrap

• In the city that started America's fresh food movement, the Ferry Building Marketplace (1 Ferry Building) on the Embarcadero is also a feast of the region's best producers: Acme bread, Cowgirl Creamery cheeses, Hog Island oysters, Frog Hollow Farm preserves, Blue Bottle coffee, and Recchiuti chocolates. Saturdays, it's home to one of the country's most irresistible farmers markets.

• California cuisine, defined by its diverse local produce and can-do attitude, is omnipresent in the city's vibrant dining scene. Chef Melissa Perello's meticulous yet gentle Frances (3870 17th St.), eclectic dishes served dim sum-style at State Bird Provisions (1529 Fillmore St), elevated organic fares at Coi (373 Broadway St.), and thoughtfully crafted plates at Parallel 37 (600 Stockton St.) are among the notables. Some credit the humble roast chicken at Zuni Café (1658 Market St.) for initiating the now world-famous San Francisco cuisine.

• There are Mexican burritos, and then there are Mission burritos. Spanish rice, beans, salsa, avocado, cheese, sour cream, and stewed chicken, grilled beef, barbecued pork, or shredded pork are all wrapped in a large flour tortilla and a swath of tinfoil for what no less an appetite than Calvin Trillin called "two or three perfect rolled-up meals." Everyone has a favorite taqueria. Start your search in the Mission at Papalote (3409 24th St. and 1777 Fulton St.), La Espiga de Oro (2916 24th St.), or Taqueria Can-Cún (3211 Mission Street). ■

Cheesemongers and other artisans commingle in the Ferry Building Marketplace.

Looking out on the
San Francisco Bay
from North Beach

THE BEST
Eco-Smart Cities

Innovation makes these urban hubs astonishing models of the future.

Songdo, South Korea

Songdo, South Korea

This über-wired suburb of Seoul has no need for garbage trucks: All household waste is sucked from individual kitchens through a huge underground network of tunnels to processing centers, where it's automatically sorted, treated, and deodorized.

Freiburg, Germany

Berkeley, California

Highly developed recycling services absorb more than three-quarters of the city's waste (2020 target: 100 percent). As the city council say, if something cannot be recycled, it should be restricted, redesigned, or removed from production.

Freiburg, Germany

This bright city has revolved around the sun since 1986, when the local government voted to focus on solar power as its main energy source. Today it boasts more than 1,700 solar installations on public buildings, and at least 100 solar businesses, making it a darling of renewable-energy fans.

Masdar City, UAE

Driverless electric "pods" whiz residents underneath this low-carbon, enviro utopia on the desert fringe of Abu Dhabi. Wafer-thin solar panels create both energy and shade, and it's never too hot: A wind tower standing 148 feet (45 m) channels a perpetual breeze through the streets.

Wind energy

Santander, Spain

In this high-tech coastal city with 12,000 hidden sensors, smartphone apps not only let you call up store specials, surfing conditions, and dumpster levels, but also upload the latest pothole locations. When no one's around, street lamps dim on their own.

Frankfurt, Germany

Home to the world's first "green" skyscraper (the 57-floor Commerzbank tower), this banking hub holds the European record for the number of ultra-low-energy, superinsulated "passive" buildings: 1,000.

Malmö

Malmö, Sweden

In this southern Swedish city, the so-called "City of Tomorrow" is Europe's first carbon-neutral neighborhood. The 600-home development collects warm summer rainwater in a thermal aquifer and pumps it up with wind energy to heat homes in winter. The city has also established minimum standards for green space in new projects.

Copenhagen, Denmark

The Danish capital not only has an offshore wind farm but also more bikes than you can shake a spoke at. Space-age complex 8Tallet—a figure eight of nearly 500 sustainable apartments—boasts a grassy insulating roof, precise layouts to maximize sunlight and ventilation, and a ramp to walk (or cycle) from ground floor to penthouse.

Vancouver, Canada

In Canada's third largest city, wastewater and raw sewage are converted to energy for apartments in the onetime industrial district. To heat their high-rises, occupants just need to pull the plug in their bathtub or kitchen sink, sending wastewater spiraling into the eco-utility plant.

Reykjavík, Iceland

Iceland is famous for its breathtaking scenery, geysers, and Blue Lagoon—and its sophisticated use of renewable energy. Hydrogen buses roam the streets of the capital, which generates all its power by tapping hydro- and geothermal resources at the island's volcanic roots.

Iceland's geothermal Blue Lagoon

DAKAR

A heady brew of color and spice at the crossroads of French-African culture

The coastal city draws on the Atlantic for its excellent seafood dishes like *cheb-ou-jen.*

VITAL STATS

- **Year of independence from France** 1960

- **French expatriates living in Dakar** An estimated 20,000

- **African cultural objects on display at the Musée Théodore Monod d'Art Africain** More than 9,000

- **Height of the minaret of Dakar Grand Mosque** 20 feet (67 m)

- **Cost of controversial African Renaissance Monument, the tallest statue in Africa** $27.2 million

- **Number of official languages** 5 (French, Wolof, Pulaar, Jola, and Mandinka)

O nce the hub of the transatlantic slave trade, Dakar blends French colonial roots and modern African spirit into an alluring peninsular city of towering high-rises and teeming markets, African drumbeats, and the muezzin's call to prayer.

À LA CARTE

Savory Cheb Joints and Dibiteries

• *Cheb-ou-jen,* a traditional Wolof rice dish, is the hallmark of Senegalese food. It's frequently made with both fresh and dried fish, sea snails, and vegetables seasoned with chili peppers. In Dakar, look for "cheb" joints—small, makeshift kitchens consisting of a huge iron cauldron resting on a brush or wood-burning fire. Le Djembe (56 Rue St-Michel) and Keur N'Deye (68 Rue Vincens) are popular local restaurants serving fresh cheb.

• Small butcher stalls found in the food markets called *dibiteries* serve freshly barbecued lamb, beef, or liver kebabs with bread and pepper sauce. If street food isn't your thing, try the *dibi* at Le Seoul II (75 Rue Amadou Assane Ndoye).

• Sample one of the many Senegalese dishes that use millet flour as the base including *chakri* (steamed millet balls eaten with sweetened yogurt), simple *lakh* (millet porridge), or the dessert *ngalakh* (millet, peanut paste, and baobab fruit sweetened with orange flower water). ∎

The Dakar Arts: From Folk to Abstract

A Senegalese sculptor

Marché Madness Head to the sprawling *Marché Sandaga* (Avenue Pompidou and Avenue du Président Lamine Guèye) for handicrafts produced by the Wolof, Senegal's largest ethnic group. Wood carving is a Wolof specialty. Figures carved out of mahogany are polished black or brown and are sometimes decorated with ivory, cattle tails, horns, or feathers. Striking Wolof pottery is formed from red clay with black or white patterns. Another good place to search for Wolof wares is the seaside *Village Artisanal de Soumbédioune* (Route de la Corniche Ouest).

Glass Paintings Frequently depicting village life or street scenes, *souwere* are bright, colorful pictures painted on the reverse side of a pane of glass. The craft likely began as a folk art introduced by Lebanese and Moroccan merchants in the late 19th and early 20th centuries. *La Galerie Antenna* (9 Rue Félix Faure) and *Le Village des Arts* (Patte d'oies off Route de l'Aéroport) creative cooperatives are a few of the places that showcase local souwere artists.

Cast in Stone Dakar has a wealth of volcanic pumice stone. Artists sculpt the soft, gray-brown stones into human figures or abstract works. Find them in outdoor workshops along the city's Western Corniche. ∎

NOVEL INTRODUCTIONS

God's Bits of Wood
Sembène Ousmane (1960) Ousmane worked as a bricklayer and mechanic in Dakar before he became the father of African cinema. His most famous novel portrays the 1947–1948 strike at the Dakar-Niger railway, detailing the African workers' struggles for equal compensation against their French employers.

Race to Dakar
Charley Boorman (2008) Actor and motorcycle enthusiast Boorman recounts his wild adventures racing from Lisbon to Dakar in the annual Dakar Rally, one of the most challenging races in the world.

Sahara
Michael Palin (2002) The Monty Python alum cracks jokes and shares humorous experiences on his travels around the Sahara while filming a documentary, including his stimulating encounter with Dakar nightlife. ∎

Bright colors and pastoral subjects characterize *souwere,* the Wolof term for reverse glass painting.

Portugal
LISBON

A charming European capital of cobbled streets, bright trams, and modern enticements

The Castelo de Sao Jorge presides over the impossibly charming Alfama, the city's oldest barrio.

Visually stunning, Lisboa tumbles over seven hills and down to the banks of the Tagus, bathed in clear Atlantic light. Its laid-back, Old World charm marries perfectly with bustling, New World vibrancy.

SHOPPING CART

Irresistible Decorations . . . and Sardines

Glazed and Gorgeous Famed Portuguese *azulejo* (glazed tile) is ubiquitous in Lisbon, decorating facades, church, palace interiors, and even metro stations. For affordable imitations try any souvenir shop, but for the genuine 17th- or 18th-century article, head to *Solar* (Rua Dom Pedro V 70), where tiles are stacked according to their age. For quality copies and original decorative panels, try the factory shop of *Azulejos Sant'Anna* (Rua do Alecrim 95). In business since 1741, their tiles are all handmade, and they are happy to arrange shipping.

Sardine Run Sardines get plenty of love in Lisbon. Cans in 125 different varieties , including sardine egg caviar and mousses, can be picked up at the *Conserveira de Lisboa* (Rua dos Bacalhoeiros, 34). The tiny bar *Sol e Pesca* (Rua Nova do Carvalho 44) sells canned sardines in a rainbow of colors. ■

Portuguese *azulejo* tile

Tower of Belém

Constructed from locally quarried, Lioz limestone, this luminescent tower stands as a legacy of Portugal's age of discovery. Its function has varied over the last 500 years, but as it perches graciously on the northern banks of the Tagus, its emblematic status as one of the country's best loved Portuguese Gothic monuments remains • The four-story tower was built between 1514 and 1520 as part of the city's defenses. • Originally built on a rocky island just off shore, coastal development later joined it to the mainland. • The tower has served as garrison, prison, customs house, telegraph post, and lighthouse in its long history. • The tower was the departing point for many of the voyages of discovery. • In 1983, it was designated as a World Heritage site and one of the Seven Wonders of Portugal in 2007. • Don't miss the statue of Our Lady of Safe Homecoming—meant to protect seafarers—and the rhinoceros carving, the first of such an animal in western European art. ■

The Belém Tower harks back to Portugal's heyday as a great seafaring nation.

Port City Pleasures: Seafood and Soufflées

Shellfish are the highlight of _cervejaria_ menus.

• Per capita the Portuguese eat more fish than any other nationality , and its *cervejarias,* or beer halls, cater to discerning seafood eaters. For the best lobster and prawns, head north of the center to Cervejaria Ramiro (Av. Almirante Reis, 1) or Cervejaria Trindade (Rua Nova de Trindade, 20c), known for its seafood as well as its atmospheric azulejo tile interior. For a modern twist, try hip Sea Me (Rua do Loreto, 21), where sushi meets Portuguese fish, such as smoked sardines and mackerel.

• Above all, Portuguese prize *bacalhau,* codfish preserved dry with salt. Rub shoulders with locals at no-frills Tasca do Jaime Rua (Sao Pedro, 40), which serves excellent *pastéis de bacalhau,* deep-fried codfish balls, to the soulful melodies of live Portuguese *fado* music. The soufflé-like *bacalhau espiritual* is worth the 45-minute wait at Cozinha Velha (Largo do Palácio). Tiny Ti Natercia Restaurante (Rua das Escolas Gerais, 54) serves up homey dishes, including *bacalhau folhado,* a pastry of cod, cream, and red pepper.

• The humble *taberna,* or tavern, is back, boasting good grub and delightful décors. Sprawling 1300 Taberna (Rua Rodrigues de Faria 103) does younger takes on Portuguese staples like lamb, duck, and, of course, fish. Taberna Tosca (Praça de São Paulo, 21) excels in the *petiscos,* or the Portuguese answer to tapas, as does Taberna Ideal (Rua da Esperança, 112). ∎

The cavernous 1300 Taberna is known for its refreshing updates to traditional Portuguese cuisine.

Admire the tiled roofs of Alfama from the terrace of the Santa Luzia church.

Washington
SEATTLE

A stimulating brew of wired and outdoorsy, booming and down-to-earth

In summer, weekly "beer can races" fill Lake Union with sailboats and their often costume-clad crews.

VITAL STATS

- **City-owned parks and open space areas** 5,003 acres (2,205 ha), or a bit over 10 percent of the total land area

- **First mobile espresso cart** 1980, under the monorail

- **Houseboats** Approximately 500, compared with more than 2,000 in the 1930s

- **Readers** 80 percent of Seattleites have library cards, the highest rate in the United States

- **Cloudy days** 226 a year

- **Starbucks** 23 per every 100,000 people, the highest rate in the United States

- **The Evergreen Point Bridge** 1.4 miles (2.3 km), the world's longest floating bridge

The city that never dries is among the most educated and active—not to mention caffeinated—in the world. A new, post-Microsoft generation of growing tech start-ups is transforming this evergreen town into a world-class hub of creativity.

LOCAL SECRETS

Wet and Weird

The Fremont neighborhood is a self-declared "Center of the Universe," and no invasion of start-up cash can erase the neighborhood's weirdness. A 1950s rocket stands atop a building, emblazoned with the neighborhood's motto, "De Libertas Quirkas" (Freedom to be Peculiar). Under a bridge at 36th Street is a giant cement troll, clutching a Volkswagen Beetle. Six aluminum people (and an aluminum dog) await a trolley that never arrives at a former streetcar stop. It's best to just amble about, taking in the neighborhood's idiosyncratic vibe.

Despite its generally cool weather, Seattle actually has a few popular beaches, like Ballard's Golden Gardens and West Seattle's Alki Beach, which affords terrific vistas of the city's skyline. If you don't want to jostle for your own piece of sand, there is a secret beach. At low tide, a shellfish-studded stretch of shore appears near the Shilshole Bay Marina. You can only get there by a kayak. ∎

Golden Gardens Park

The Space Needle

The Space Needle, built for the 1962 World's Fair, is at once a relic of history and an homage to the bright future. Once the tallest structure west of the Mississippi, the 605-foot (184 m) tower is a graceful and unmistakable symbol for a city that dares to think ahead of its time. • The construction took just over a year, earning it the moniker "The 400 Day Wonder." • The tower grows up to an inch (25 mm) on a hot day. • Three years after the Space Needle's completion, a strong earthquake shook Seattle. The Needle's only reported problem was water sloshing out of the toilets, as it can withstand up to 9.1-scale earthquakes without damage. • It's 848 steps from the basement to the top, or a 43-second elevator ride. • The plan to build a stork's nest on top was abandoned, as storks cannot live in Seattle's damp climate. ∎

Seattle's Pike Place Market,
cornucopia of Northwest produce

Seattle Tastes: Pacific Bounty

A city for coffee hounds

• Is there such a thing as Seattle cuisine? Marrying abundant natural ingredients with pan-Pacific flavors, the food of Seattle is healthy and unique. **Spur** (113 Blanchard St.) adds gastropub impulses to Northwest outdoorsiness. (Think sockeye salmon crostini.) The supper club **Sutra** (1605 N. 45th St.) serves sumptuous five-course vegetarian feasts that make the most of the state's fauna, and **The Walrus and the Carpenter** (4743 Ballard Ave.) playfully elevates the region's bounty, like scallop tartare and seasoned pea vines. To eat like a local, order humble teriyaki: Seattle's de facto official lunch is everywhere, especially on youthful University Avenue.

• You're never far from the water so it follows you'll find amazing seafood. Stop for happy hour at **Elliott's Oyster House** (1201 Alaskan Way), where you'll find freshly shucked shellfish galore. Roll up your sleeves and dig into buckets of clams at **Etta's** (2020 Western Ave.). Flash-fried in various sauces, Cantonese-style Dungeness crab takes the spotlight at **Sea Garden** (509 7th Ave. S.) in the International District. Try sashimi of geoduck (pronounced gooey-duck), an elephant trunk-shaped clam native to the region, at **Shiro's** (2401 2nd Ave.). **Tanglewood Supreme** (3216 W. Wheeler St.) offers seasonal delicacies like weathervane scallops or albacore loin. ∎

Briny bivalves, the fruit of the Pacific

NOVEL INTRODUCTIONS

Indian Killer
Sherman Alexie (1996)
Part thriller, part social critique, this chilling novel by one of the most celebrated local writers follows a chain of serial murders taking place in Seattle.

The Other
David Guterson (2008)
Old-school Seattle before the Internet boom provides a nostalgic backdrop for this story of friendship between a hermit and his childhood buddy.

Hotel on the Corner of Bitter and Sweet
Jamie Ford (2009)
A relic from the 1940s unveils a story of friendship and betrayal in Seattle's Japantown during World War II.

Where'd You Go, Bernadette
Maria Semple (2012)
When an insufferable transplant from California goes missing, her daughter embarks on a comic journey to find her in this scathing satire of Seattle. ∎

Minnesota

MINNEAPOLIS

A friendly, inviting Midwest hub and the cultural capital of the Plains

The photogenic shores of Lake Calhoun are a natural attraction for walkers and joggers.

VITAL STATS

- **Parks** 170 covering 5,542 acres (2,243 ha), ranking no. 1 in U.S. cities with best green space

- **Year Walker Art Center established** 1927, the oldest public art gallery in the upper Midwest

- **Stores in the Mall of America (in Minneapolis suburb Bloomington)** More than 520

- **Number of lakes** 22

- **Driving distance to the center of sister city, St. Paul** 14.1 miles (16 km)

- **Miles of Skyway** 8 (13 km)

Quality of life ranks high in this upper Midwest center, which boasts top-notch theater companies, sports teams, and a thriving art scene. Residents love skating, biking, and kayaking around their city whenever possible.

LOCAL SECRETS

Urban Boating and Artsy Outings

The mighty Mississippi River starts its long wind to the Gulf of Mexico in Minnesota, offering visitors a chance to paddle the famed waterway through the middle of a city. Urban outfitter Above the Falls Sports (120 3rd Ave. N.) provides boats and guides for a leisurely Minneapolis kayak trip.

The city's renowned Walker Art Center (1750 Hennepin Ave.) is definitely worth a visit, but there are tons of lesser known artsy nooks and crannies. Check out The House of Balls (212 3rd Ave. N, Suite 108) where you can touch the sculptures and offer comments. Once you're inspired, make some art yourself: Mold glass at Potekglass (2205 California St., NE), where torch and safety glasses are included. ∎

A Midwest Hub of Global—and Homegrown—Eats

Sushi on Eat Street, the city's aptly named dining district

• What you might know as a casserole is what Minnesotans call a *hotdish.* A favorite variation: the Tater Tot hotdish. For a fancy take on this staple, head to the punny Haute Dish (119 Washington Ave. N.), whose "Tater Tot Hautedish" features additional ingredients—porcini, short rib, and green beans—sure to please foodies. Also try their "Meatloaf in a Can," which comes with mushroom gravy, veggies, and "mashers."

• Forget the stereotypes about bland midwestern food. Minneapolis is a global melting pot, as a walk down Eat Street shows. The 17-block commercial district, centered on Nicollet Avenue in South Minneapolis, attracts visitors drawn to cheap flavorful dining, with German, Greek, Malaysian, Caribbean, Japanese, Tibetan, and Vietnamese cuisine all on offer. For an unforgettable ethnic eating experience, visit nearby Safari Express in the Midtown Global Market (920 E. Lake St.), for an American take on a East African delicacy: a burger made with camel meat and served with fries. ■

Nicollet Avenue is lined with popular eateries, including Icehouse.

Make It, After All
The Mary Tyler Moore Show, the hit 1970s TV sitcom about a single, Minneapolis TV reporter, immortalized the city. Even today, fans mimic the actress's joyous opening-sequence hat toss, immortalized in a downtown bronze statue (700 Nicollet Mall), or visit 2104 Kenwood Parkway, the house where Mary supposedly lived for the first five years of the show.

Final Curtain
Pay tribute to circus and carnival workers at Showmen's Rest, a Lakewood Cemetery section for veterans of the outdoor entertainment industry. The monument's epitaph says it all: "No Ferris wheel with circling lights, glitters across the quiet nights. Bird music has replaced the sound, of barker's calls and merry-go-rounds. Tent canvas folded, stored away, steeps in no sun for us, this day."

Insanely Quiet
The anechoic chamber at Orfield Labs absorbs 99.9 percent of sound, making it the quietest place in the world, according to *Guinness World Records.* The room's background noise measures below the minimum sound human ears are capable of processing and is so disorienting that few people can tolerate the silence for more than 45 minutes. For tour information, email *info@ orfieldlabs.com.* ■

HAVANA

An artsy, soulful, and strikingly enchanting Caribbean capital

Thanks to building ordinances in the 19th and 20th centuries, much of the baroque and neoclassical physique of Old Havana remains intact.

VITAL STATS

- **Number of classic American cars** An estimated 60,000 that pre-date the 1960 U.S. embargo

- **Ice cream served** More than 25,000 customers a day at Coppelia, the "cathedral" of Cuban ice cream, where a scoop costs only four cents

- **Number of statues featuring the visage of Fidel Castro** 0

My City: Iliam Suárez

I can deal with airport stress—the long check-in lines, lockstep marches to connecting flights, and claustrophobia—all for the pleasure of being transported to new places and exposed to different cultures. Today, I'm returning. Hours, planes, fascination, connecting flights, check-in, stress, and a question: Why am I going back? Havana provokes addictive uncertainties in me . . .

The taxi zigzags along Avenida Boyeros, and I count and recount the homes where multiple generations of us coexist among the ordinary, like the *paladares* serving Cuban-style food for Cubans. These humble family businesses are in every neighborhood—more a draw for the thrifty than those seeking delicacies. If exquisiteness is your goal, my suggestions are La Guarida (Centro Habana) or Atelier (Vedado).

Midnight: Time for nicotine and a bar! I debate between Bohemio (Vedado), Madrigal (Vedado), or El Chanchullero (Habana Vieja). Bohemio wins! Oyá (the Yoruba goddess of the wind) blows through its open doors, and I can light up my H. Upmann cigar without bothering my neighbors who, amid their rum and cocktails, cheerfully, loudly announce an off-line cultural calendar. (Oh, Internet, how I miss thee! The bad taste of reentry emerges.) They clue me in: Various jazz musicians are playing at the Teatro Mella (Vedado); Danza Contemporánea de Cuba is performing at the Teatro Nacional (Plaza de la Revolución); and Ezequiel Suárez is opening at Galería Habana (Vedado). I throw in a fantasy: an I.A. (an electronic music duo I co-founded) concert at the Museo Nacional de Bellas Artes (Habana Vieja), but instead I motion for the check.

Home again, strolling along the Malecón, one of the world's most beautiful roads. Ocean air! Havana is best summed up cruising along the Malecón—but walking it is even better than driving. Archetypically Cuban, the seawall holds our island idiosyncrasies like it does the salt from the sea. It's also home to all types of architecture, sounds, smells, parks, monuments, hotels, stores, fishermen, musicians, lovers, cafés such as Café Neruda (Centro Habana), and arts and crafts markets that draw tourists and Cubans such as Feria de San José (Habana Vieja). Plus, the Malecón is a gateway for those who don old sneakers to navigate the craggy reef for a dip along "the Coast" (Playa), or swim barefoot at El Mégano beach (Playas del Este). The Malecón ends at Calle 20, tempting us to head uphill and collapse into a tree-shaded hammock at the Cuba Libro literary café and English-language bookstore (Vedado).

The taxi driver looks at me and asks if I'm Cuban. "Yes!" I admit. He tells me that he's a 57-year-old lawyer from Camagüey. "First time you've traveled?" "No," I answer. "Whenever I pick up a Cuban at the airport, I ask, 'Why did you come back?'" We already know why. Still, I ask, "How much do I owe?"

Iliam Suárez is a Cuban actress, film editor, and co-creator of I.A., a Cuban electronic music duo. She is conceptual, artistic, and musical director of Cuba's annual Pro-electrónica Festival. ∎

Playas del Este, less touristy than other Cuban beaches

"You have collected images of old balconies and shady corners of the ancient city . . . The moment has come for the visitor to set off through the streets and neighborhoods, embarking on their own discovery of the city."
—Swiss novelist Alejo Carpentier, who was raised in Havana (1939)

ICON

The Malecón

The Malecón is often the first (and last) place visited on any Cuba trip. The pull of Havana's seawall is irresistible, no matter where you hail from or how you roll: the exile after decades abroad; the first-time tourist; or lovers entwined on a hot summer's night. After 40 years away, journalist Martha Gellhorn said: "The first morning in Havana, I stood by the Malecón, feeling weepy with homesickness for this city." • It's nearly 5 miles (8 km) long. • Cuban-designed, but American-built, it was started in 1901 and finished in 1959. • For an eight-block stretch, the Malecón is called Avenida Washington—a holdover from prerevolution days when the U.S. Embassy was located here. • Nicknames for the seawall include "Havana's sofa" and "silver lamé." • Surging waves frequently crash over the wall in the winter, forcing closure of the seaside road. • Fishing, kissing, flirting, and music making vie for favorite pastimes on the Malecón. ∎

When in Havana: Cigars, Rum, & Rumbas

Havana staples—rum and cigars

Have a Cigar Cuba's world-class Habanos can be bought at the **Real Fábrica de Tabacos Partagás,** which offers tours (Industria #520, between Barcelona & Dragones); **Casa de Habano,** with a cozy bar/smoking lounge (5ta Avenida & Calle 16); and in the mobster-era **Hotel Riviera** (Paseo, corner Malecón). Everyone but serious aficionados will find the one-peso (four-cent) cigars sold at cafeterias like **Café Hatuey** (corner of Avenida 41 and Calle 10) an acceptable smoke.

Rum It Up Cuba is also known for its rum. Although Havana Club enjoys brand recognition, the smoothest, tastiest mainstream rum is Santiago. Have a tour and taste of Cuba's leading rums at the **Museo del Ron** (Avenida del Puerto #262), or head straight to the market in **Dos Gardenias** (7ma Avenida, corner Calle 28) for a wide selection. For fun, try Cuba's popular rotgut rum, Planchao, sold in individual Tetra-Pak boxes everywhere.

Sounds of the City Havana is a wholly musical town. Bring that tropical soundtrack home with CDs purchased at **La Habana Sí** (Calle L, corner Calle 23), the **Album** music store in the Casa de la Música Miramar (Calle 20 #3308, corner Calle 35), where CDs are also sold dirt cheap, or the **duty-free shop** (José Martí International Airport, Terminal 3), more expensive but with an impressive selection. ■

Musical notes fill the city, from acoustic street tunes to world-class performances at the Gran Teatro de la Habana.

Cuban Comfort Food and Ethnic Eats

Flavor-packed *ropa vieja* in tortillaspies

• Savvy travelers know the best meal deals in town are *cajitas*—"little boxes" packed with rice, salad, and your choice of protein (pork, chicken, shrimp, or fish). Dig into a $1 to $3 meal at Las Dueñas (Calle 19 #1102, between Calles 14 & 16) or El Chanchullo (Calle 17 #1357, between Calles 24 & 26).

• Traditional Cuban dishes including *ropa vieja*, tamales, and roast pork with yucca are known as *comida criolla*. It's deceptively simple food that's easy to botch, but you won't go wrong at lovely Doña Eutimia (Callejón del Chorro #60-C) or El Buganvil (Calle 190 #1501, between Calles 15 & 17)—with 24 hours' notice (and a big group), they'll do spit-roasted pork with all the trimmings.

• When you get tired of rice, beans, pork, and pizza, head to one of Havana's new ethnic restaurants. El Beduino (Calle 5 #607, between Calles 4 & 6) serves authentic falafel, tabbouleh, and the like in a trompe l'oeil Middle Eastern oasis, while Los Compadres (Calle 66A, corner Avenida 41) specializes in upscale Mexican food; grab one of the rooftop tables at sunset for added atmosphere. ■

Hidden Havana: Romance, Art, and R&R

Paris, Venice—some cities are synonymous with romance, and Havana has moved many to propose matrimony. You can make it extra memorable in the coral and shell labyrinth of the Jardín Japonés (Malecón & Calle 22); over a bottle of wine in the bathtub for two at darling Café Fortuna (3ra, corner Calle 28); or sitting side by side, beholding the Havana skyline from the viewing platform of the lighthouse at El Morro (across Havana Bay).

You cannot turn over a rock without discovering six artists, and Havana embodies the axiom with open studios throughout the city. For fantastic renderings of Cuban "apostle" José Martí, make a beeline for Estudio 5 (Compostela #5, between Cuarteles & Chacón), working space of painter/sculptor Kamyl Bullaudy Rodríguez. One-stop appreciation of a handful of the city's most talented artists, including the inimitable Ernesto Rancaño, can be had at La Mina Galleries (Calle Oficios #6, corner Obispo).

Certain parts of Havana—Cerro, Centro Habana—are the definitive "concrete jungle." For some shade and quiet, head to magical Parque Almendares (Avenida 41 & Calle 49C) for rowing on the river or a forest trek; Parque Ecológico Monte Barreto (7ma Avenida & Calle 70), with pony rides and picnic spots; and Parque Lenin (Calzada de Bejucal, Arroyo Naranjo) that has it all: a rodeo, horseback riding, barbecue pits, and a zoo. ■

The sun-bleached Castillo El Morro guards the entrance to Havana Bay.

La Bodeguita del Medio's famous visitors, Hemingway included, are honored on the bar's memorabilia-packed walls.

Oceanfront Cities

Glittering seascapes provide both the backdrop and the beat of these waterfront urban meccas.

Tallinn, Estonia's old town

Tallinn, Estonia

From its picturesque perch on the Baltic, this is one of the most intact medieval towns in Europe. Visitors love to wander Old Town and explore Lennusadam Seaplane Harbour, an interactive maritime museum with ships and a submarine to explore.

Tel Aviv, Israel

Tel Aviv, Israel

There's plenty of room for beach bathing in this modern Israeli city on the Mediterranean. The historic port of Jaffa has found new life in recent years with a vibrant gallery, café, and restaurant scene.

Durban, South Africa

The continent's busiest seaport blends African and Indian cultures and influences in its beaches, restaurants, and spectacular seaside promenades.

St. John's, Canada

With Irish folk music floating from seafront bars, Newfoundland's largest city feels more like Dublin. But when icebergs float into the harbor and whales spout offshore, the city struts its own frontier personality.

Portland, Maine

This lively but laid-back city boasts both top-end galleries and waterfront lobster shacks. But perhaps nothing speaks to its nautical heritage more than the postcard-ready Portland Head Light, authorized by George Washington.

Perth, Australia

Western Australia's largest city sits on the edge of the continent, taking full advantage of its Indian Ocean roost. From Marmion Marine Park, it's easy to spot Australian sea lions, bottlenose dolphins, and migrating humpback whales.

The Pacific rolls onto the San Diego shore

San Diego, California

While surfers hit Pacific Beach for some of the best wave riding this side of Maui, others wander the boardwalk, stopping at shacks for fresh fish tacos. A bit south, cruise ship visitors wander a strikingly clean downtown and tour the 1945 World War II U.S.S. *Midway*, the country's long-serving aircraft carrier.

Marseille, France

This historic port city has long served as a crossroads between continents, a case made by its stunning new Museum of European and Mediterranean Civilisations, a giant box covered with latticework. Rooftop seating offers views of the passing parade of yachts heading out to sea.

Vladivostok, Russia

Russia's remote window to the Far East is home to the country's Pacific Fleet, which visitors can see while walking along Golden Horn Bay. It's also the terminus for the famed Trans-Siberia Railway, which links it to distant Moscow, more than 5,000 miles (8,047 km) away.

Brisbane, Australia

Laid-back Brizzie offers the best of both worlds: a sophisticated global city with easy access to beaches, rain forests, and even the world's first koala preserve. Visitors cruise the Brisbane River, explore the South Bank parklands, and take in the cosmopolitan panorama on the towering Story Bridge climb.

North Stradbroke Island, a popular holiday jaunt just across Raby Bay from waterfront Brisbane

Oregon
PORTLAND

A buzzing Pacific Northwest city and capital of quirky

Rowers glide across the Willamette River.

VITAL STATS

- **Breweries** 53

- **Volcanoes** 1 within the city limits, although it's dormant

- **Percentage of bike commuters** 6, the highest proportion in the United States

- **Bridges crossing the Willamette and Columbia Rivers** 12 (as of the end of 2015)

- **Percentage of waste Portlanders recycle** 63, one of the highest rates in the nation

- **Varieties planted in International Rose Test Garden** More than 500

With fleets of food trucks, slacker-filled coffee shops, and a happy hipster mind-set, Portland gets the last laugh with a quality of life that emphasizes enjoying the day—and not taking it too seriously.

SHOPPING CART

Indie and Craftsy, Portland-Style

Indie Spirit Portlanders follow their own path, instinctively steering clear of national retailers. *Powell's City of Books* (1005 W. Burnside St.) is an extreme example, the world's largest independent bookstore with more than a million volumes. At the other extreme is *Annie Bloom's Books* (7834 SW Capitol Hwy.), a cozy little neighborhood shop with a helpful staff, comfortable chairs for browsing, and the requisite cat. For indie sounds, check out *Mississippi Records* (4007 N. Mississippi Ave.), a vinyl shop with its own label specializing in local artists.

Get Crafty A pioneer in the DIY movement, Portland indulged its creative side long before anyone had heard of Etsy. The *Oregon College of Art and Craft shop* (8245 SW Barnes Rd.) features cutting-edge designs from faculty, students, and alumni. Along with jewelry and photography, you can find fiber, handmade books, and multimedia works. ■

Bodacious Donuts and Chill Brews

• Maybe it's fueled by late-night carousing, but Portlanders love their donuts. Voodoo Doughnut (22 SW Third Ave.) launched the national trend for whacky circular treats. The shop has been churning out maple bacon– and Cap'n Crunch–flavored versions for more than a decade, 24 hours a day. Its signature treat: a voodoo doll donut filled with blood-red raspberry jelly, complete with a pretzel-stick stake. Other shops have their own take. Blue Star Donuts (1237 SW Washington St.) offers a fried chicken donut, and a crème brûlée one served with a shot of Cointreau. Pip's Original (4750 NE Freemont St.) keeps things (relatively) simple with a glazed honey and sea salt confection.

Voodoo Doll doughnut

• In a city with more than 50 craft brewers, your favorite spot will depend on your taste. IPA or lager? Stout or pilsner? Commons (1810 SE 10th Ave.) has eight brews on tap in its tasting room; Gigantic (5224 SE 26th Ave.) features a lounge, and growlers are available; and Upright (240 N. Broadway) serves up French- and Belgian-inspired farmhouse brews. Wine lovers are in luck, too. Oregon's famous young vintners from the Willamette Valley have brought their craft to the city. Southeast Wine Collective (2425 SE 35th Pl.) offers tastings of the latest vintages with movie nights. ∎

Willamette Valley wines are up for the tasting in downtown Portland.

ODDITIES

A Pretty Penny
This Oregon 'burg owes its names to the flip of a coin. Two city founders, Asa Lovejoy and Francis Pettygrove, wanted to name the settlement after their hometowns, Boston, Massachusetts, or Portland, Maine, respectively. The disagreement was finally decided with the toss of what is now called the Portland Penny, on display at the Oregon Historical Society.

D'oh!
Don't have a cow if the street names remind you of the television show *The Simpsons*. Matt Groening drew inspiration from his hometown for his cartoon creation. Many characters take their names from city streets, like Flanders, Quimby, Lovejoy, and Kearney. You'll even find a 743 Evergreen Terrace, the cartoon family's home address.

Sleep Small
Caravan, the world's first "tiny house" hotel, lets visitors live large. Each of its four units in the Alberta Arts District is less than 200 square feet (19 sq m) and includes a kitchen, a full bath, and a room that sleeps one to four people. ∎

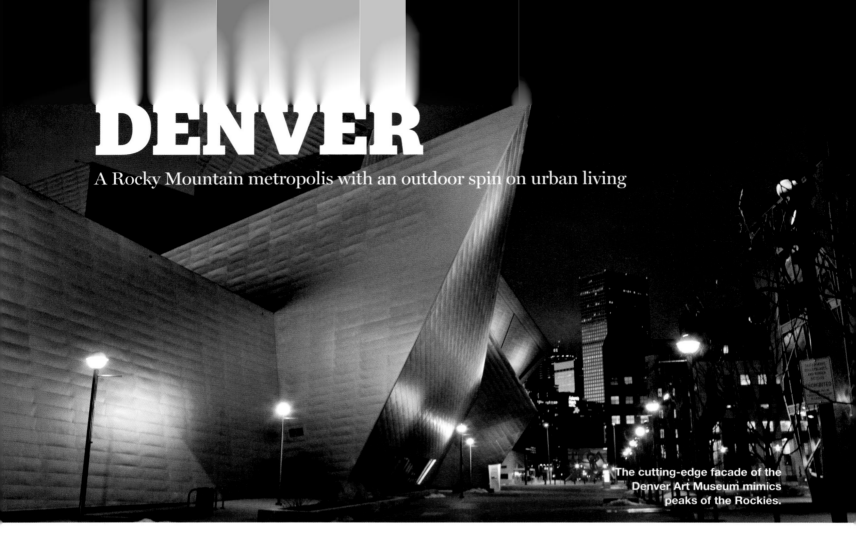

DENVER

A Rocky Mountain metropolis with an outdoor spin on urban living

The cutting-edge facade of the Denver Art Museum mimics peaks of the Rockies.

VITAL STATS

- **Named mountain-tops visible from the city** 200

- **Off-street bike paths** 850 miles (1,368 km), making it one of the nation's largest urban trail systems

- **Annual days of sunshine** 300

- **Length of Colfax Avenue** 26.5 miles (42.6 km), said to be the longest continuous street in the United States

- **Parks** 205 in the city limits and more than 20,000 acres (8,094 ha) of parkland in nearby mountains

- **Ounces of gold on state capitol dome** 72, mined in Cripple Creek, Colorado

Known for its athletic, outdoor-centric lifestyle, Denver considers the Rockies its personal playground, with resorts attracting skiers and hikers year-round. The city puffed up its laid-back reputation in 2014 when it became the first major municipality in the world to legally sell marijuana for recreational use.

SHOPPING CART

Denver Duds and Mile-High Gear

Snappy Dressers Western wear is de rigueur in Denver, and the city offers great spots to gussy up. *Rockmount Ranch Wear* (1626 Wazee St.) in now hip Lower Downtown is famed for inventing the flashy snap-button shirt in the 1940s. (Past customers include Elvis, Bob Dylan, Paul McCartney, and Bruce Springsteen.) *Cry Baby Ranch* (1421 Larimer St.), carries pointy and pricey handmade Liberty cowboy boots in every imaginable color, along with classic cowboy hats and belts.

Gear Up Denver is a city of outdoor lovers and an ideal spot to outfit your open-air adventures at a discount. Find closeout deals and consignment items like Gore-Tex jackets and backpacks at *Wilderness Exchange Unlimited* (2401 15th St. #100), while *Sports Plus* (1055 S. Gaylord St.) specializes in used and new athletic equipment for golf, tennis, and more. ■

Medical (and recreational) marijuana

THEN & NOW

The Mitzpah Arch

This photo of Denver's famous welcoming span, the towering Mitzpah, or Welcome, Arch was taken in 1910, just four years after its formal dedication on Independence Day. The arch, which crossed 17th Street, got its name from a Hebrew word describing the emotional bond between people who are separated. Constructed from 70 tons (64 tonnes) of steel and illuminated with 2,194 lightbulbs (historians say), the friendly arch wore out its welcome by 1931, when it was dismantled as a traffic hazard.

Today, the famous archway stands some 25 miles (40 km) away from the city's modern gateway, Denver International Airport. But crowds still converge on Union Station during the December holiday season when the building and surrounding structures sparkle with more than a half million energy-efficient LED lights. The glowing promenade stretches along the 16th Street pedestrian mall and then radiates through LoDo (Lower Downtown). ∎

Shop Rocky Mountain chic
in Larimer Square.

Art and Bucking Broncos

The Clyfford Still Museum (1250 Bannock St.) houses 2,000 pieces by the American abstract artist. Still refused to sell his work during his lifetime and offered to leave nearly all of it to any city that would create a gallery for the work. Several municipalities bid for the opportunity. Denver won, and then sold four works for $114 million to fund the museum.

Herds of wild buffalo no longer roam the Great Plains, but ranch-raised animals still are served in city eateries. Sample the lean red meat at Buckhorn Exchange (1000 Osage St.), the city's oldest restaurant, decorated with 575 stuffed animals, guns, and Old West artifacts, or The Fort (19192 Colorado Hwy. 8), a re-creation of an 1830s trading post.

The bucking, bright blue bronco that towers three stories high at Denver's airport has been stopping traffic and raising eyebrows since it was installed in 2008 as part of the city's public art program. Not everyone approves of the towering stallion. Among Blue Mustang's nicknames: "Blucifer" and "Satan's Steed." Still, it has its defenders and its own Facebook fan page. ∎

The 32-foot (9.8 m) "Blue Mustang"

The Clyfford Still Museum showcases the (nearly) complete oeuvre of the late abstract expressionist.

ODDITIES

Mile High
Although the city really is 5,280 feet (1,610 m) above sea level, it's hard to say exactly where it hits that mile-high mark. Each of three steps leading up to the Colorado Capitol claims it's a mile up. Ignore the words carved into the first brass marker. Latest GPS measurements show the 13th step, indicated by a second brass marker, is the real deal.

Fit Pets
Not only are residents among the skinniest in the United States, its pets exude health too. The metro area has the most veterinarians per capita—and the fewest fleas.

Fervent Fans
The Colorado Rockies baseball team has a passionate following. Its first game in 1993 attracted 80,277 fans, the most to ever witness an opening game in baseball history. The team attracted nearly 4.5 million spectators that year, the largest single season attendance of any sports team. ∎

A kaleidoscope of color at
Denver's Cinco de Mayo celebration

THE BEST
High-Altitude Cities

The urban mile-high club spans a stunning and far-flung array of cities.

Lhasa, Tibet's Potala Palace

Lhasa, Tibet, China

At an altitude of 11,975 feet (3,650 m), Lhasa is higher than any other city on our list. The 17th-century Potala Palace, former home of the Dalai Lama, hovers above the city like a giant Buddhist scroll.

Sana'a, Yemen

Cusco, Peru

The onetime capital of the Inca Empire—laid out in the shape of a puma—is a vivid contrast in styles. Spanish colonial churches sit side by side with the ruins of Inca temples and palaces.

Sana'a, Yemen

The highest capital city in the Middle East is also one of the world's oldest continuously inhabited cities, founded around 2,500 years ago. The Old City, celebrated for its mud-brick dwellings decorated with geometric designs, is a UNESCO World Heritage site.

Windhoek, Namibia

Set between the Kalahari and Namib Deserts, Namibia's capital roosts on an arid 5,600-foot (1,707 m) plateau. The isolated Afrikaner settlement grew into a thriving modern city after independence in 1990.

Thimphu, Bhutan

A throwback to the bygone Himalaya, Thimphu flaunts medieval palaces and Buddhist festivals with drumming, dancing, and lurid masks. Its 17th-century fortified monastery houses Bhutan's government.

San Miguel de Allende, Mexico

Tucked into the arid mountains northwest of Mexico City, San Miguel's bohemian vibe and pleasant highland climate has attracted artists and writers both domestic and foreign since the 1930s.

Bhutanese masks

Innsbruck, Austria

Innsbruck, Austria

Host of the Winter Olympics in 1964 and 1976, Innsbruck is surrounded by skiing and snowboarding slopes. Its medieval Old Town bustles with shops and cafés, while its baroque palaces channel the long-lost Habsburg empire.

Santa Fe, New Mexico

Founded the same year as the original Jamestown colony (1607), Santa Fe is both the highest (7,260 ft/2,213 m) and oldest U.S. state capital. With the snowcapped Sangre de Cristo Mountains as a backdrop, this famously artsy city blends Spanish, Pueblo Indian, and modern American traditions.

Addis Ababa, Ethiopia

The queen of the Ethiopian Highlands was born of an 1886 decision by Empress Taytu Betul to establish a royal palace near sacred Mount Entoto. As base of the African Union and other organizations, Addis is the "Geneva of Africa."

Quito, Ecuador

As the best preserved Spanish colonial city in Latin America, Quito's entire old town is a UNESCO World Heritage site—though shortness of breath and headaches are common for newcomers to the city, perched at 9,350 feet (2,850 m) in the Andes.

Quito, the allure of the Andes

Hungary
BUDAPEST

A gem on the Danube where images of the past mix with world pleasures of the present

The lit-up terraces of Fishermen's Bastion rise over the Danube.

Once a retreat for the toffs of the Habsburg Empire, Budapest is actually two cities: Buda and Pest, divided by the Danube River. That division has always made the city something different: East meets West, past meets present, royal grandeur meets bohemian sidewalk cafés.

À LA CARTE

Irresistible Comfort Food, Budapest-Style

• Cheap, good Hungarian food, the kind you get at a local *etkezde,* or diner, starts with a simple idea: goulash, paprika-flavored stews. For goulash done right, Kárpátia (Ferenciek tere 7-8) has been serving Hungarian and Transylvanian specialties, including carp goulash and goulash soup, since 1877. It's one of the few restaurants around that recognizes vegetarians as a species, plus there are gypsy and folk music performances nightly. Spinoza (Dob utca 15, 1074) is a traditional Hungarian sidewalk café, where you can enjoy people watching for an afternoon with your beef goulash and homemade spätzle. It also features live music, a theater, and an art gallery, a one-stop shop for the arts crowd. Moving up the fancy scale, chandeliered and Michelin-starred Onyx (Vörösmarty tér 7-8), features its own nouvelle spin on goulash. ■

Goulash spiced with paprika

The Chain Bridge

Construction on the Széchenyi Chain Bridge, the first permanent stone bridge to connect Buda and Pest, started in 1840 and took nearly a decade to finish. When it opened, it had one of the longest suspension spans in the world, held in place by the huge chains that give the bridge its name.

As the Nazis retreated toward the end of World War II, they blew every bridge crossing the Danube. All that remained of the Chain Bridge were the pillars, its massive chains limp in the river.

Rebuilding started almost immediately; the bridge was rededicated November 20, 1949, exactly 100 years after it first opened.

Today, the bridge is the site of almost continuous summer festivals and parties. On the Buda side is Clark Adam Square, where you can catch the funicular up Castle Hill; on the Pest side, Széchenyi Istvan Square leads to the city's swanky neighborhoods, including the pedestrian Zrínyi Street. ∎

The Roman Catholic St. Stephen's Basilica features
neoclassical design with Renaissance accents.

Budapest Finds: From Paprika to Porcelain

Paprika, Plus Hungary's famed deep-red paprika is sold at any grocery store. Still, a great place to start in Budapest is the *Great Market Hall* (Vámház körút 1-3), the city's largest and oldest market. You can find half a dozen different types of paprika powder in beautiful, easy-to-pack pouches and small jars of spicy paprika paste, all made in southern Hungary. The huge neo-Gothic structure also has plenty of Hungarian crafts and souvenirs, but the real attractions are the edibles you can take home: sweet Hungarian Tokaji wine and pálinka brandy, artisan chocolates, dried red peppers, and marzipan delights.

Porcelain from Herend

Tune Town As one of the cradles of classical music (see Bartok and Kodály), Budapest has a rich musical heritage that continues today. *Liszt Ferenc Zeneműbolt* (Andrássy utca 45) is a wondrous old music shop that specializes in sheet music, CDs, and books on Hungary's musical legends. *Hungaroton* music releases around 150 new albums each year, available at its Budapest factory outlet (Rottenbiller utca 47).

Fragile Finds For something more upscale, *Herend Porcelain* offers a chance to eat off the same dishes the Habsburgs used. Herend is hand-painted, very fine porcelain; many of the patterns have not changed since the company first began producing ware in 1826. It's available in many stores, but for the best deals, head to a factory shop, like the one at József nádor tér 11. ∎

Mystery Writer
The author of *Gesta Hungarorum,* a history of early Hungary penned during the Dark Ages, identifies him- or herself only as "Anonymous" and has never been identified. A cryptic statue of Anonymous in front of Budapest's Vajdahunyad Castle is a mecca for modern scribes who believe that simply touching the statue's pen improves your prose.

Puzzle Man
Ernő Rubik was teaching at the Budapest College of Applied Arts when he invented the Rubik's Cube in 1974; between 1980 and 1982, about 100 million were sold.

Celluloid Secret
Despite its name, *The Grand Budapest Hotel* (2014) was filmed in Germany rather than Hungary—although director Wes Anderson admits that he used the Hotel Gellért in Budapest as a model for his fictional abode. For a real glimpse of Budapest, watch the 2003 comedy thriller *Kontroll* from director Nimród Antal. ∎

Paprikas, bell peppers, and other colorful Hungarian bounty fill the stalls of the Great Market Hall in central Budapest.

Austria
VIENNA

An Old World paradise teeming with culture, confections, and coffeehouses

Graben, a famous Viennese shopping street

VITAL STATS

- **Graves in the Vienna Central Cemetery** 330,000, including Beethoven's

- **Viennese balls** More than 450 a year

- **Varieties of roses in Volksgarten** 400 species

- **Stairs to the top of St. Stephen's Cathedral** 343

- **Height of the famous Riesenrad Ferris wheel** 212 feet (65 m)

- **Museums** More than 100

Entrancing Vienna still has the corner on the global market when it comes to cultural magnificence, dating back to Mozart, replete with elegant concert halls and irresistible eateries. But the Austrian city also brags bohemian neighborhoods, trendy restaurants, and edgy exhibitions.

À LA CARTE
From Sublime Schnitzels to Must-Sit Cafés

- Wiener schnitzel, the national dish of Austria—a veal cutlet pounded thin, coated in bread crumbs, fried until crisp, and served with a wedge of lemon—is a must-eat. You can find schnitzel on almost any *beisl* menu. (The "beisl" is Vienna's answer to the "bistro.") But bigger is better: Century-old Figlmüller (Wollzeile 5) promises schnitzel almost a foot (30 cm) in diameter.
- For a taste of Vienna's coffeehouse culture: Café Central (Herrengasse 14) is the frozen-in-time classic; Café Landtmann (Universitätsring 4, A-1010) has been a politico haunt since 1873; and Demel (Kohlmarkt 14) tempts with a window full of wondrous confections. Savor a slice of apfelstrudel, paper-thin layers of buttery pastry wrapped around tender apples and raisins. ■

Inside (and Outside) Vienna

Vienna's opulent State Opera House

Nothing will get you closer to 18th-century Vienna than a peek into one of the city's *Pawlatschen*, or courtyards, where residents would gather and household chores took place. Find several of these hidden (but publicly accessible) courtyards along Singerstrasse and Bäckerstrasse.

A night at the opera is a Vienna must-do, but if you didn't book your tickets in time, you can still take a guided backstage tour of the majestic State Opera House (Opernring 2) or, during the summer months, watch live opera for free on the large video screen outside the building.

Naschmarkt (Rechte Wienzeile 35), Vienna's historic food and flea market, can be overwhelming on a Saturday. Instead, join Vienna's home cooks and chefs on a weekday when the flea market portion is closed to shop for regional honeys, unique oils and vinegars, and Austrian sweets. ∎

Sample small-batch oils and vinegars at the Naschmarkt.

NOVEL INTRODUCTIONS

Setting Free the Bears
John Irving (1968) Many Irving novels travel to Vienna, where the author studied. *Setting Free the Bears* is his first, set in the social upheaval of 1960s Vienna, as the characters plot to liberate the animals in the Vienna Zoo.

The Forever Street
Frederic Morton (1984) Nineteenth-century Vienna was a desolate gypsy camp to Berek Spiegelglass, until a legendary fragment of Jerusalem's Wailing Wall changed his life. Morton explores six decades of Vienna through this Jewish family.

The Painted Kiss
Elizabeth Hickey (2005) Amid the lively cafés and opera houses of 19th-century Vienna, young Emilie Flöge meets painter Gustav Klimt. Hickey reimagines the meeting that inspired a lifelong relationship and Klimt's masterpiece "The Kiss." ∎

Vienna's imperial splendor on the Danube

FLORENCE

A Renaissance feast with delectable modern flourishes

The redbrick Duomo lords over the city.

VITAL STATS

- **Year in which Julius Caesar is believed to have founded Florentia** 59 B.C.

- **Bricks in Brunelleschi's Duomo** 4 million, making it the world's largest brick-and-mortar dome

- **Tickets sold at the Uffizi** 1.6 million a year, more than four times the population

- **Size of Boboli Gardens** 111 acres (45 ha)

My City: James M. Bradburne

I am not Florentine, but after living here for eight years I call Florence my city. Even so, I still see it through the eyes of a foreigner. Every time I cross the Arno on one of the bridges, I fall in love, again, with the perfect harmony between nature, art, and architecture.

Florence is a compact city; I walk everywhere; as long as you watch out for cyclists and don't fall into a trance gazing at Brunelleschi's *cupolone* ("big dome"), it's the best way to experience the city. However, unless you enjoy a brisk stroll at dawn, you will rarely be alone. Florence is a cultural magnet, which means tourists are hard not to notice, especially if you live here.

The real character of Florence reveals itself in its finer grain, away from the blockbuster Uffizi and Accademia. I love revisiting the smaller museums, such as the Museo Horne for its paintings by Giotto, Masaccio, and Filippino Lippi, and the Museo Stibbert for its remarkable collection of armor and Japanese art. I especially like to take visitors over the Arno to the Museo Bardini for its Donatello, Guercino, and the original of the "Porcellino" (or piglet, the famed bronze boar fountain, a copy of whose nose gets shined daily by visitors passing through the Mercato Nuovo). The neighborhood also boasts the world's best bespoke perfumer, Lorenzo Villoresi, whose studio combines an alchemist's laboratory with an apothecary shop.

Although not lacking luxury brands, Florence is still a thriving hub of traditional crafts. The leather goods at Il Bisonte on Via del Parione represent the best of "Made in Italy" (I never travel without my Bisonte satchel), while nearby Visconti continues to make extraordinary pens by hand (I own over a dozen).

I too was once a tourist and returned faithfully to Trattoria Sostanza, Coco Lezzone, or Ristorante Natalino for *bistecca Fiorentina* (Florentine steak). Now that I live here, I head for Ristorante Cibrèo, near the Sant' Ambrogio market. Chef Fabio Picchi is one of the founders of the slow food movement, so the dishes are authentic, delicious, and, of course, locally sourced. In season, the tomato gelée is out of this world. For a truly Florentine experience, I go across the street to the Teatro del Sale, where larger-than-life Picchi cooks in an open kitchen followed by theater or music.

Then there is the Palazzo Strozzi, my favorite place in Florence (but as its director I admit I am biased). It's become a symbol of the city's "new Renaissance," with marvelous contemporary exhibitions, a center for concerts, screenings, lectures, and educational activities, and a trendy café run by the Caffè Giacosa—which serves one of the city's best espressos.

To live and have a job I love in the heart of this cultural mecca—who could ask for more?

James M. Bradburne is an Anglo-Canadian architect, designer, and museologist whose portfolio includes expo pavilions, science centers, and art exhibitions. In 2006, he became director general at Palazzo Strozzi, one of Florence's leading cultural centers. ∎

Chef Fabio Picchi of Ristorante Cibrèo

"What irritates the modern tourist about Florence is that it makes no concession to the pleasure principle. It stands four-square and direct, with no air of mystery, no blandishments, no furbelows—no Gothic lace or baroque swirls."
—Mary McCarthy, *The Stones of Florence* (1956)

Michelangelo's "David"

Michelangelo's masterpiece caused a sensation when it was unveiled in 1504. Intended for a niche on the cathedral tribune, "David" was placed instead in front of the Palazzo Vecchio as a symbol of Republican liberty. Beautiful, virtuoso—and enormous—no work better typifies the artistic and intellectual aspirations of the Renaissance.

• Another artist had already started the David when Michelangelo received the marble. The first sculptor rejected it because he thought the marble was flawed. • Standing almost 17 feet (517 cm), David was the largest nude sculpted since antiquity—proof to the Florentines of the Renaissance, as they had surpassed even ancient Greece

and Rome. • To compensate for the statue's intended lofty but difficult-to-see position, Michelangelo distorted the proportions of the head and neck. • David's hair was originally gilded, but rain washed away the gold. • In 1527 during an uprising, someone threw a chair out of a window in Palazzo Vecchio and broke David's left arm in three places. ■

Florentine Finds – From Edibles to Wearables

A delicate *pietra dura* "flower"

Leather Best Strolling down chic Via de' Tornabuoni is a reminder that the postwar Italian design craze started in Florence with *Gucci* (No. 73r/81r), *Roberto Cavalli* (83r), *Pucci* (No. 20-22/r), and *Salvatore Ferragamo* (No. 16). Florentines have been famous for leather since Dante's day. Watch them work at the *Scuola del Cuoio* (Leather School) in the Monastery of Santa Croce, then hunt for boots or bags at *Casini Firenze* (Piazza de Pitti) and men's and women's jackets at *Davide Cerasi* (Lungarno Acciaiuoli 32/r).

Florentine Originals The city's Renaissance tradition of *pietra dura* (semiprecious stone mosaics) still thrives near the Accademia at *Scarpelli* (Via Ricasoli 59/r), where craftsmen make everything from tables to intricate jewelry. For something lighter, pick up a historic print of Florence at a historic shop: *Baccani* (Via della Vigna Nuova 75r).

Tuscan Treats Built in 1874, the city's food palace, the *Mercato Centrale* (Via dell'Ariento 10), is jam-packed with delectable Tuscan olive oils, olives, pasta, and spices to take home, as well as picnic goodies; visit *Conti's stall* for truffles and dried mushrooms. Across the Arno, the wine shop *Fiaschetteria* (Via dei Serragli 47/r) is the place to seek out a special Brunello or super Tuscan bottle. ∎

NOVEL INTRODUCTIONS

A Room With a View
E. M. Forster (1908) The classic description of Florence at the dawn of mass tourism, as Lucy Honeychurch defies her Edwardian family's straightlaced snobs to find true love.

The Agony and the Ecstasy
Irving Stone (1961) Based on Michelangelo's own letters, this biographical novel vividly evokes the turbulent Florence of his time.

The Enchantress of Florence
Salman Rushdie (2008) Rushdie depicts the city during its golden age under the Medici as part of a sumptuous Arabian Nights tale.

Inferno
Dan Brown (2013) Discover some of contemporary Florence's links with Dante and the Palazzo Vecchio's mysteries as Robert Langdon hunts for clues, using Botticelli's map of the *Inferno*. ∎

At the Scuola del Cuoio apprentices are trained in the art of leather tanning.

Signature Steak, Seafood, and Spirits

Home of the tangy Negroni

• The fabled *bistecca alla fiorentina* (Florentine steak) is a two-finger-thick, charcoal-grilled T-bone steak sourced from Tuscan Chianina cattle, perhaps the world's oldest and largest breed. Always served rare and by weight, try it by the Mercato Centrale at the Trattoria Mario (Via Rosina 2), or at Trattoria Sostanza (Via del Porcellana 25) near Santa Maria Novella, which has been serving sizzling slabs since 1869.

• Florence's signature street food is something of an acquired taste: *trippa alla fiorentina*, stewed honeycomb tripe, or *lampredotto* (from the cow's fourth stomach), served with a zesty, caper-rich *salsa verde* in a crusty bun dunked in the broth. Join the mid-morning crowd at L'Antico Trippaio (Piazza dei Cimatori) or Orazio Nencioni (Loggia del Porcellino, by the Mercato Nuovo) or Da Nerbone in the Mercato Centrale, which also makes great boiled beef *panini*.

• In 1919, Count Camillo Negroni asked bartender Fosco Scarselli at the Caffè Casoni, now Caffè Giacosa (Via della Spada 10/r and Piazza degli Strozzi 1), to juice up his favorite cocktail, the Americano (Campari, sweet vermouth, water, and lemon). Scarselli substituted gin for soda water and orange for lemon, and Florence's beloved Negroni was born—and is still best at its swanky birthplace. ∎

Hidden Piazzas and Palazzos

Escape Florence's stony heart in minutes on foot. From Piazza di Santa Felicità, walk up Costa San Giorgio to one of the city's best kept secrets: the quiet, recently restored Giardino Bardini (Bardini Garden), created in 1309, with terraced lawns, statues, and even a canal. Nearby, take in the spectacular views from the Fortezza di Belvedere. Follow the banks of the Arno west to the Medici's old dairy farm, now leafy Le Cascine, the locals' favorite park for a jog or picnic.

Florence's rich history includes many surprises. The medieval Palazzo Vecchio is worthy of Machiavelli, who worked in an office here, and rife with hidden passageways, stairs, and chambers—accessible on a Secret Passages tour. Elsewhere, the historic Officina Profumo Farmaceutica di Santa Maria Novella (Via della Scala 16), founded in 1612, still sells elixirs from ancient recipes. And stop by the church of Santo Spirito where Michelangelo studied cadavers in the morgue and donated the wooden *Crucifixion*, one of his earliest works, as thanks. ∎

Giardino Bardini, a soothing escape from the city

The medieval Ponte Vecchio arches gracefully over the Arno River.

STOCKHOLM

A sparkling, historic city with a creative spin on modern living

View of Gamla Stan,
the historic old town

VITAL STATS

- **Islands that make up Stockholm** 14

- **Average daylight in July** 19 hours, 20 minutes

- **Average daylight in January** 6 hours, 40 minutes

- **Residents who live less than 984 feet (300 m) from green areas** 95 percent

- **Diameter of the Ericsson Globe Arena** 361 feet (110 m), the largest hemispherical building in the world

Built on a series of connected islands, Stockholm offers panoramic views of city and waterways. Between its coastal setting and abundant parks, Sweden's capital city embraces top-notch urban attractions that are never far from nature's splendors.

LOCAL SECRETS

Outdoor Escapes

Experience Stockholm's beauty from on high. The photography museum Fotografiska (Stadsgårdshamnen 22) in the Södermalm district is worth visiting for its panoramic view of Old Town from the bistro on the top floor. Also in Södermalm is the nearby Fåfängan Café (Klockstapelsbacken 3). It sits atop a cliff, so it requires traversing a steep road, but the view far out over the water makes it worthwhile. Once you've got the aerial view, descend back to earth and visit Stockholm's wealth of parks, waters, and ski areas. During winter, Stockholmers head to Hammarbybacken's slopes and snowboard park. For off-the-beaten-path parklands, visit the island of Djurgården, which has thick woods, duck-filled canals, and a maze of bicycle paths. A particular Djurgården highlight is Rosendals Traädgård, an organic garden. ∎

Wet and Wild Stockholm Staples

Gravlax with mustard sauce

• With so much water coursing around and through the city, you'd expect to find fantastic seafood. Stockholm doesn't disappoint with famed Nordic dishes. Try its unique preparations of herring and trout in restaurants around Stureplan, a public square, in Gamla Stan (Old Town), and Kungsträdgården, a centrally located park dotted with outdoor cafés. Other must-eats: *gravlax,* or raw salmon cured with sugar, salt, and dill, and *skagen,* prawns with lemon, dill, and mayonnaise, served atop toast. Stockholm's taste for curing and pickling developed from its short summers and long winters, which called for innovative modes of food preservation.

• At the other end of the protein spectrum is Stockholm's wide variety of traditional meat dishes, including meatballs, or *köttbullar,* made of mincemeat combined with egg, spices, and other ingredients; moose steak; and reindeer casserole. (Yes, reindeer are real.) Try the meatballs at Ulla Winbladh (Rosendalsvägen 8), which will give you an idea of what Ikea is aiming for. At Bakfickan Djuret (Lilla Nygatan 5)—the word translates as "the animal"—sample a terrific range of meats, paired with wine. At Östermalms Saluhall (Östermalmstorg), a beautiful indoor market that dates from the 1880s, try the smoked reindeer heart or moose salami at B. Andersson Fågel & Vilt. ∎

Outdoor cafés in Gamla Stan and other Stockholm neighborhoods are perfect locales to try authentic Swedish foods.

The Red Room
August Strindberg (1879) This seminal work, considered the first modern Swedish novel, satirizes 19th-century Stockholm through the story of young bohemian Arvid Falk.

City of My Dreams
Per Anders Fogelström (1960) The first in a five-part series centering on Stockholm follows a family from 1860 through 1880. The leading modern writer sheds light on the city's history through the experiences of the poor.

The Girl With the Dragon Tattoo
Stieg Larsson (2005) Stockholm saw its sunny image change forever thanks to Larsson's violent thriller, an international best seller and the first in a trilogy of sex, corruption, and revenge. The city now runs organized tours visiting sites from the books. ∎

PRAGUE

The "heart of Europe," beating with a hallowed history and youthful vibe

Old Town Square lies at the medieval heart of Prague.

VITAL STATS

- **Spires** 500. Prague's nickname, the City of 100 Spires, dates back to the early 19th century, when there were only 103.

- **Year Old Town City Hall clock built** 1410, said to be the oldest working astronomical clock in the world

- **Beer consumption** 42.5 gallons (161 L) a year. Czechs are by far the world's biggest beer drinkers.

My City: **Marsha Kocab**

I suppose I would never have ended up in Prague for 30 years if I were one to walk the beaten path. And walking off the beaten path is when you find the uniqueness of Prague.

The Gothic and baroque splendors you see along the Royal Way, the two-mile (3.2 km) coronation route of Bohemian kings that runs from the Powder Tower in the Old Town to Prague Castle, are stunning. But when I stand in Old Town Square, I am as much fascinated by what I cannot see as what I can. Below the cobblestones are remains of Romanesque buildings covered to prevent flooding in the 13th century. There may even be remnants of underground tunnels leading to the castle, far away. The square hasn't changed much since then. The feeling of living history is overwhelming.

This feeling pertains to more recent history too, as when you walk a little off the route to Café Montmartre, where Franz Kafka used to sit. Here you can visit the Václav Havel Library, a tribute to a great man of my own time. It's hard for me to think of him without mentioning the Café Slavia, near the Vltava River in the Old Town, where many political discussions were held during the 1989 Velvet Revolution that swept away communism. Café Louvre, on Národní Street nearly across from the Slavia, captures the literary and cultural scene of both the 1920s and today.

I have three favorite restaurants in Prague, but there are many excellent ones. For a quick lunch, I love to visit Country Life in the Old Town, which is more of a cafeteria of vegetarian food. Not far away is Café Imperial, a perfect example of the "grandness" of early 20th-century art nouveau. For more elegant dining, I prefer V Zátiší, on a quiet corner near Charles Bridge.

The Czechs say everyone should visit the National Theatre at least once in their lives, and with that statement, I easily talk my guests and children into attending a ballet or opera. For lovers of jazz, the Ungelt Jazz & Blues Club in the Old Town has live music every night, and what always impresses me is that the building has been there since 1101. It's located in the Ungelt Courtyard, behind Týn Church.

This area is also a good place to shop. One well-known and popular shop, Botanicus, sells all-natural soaps, oils, spices, and teas of the highest quality.

After days of absorbing the grandeur of the castle and the Royal Way, I like to take my guests north of the center to Troja and the Botanical Gardens. The first order of business is to walk among the outdoor exhibitions, chapel, and vineyards. Then we sit down to drink some of the wine made there and to look out onto the Vltava River and majestic Troja Chateau.

American writer Marsha Kocab has lived in Prague for 30 years and is author of Neither Here Nor There, *a memoir of life in central Europe before and after the fall of the Iron Curtain.* ∎

Collection by Czech fashion designer Klára Nademlýnská

> **"Prague doesn't let go . . . This old crone has claws. One has to yield, or else. We would have to set fire to it on two sides, at the Vyšehrad and at the Hradčany; then it would be possible for us to get away."**
>
> —Prague-born writer Franz Kafka

Charles Bridge

For a city that prides itself as a link between eastern and western Europe, it's fitting the most memorable sight is a bridge. A wonder of the Middle Ages, this graceful Gothic structure (adorned by 30 baroque statues) links Old Town to Malá Strana while affording a view of Prague Castle both awe-inspiring and humbling. • There are 30 statues lining the sides of the bridge. • Though construction of the bridge dates from 1357, the baroque statuary was added mostly in the 17th and 18th centuries.• Total length is 1,692 feet (516 m), nearly the length of five football fields.• The best view of the bridge (and Prague Castle in the distance) is from the Old Town Bridge Tower.• The bridge was nearly destroyed by flooding in 1890. The tragic 2002 flood got close but never breached the top. • Legend holds that raw eggs were used in the mortar to give the bridge extra strength. ■

Crystal, Marionettes, and Prague Chic

A mecca for glass and stemware

Glass Menagerie Czech glass and crystal is famous around the world for the quality of the design and craftsmanship. There are no shortages of crystal shops around the Old Town. For classic elegance, try *Moser* (Na příkopě 12). Artěl (Celetná 29), owned by an American expat, specializes in stylish reproductions of the best Czech designs from the 1920s and '30s.

Pulling Strings A hand-carved, wooden marionette makes an authentic, original gift. Prague puppeteers have been carving dolls for centuries, and the most popular designs evoke medieval demons and witches. Check the eclectic selection at *Truhlář Marionety* (Týnský dvůr 1), from DIY kits to instrument-playing beetles.

Ready to Wear Don't dismiss Prague as a fashion destination. Although the city lacks the cachet of a Milan or Paris, young Czech designers have established a niche in simple, affordable women's clothing for fun or office. Most boutiques are near Old Town Square, such as *TEG* (V kolkovně 6), *Bohème* (Dušní 8), and *Klára Nademlýnská* (Dlouhá 3). ∎

Prague bursts with luxury, and even has its own Pařížská, or "Paris street," near the Old Town square.

New Prague Cuisine and Plein-Air *Pivo*

Traditional fare in belle epoque style at Café Savoy

• The best local chefs are giving stodgy traditional Czech food an overdue makeover, retaining local favorites like pork and duck but cutting out the fatty sauces and glop. To gauge their progress, try Kalina (Dlouhá 12), where head chef Miroslav Kalina works his magic on wild boar or veal sweetbreads. Elegantes (Letenská 12) in the Augustine Hotel is another worthy purveyor of what's being called—with pride—the "new Prague cuisine."

• *Vepřo-knedlo-zelo* (VEP-choh-KNED-loh-ZEH-loh), usually lumped together in speech as one long word, is Czech slang for roast pork, dumplings, and sauerkraut—the de facto national dish. Unfortunately more than a few uninspired versions are served up around town. For a superior effort, try Café Savoy (Vítězná 5) in Malá Strana, or Mistral Café (Valentínská 11) in Old Town.

• Czech beer—*pivo*—is arguably the best in the world, and there's no better place to enjoy it than at a bustling summer beer garden. Climb the stairs at the northern end of Revolucni Street to find the Letná Beer Garden in Letná Park where you can also stroll or in-line skate and take in sweeping views of the Old Town below. Parlament (Korunní 1), in Vinohrady, is similar but offers a greater choice of brews. ■

Vltava Nights Plus Prague Pho

Warm summer evenings draw thousands to Náplavka, an energetic stretch of the Vltava River, for live music, lots of ambling, a wistful gaze over the water, or an impromptu picnic with open-faced sandwiches, called *chlebíčky* (KLEH-beech-kee), and a bottle of local beer.

A recent renaissance in all things 1980s includes those simple communist-era pubs and restaurants where the prices were low, the food honest, and the beer decent. These retro pubs can be great fun (and good value). Our favorite is Lokál (Dlouhá 31), in the Old Town, where a perfectly prepared schnitzel and a glass of Pilsner Urquell beer will set you back just $10.

The Vietnamese are the third largest ethnic minority in the Czech Republic. When you tire of the hearty Czech fares, head out to Sapa (Libušská 319/126), a sprawling Vietnamese market, where you can have some of the most authentic Vietnamese food in Europe or stock up on spices, herbs, and trinkets. ■

Excellent vantage point from Letná Park

Staré Město (Old Town) has marched to the beat of the Astronomical Clock for centuries.

AMSTERDAM

Progressive and cosmopolitan, a charmed historic capital forever reinventing itself

Terrace cafés soak up the sun
along Amsterdam's many canals.

VITAL STATS

- **Bicycles** 881,000, more than one per resident

- **Houseboats** An estimated 2,500

- **Number of van Gogh drawings and paintings in his namesake museum:** More than 200

- **"Coffee shops" licensed to sell cannabis and other soft drugs** More than 200

- **Navigable canals** 165, more than Venice

Incredibly, Amsterdam still shines like a buffed, golden age jewel. You can cycle along canals lined with 17th-century gabled houses, or view old masters in the Rijksmuseum. Yet this supremely confident city is always looking ahead, and recently emerged as a cutting-edge design center.

LOCAL SECRETS

Eclectic Hideaways to Drink and More

Brown cafés, venerable drinking holes once stained dark with nicotine, are all over town. In the medieval center, Café Hoppe (Spuistraat 18-20) has beautiful lead-lined windows, heavy velvet curtains, and purportedly the highest beer sales in town. Over in the Jordaan, patrons moor boats at the tiny terrace of Café 't Smalle (Egelantiersgracht 12) and order a foamy beer with diced Gouda cheese.

Tucked away in a side street of leafy Vondelpark, the Hollandse Manege (Vondelstraat 140) is the oldest riding school in the Netherlands, dating from 1744. A stairway behind the stables leads to a café, where you can sit on the balcony and watch the magnificent beasts trot their stuff. ∎

High Dutch Design, Tantalizing Tulips, and Royal Jewelry

Tulip mania endures in the Flower Market.

Home Makeovers Innovative, practical, and suffused with dry wit, Dutch design is instantly recognizable. Trendsetter *Droog Design* (Staalstraat 7b) carries tongue-in-cheek items like a cow chair or a doorbell of clinking wineglasses. The sprawling showroom of *Moooi Gallery* (Westerstraat 187) is the brainchild of star designer Marcel Wanders, famous for his blow-on/off electric lamp. Not to be outdone, *Frozen Fountain* (Prinsengracht 645) stocks a natty pig light in its trove of furniture, textiles, and home accessories.

Flower Power Catch a dose of Dutch tulip mania at the celebrated "floating" *Bloemenmarkt,* on the Singel Canal near Muntplein. The bulb shop at the *Amsterdam Tulip Museum* (Prinsengracht 116) also sells impossibly colorful, frilly varieties. Check labels for USDA approval to get through customs.

Best Friends Amsterdam does diamonds like no one else, a jewelry-making craft that stretches back to the later 16th century. *Gassan* (Nieuwe Uilenburgerstraat 173-175) gives free tours of its diamond polishing and cutting works inside a wondrous reddish brick factory built in 1897. Another old and venerable diamond cutter is *Coster,* famed for refashioning the British royal crown in 1852. Coster's boutique is opposite the Rijksmuseum (Paulus Potterstraat 2-8). ∎

Monochromatic accents at Droog Design

Music Afloat

In a city renowned for eccentrics, one of the most beloved is Reinier Sijpkens, a musician who tools around the canals in a colorful little boat named *Notendop* (nutshell), playing a pipe organ with one hand and a flügelhorn with the other.

Masters' Cats

Amsterdam's quirkiest art museum, the Kattenkabinet (Herengracht 497), is devoted to the feline presence in the esthetic. The collection includes Picasso's "Le Chat" and a small Rembrandt painting—a Madonna and child, with a cat and snake.

Early Christmas

Every December 6, the Dutch celebrate Sinterklaas, or St. Nicholas's Day. A few weeks earlier, the white-bearded saint, dressed as a bishop with miter and staff, arrives in Amsterdam by steamboat "from Spain." Impish helpers called *Zwarte Pieten* (Black Peters) toss sweets and carry sacks to nab naughty children. ∎

The city's overflowing population of bicycles adds to the Dutch charm.

THE BEST
Canal Cities

Move over, Venice: There's a host of other alluring, world-class waterway towns.

Medieval edifices shimmer along Brugge's canals.

Brugge, Belgium

One of Europe's best preserved medieval cities, Brugge is laced with centuries-old waterways that twist under arched stone bridges and past step-gabled houses. At night everything takes on an ethereal quality: Ancient towers are bathed in golden light, while white swans glide past like silver ghosts.

Hoi An, Vietnam

Hoi An, Vietnam

A prosperous trading port until the 19th century, Hoi An's graceful architecture has a Chinese-Japanese accent. On the Thu Bon River, fishermen in traditional round Thung Chai (basket boats) ply the waves alongside modern tourist vessels.

Delft, Netherlands

Known for its distinctive blue-and-white porcelain, Delft also boasts some of Holland's most magical canals. Grainy morning haze recalls Vermeer's celebrated landscape of the 17th-century town and harbor.

Tigre, Argentina

Named for the *tigres*, or jaguars, that once hunted here, Tigre draws weekend breakers from nearby Buenos Aires with its unique mix of stilted houses and colonial manses. The chocolate-colored canals are the lively province of rowing clubs.

Annecy, France

Wander off its glassy centerpiece, Lac d'Annecy, to take in the quaint porticoes, flower-draped bridges, and cobblestone quays along the town's winding canals. The waters part dramatically at the Palais de l'Isle (Island Palace).

El Gouna, Egypt

Small stone bridges span the tidy canals of this Red Sea yachting and diving resort, the pet project of Egyptian billionaire Onsi Sawiris. Virtually every sun-kissed abode has its own strip of sandy beach.

Delft houses

Aveiro, Portugal

Aveiro, Portugal

This Renaissance port city dubbed the "Venice of Portugal" has gorgeous waterways just a few minutes' drive from the beach. Brightly painted, gondola-like moliceiros bob with tourists along the picturesque canals.

Birmingham, England

Its history as a bustling hub of Victorian commerce left a canal network running 114 miles (183 km), possibly more than even Venice. Nowadays, the barges that inch along the photogenic Main Line canal are heavy with weekend breakers. Order a pint of beer at the waterside Tap & Spile pub and feel transported back in time.

Suzhou, China

Founded on the Yangtze River in the fifth century B.C., Suzhou is renowned for its manicured gardens and waterways festooned with red lampions. Silk traders flourished close to the 1,100-mile (1,770 km) Grand Canal, one of the world's longest inland shipping routes.

Alappuzha, India

You can drift for days through a labyrinth of canals, lagoons, and estuaries in this lush, palm-shaded south India city. It's best to explore in a rattan-covered, wooden-hulled *kettuvallam*, a converted houseboat.

An Indian *kettuvallam* (wooden houseboat) in Kerala's backwaters

NEW ORLEANS

A revived city where the famed Big Easy never left

The Crescent City Connection spans the mighty Mississippi River.

VITAL STATS

- **Population growth since 2007** 28.2 percent, greater than any other American city

- **Festivals** 120 a year

- **Cups tossed from Mardi Gras floats every year** 1.5 million

- **Charbroiled oysters served at Drago's Seafood Restaurants** Up to 900 dozen a day

My City: Dwayne Breashears

In 1993 I left New Orleans for what I thought were greener pastures. I lasted five years away from home. I realized that the sights, sounds, smells, tastes, people, and vibe couldn't be replaced. There was no place like home. We're a family of 370,000 (give or take a few tourists) with only two degrees of separation at best. How could I not love it?

It's a green city. Esplanade, Carrollton, and Saint Charles avenues, like so many other streets in the city, are lined with oak trees that give us shade and protection by day, yet by night add an air of mystery. If these old oaks could talk, what secrets would they share of the mansions that face them? Sure, we have a Garden District, but the entire city is a garden. Who can resist the smells of honeysuckle, gardenias, Brugmansia, crape myrtle, or night-blooming jasmine?

Everybody talks about the food in New Orleans, whether it's a home-cooked meal or a delectable dish from one of the hundreds of restaurants. Or is it thousands? How can you pass up breakfast at Mid-City's Wakin' Bakin' (the best bacon in town)? They even deliver when you're not in the mood to get dressed and go out. Brunch with bottomless mimosas at the Country Club in the Bywater? Yes, please. Bleu cheese and bacon pizza at a Theo's? A burger at Yo Mama's in the French Quarter (who knew peanut butter is good on a burger?)? The best Reuben in the city can be found at Buffa's in the Marigny, along with live music at night. Dinner? Vacherie (roasted half duck with Steen's cane syrup glaze), Olivier's (Mama Cheryl's Crawfish Etouffee), Muriel's (seafood Bayoubaisse). My mouth waters thinking about what their menus have to offer.

Is there a party season? Of course. It's called the entire year. New Year's Eve, Twelfth Night, Mardi Gras, French Quarter Fest, and Jazz Fest warm you up for the rest of the year. And I do believe most of the populace of the city has a trunk full of costumes.

Music is everywhere. The Prime Example and the Mother-in-Law Lounge in the Seventh Ward, and the Candlelight Lounge and Kermit's Treme Speakeasy in the historic Treme are off the beaten path and as real as it gets. If you want to sample a variety of the sounds of New Orleans, then Frenchmen Street is the place to be. Blue Nile, Snug Harbor, d.b.a., Yuki Izakaya, and Three Muses are all haunts of mine. And if there's ass-shaking to be done, a deejay set on St. Claude Avenue at the Hi-Ho Lounge or a Twisted party at the AllWays Lounge is the place to be. There's something for everyone. You just need to know who to ask to find it. Ellis Marsalis. The Treme Brass Band. Irma Thomas. Big Sam's Funky Nation. Walter "Wolfman" Washington. Find them. We'll welcome you.

Dwayne Breashears is the program director of WWOZ, a community-supported jazz and heritage radio station, where he produces the internationally syndicated New Orleans All the Way Live. ■

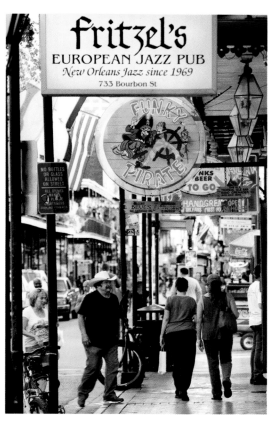

The French Quarter, epicenter of jazz

"New Orleans, more than many places I know, actually tangibly lives its culture. It's not just a residual of life; it's a part of life. Music is at every major milestone of our life: birth, marriage, death. It's our culture."
—New Orleans-born actor Wendell Pierce

Watching the world go by from a New Orleans streetcar

Beignets in a Box Plus Alcohol-Free Art

Folk artist Dr. Bob's motto

Easy Eats Take home morsels of New Orleans' legendary cuisine. Pick up beignet mix or cans of its namesake coffee at the *Café du Monde Gift Shop* (1039 Decatur St.). Cajun spices and hot sauces line the shelves at *World Famous N'awlins Cafe & Spice Emporium* (1101 N. Peters St.). For Big Easy confections, head to *Aunt Sally's Praline Shop* (818 Chartres St.) and buy pecan-studded candies made right in front of you; or stop at *Laura's Candies* (331 Chartres St.) and ask for the Mississippi mud, chocolate spiked with caramel.

Art Stops The ubiquitous "Be Nice or Leave" signs, seen on porches and in bars around the city, are made by folk artist *Dr. Bob,* who creates unmistakable paintings with beer bottle caps. Visit his studio in the Bywater (3027 Chartres St.) to hear the man himself spin yarns about New Orleans. *Stone & Press Gallery* (238 Chartres St.) stocks intricate mezzotint prints and drawings from the early 20th century. Pick out the colorful paintings of New Orleans buildings by *James Michalopoulos* at his eponymous gallery (617 Bienville St.). ∎

Stock up on Crescent City specialties like beignet mix and coffee with chicory.

The Awakening
Kate Chopin (1899)
The novel looks at societal and gender roles against the backdrop of New Orleans and the southern Louisiana coast.

The Moviegoer
Walker Percy (1961)
Mardi Gras catalyzes a young stockbroker to break out of his monotonous life and embark on a philosophical journey through New Orleans and beyond.

A Confederacy of Dunces
John Kennedy Toole (1980) The comic novel follows the curmudgeonly Ignatius J. Reilly in 1960s New Orleans. Using the Yat dialect and a host of comic characters, Toole satirizes and champions the city's idiosyncrasies.

Almost Innocent
Sheila Bosworth (1996) The evocative novel brings the splendor and decay of New Orleans to life through the eyes of a young girl growing up in the 1950s. ∎

Big Easy Eats: Comfort Cajun to Bayou *Bánh Mi*

Snout-to-tail snacks at Cochon

• **Cajun All the Rage** With generous amounts of what locals call "the holy trinity" of green peppers, onions, and celery, the traditional cuisine draws from French cooking and abundant bayou ingredients. Cochon (930 Tchoupitoulas St.) elevates Cajun cookery with its refined charcuterie plate, fried alligator, and crawfish pie. Mr. B's Bistro (201 Royal St.) in the French Quarter does comfort food justice with its andouille-rich gumbo. Since 1840 the French-Creole dishes at Antoine's (713 Saint Louis St.) have been perennial favorites among visitors like Pope John Paul II.

• **Bayou Vietnamese** Thanks to the city's vibrant Vietnamese community, pho, and *bánh mì* are part of the mainstream parlance in New Orleans. Most restaurants are in the ethnic enclaves on the West Bank, Pho Tàu Bay (113 W. Bank Expy.) among the most celebrated. A respected institution, Dong Phuong Bakery (14207 Chef Menteur Hwy.) draws from Indochina's French heritage to create superb crisp baguettes and buttery croissants. Closer to city center, Magasin Café (4201 Magazine St.) serves authentic fare in an airy, modern bistro, while in the bohemian haven of the Bywater, trendy Booty's Street Food (800 Louisa St.) excels in what locals dub Vietnamese po' boys, as well as other street food favorites from around the world. ∎

Backstreet and More

A life-size statue of Ignatius Reilly on Canal Street celebrates the unforgettable protagonist of the novel *A Confederacy of Dunces*. Since 2002 the bronze figure has been gaping at the passersby, sporting his signature hunting cap with earflaps. Because pranksters have tried to steal it several times, it's removed and safely stored each year during Carnival.

Near the Convention Center, you might happen upon an artificial tree made of oil drums, with a small shack suspended on top. Titled "Scrap House," the work by artist Sally Heller is entirely made of Hurricane Katrina debris to commemorate the victims of the 2005 storm that devastated the city.

The French fur trappers are long gone, but you can still kayak in New Orleans. Head to the historic Bayou St. John next to the city park, where you can rent a boat and paddle the four-mile (6.4 km) length of the water past historic buildings and cemeteries. ∎

"Scrap House" honors Hurricane Katrina victims.

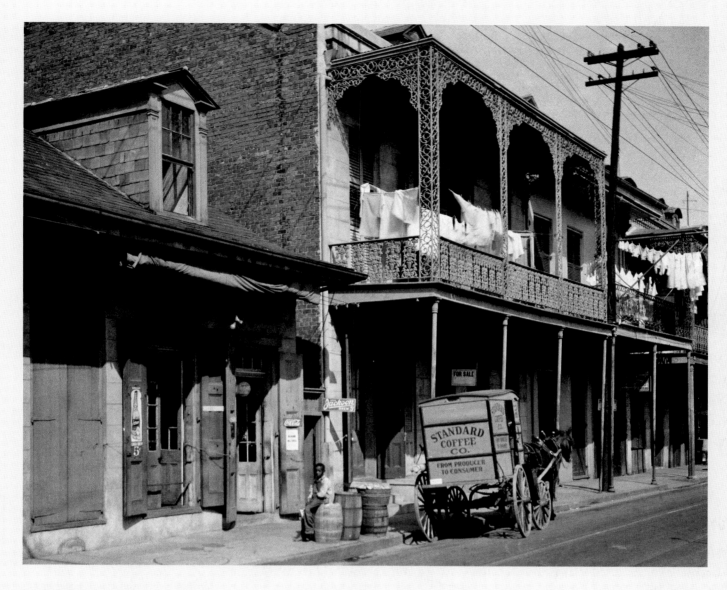

The French Quarter

Plus ça change . . . New Orleans honors its rich past by preserving its architectural marvels, and the French Quarter is a shining example. Like any good southern belle, the ornate Creole homes have not only weathered the test of time, but have also become even more beautiful with age (and some face-lifts).

In the 1929 photograph, a boy sits on a barrel next to a humble French colonial building that housed a brewery. (Only a few of such edifices remain today, including the Quarter's 18th-century Lafitte's Blacksmith Shop that boasts to be the oldest American building serving as a bar.) Next to him is a horse cart that belongs to Standard Coffee, a local company that continued to operate independently until it was acquired in 2012.

The immaculately restored 19th-century homes of the French Quarter are unmistakable for their spacious wrought-iron balconies—perfect for catching a breeze and admiring the historic beauty of the neighborhood. ∎

Laissez les bons temps rouler
on Bourbon Street.

Nevada
LAS VEGAS

A bastion of neon, sequins, and 24/7 adrenaline

The Bellagio's fountains put on a beautifully choreographed nightly spectacle.

VITAL STATS

- **Year founded** 1905, near an old Mormon fort erected in 1855

- **Year gambling legalized** 1931

- **Annual gaming revenue** More than $6.2 billion

- **Number of hotel and motel rooms** 150,436

- **Annual number of couples who get married in Las Vegas** An estimated 100,000

- **Number of conventions per year** 19,029

- **Tallest building** Stratosphere Hotel and Tower, one of the tallest buildings west of the Mississippi at 1,149 feet (350 m)

- **Number of churches and synagogues** More than 500

Few cities are more loved and loathed than this brash oasis in the Nevada desert. None boasts a more madcap past, a blend of Mormon missionaries and mafiosi, eccentric billionaires and last-chance gamblers drawn by a collective dream of making something out of nothing.

À LA CARTE

Throwback Vegas: Cocktails and Rat Pack Steaks

• Classic restaurants from the Rat Pack era are still popular with Vegas old-timers. Frank Sinatra, Dean Martin, and Sammy Davis, Jr., were regulars at the Golden Steer (308 W. Sahara Ave.), where surf and turf, chateaubriand, and New York strip count among the specialties. Another Rat Pack hangout was Bob Taylor's Original Ranch House & Supper Club (6250 Rio Vista St.), with its mesquite grilled meats and free dessert for anyone who can down an entire 32-ounce Diamond Jim Brady steak. Scenes from the 1995 film *Casino* were filmed at Piero's Italian (355 Convention Center Dr.), where the pasta goes well with a glass of Chianti.

• Las Vegas is world renowned for cocktails—and bartenders trained to make them. Among the notable local libations are the Mango Passion Bellini at the Bellagio (3600 S. Las Vegas Blvd.), the Tiki Bandit at Frankie's Tiki Room (1712 W. Charleston Blvd.), Blood and Sand at the retro Downtown Cocktail Room (111 S. Las Vegas Blvd.), Pineapple Mojito at the Wynn (3131 S. Las Vegas Blvd.), and Inhale and Exhale at the Luxor's Flight Bar (3900 S. Las Vegas Blvd.). ■

Fremont Street (aka "Glitter Gulch")

Let there be light! And let that light be neon (first displayed in 1910). By 1948—17 years after gambling was legalized and Nevada's divorce laws were loosened—Glitter Gulch flashed bright with the promise of fun and the fast buck. Fremont Street, the city's main drag, was an inviting parade of shops, hotels, bars, and small casinos.

Millions of bets later, neon and hopes of a quick dollar dazzle on.

Annual gaming revenue is over $6 billion, and Glitter Gulch is now a roof-covered pedestrian precinct called the Fremont Street Experience. At places like the neon-frenzied Fremont Hotel & Casino you can wager, sleep, and eat for days without ever going outside or otherwise see the light of day. "With all the pulsing neon and all the color in Las Vegas, it's a bit like being in an aquarium," says photographer John Kernick. ■

Beyond The Strip

Spring Mountain Ranch State Park

Las Vegas gets a light dusting of snow every few years—barely enough to build a snowman. But nearby Mount Charleston is usually snow-covered from November through March. Located just 30 minutes' drive from the Strip, the Las Vegas Ski and Snowboard Resort offers four lifts, a terrain park, and 30 trails ranging from beginner to advanced.

Ignoring the tourist-packed areas, Las Vegans flock to "local" casinos far away from the Strip and Fremont Street. Places like Sam's Town (5111 Boulder Hwy.), Red Rock (11011 W Charleston Blvd.), and The Orleans (4500 W Tropicana Ave.) offer lower stakes table games, bargain buffets, and even child care.

Nevada's crucial role in the Cold War is the focus of the National Atomic Testing Museum (755 E. Flamingo Rd.), which documents the development of America's nuclear arsenal from the early 1950s to present. Among the artifacts are defused atomic bombs and Geiger counters, while the Ground Zero Theater simulates an atmospheric blast.

Perched on the city's western edge, Spring Mountain Ranch State Park (6375 Hwy. 159, Blue Diamond) preserves a wonderful patch of unspoiled desert once owned by millionaire Howard Hughes. Activities include evening astronomy walks, summer outdoor theater, living history programs, and guided tours of the old ranch house. ■

Explosive exploration at the National Atomic Testing Museum

NOVEL INTRODUCTIONS

Fear and Loathing in Las Vegas
Hunter S. Thompson (1971) This cult classic traces the exploits of Raoul Duke and Dr. Gonzo during a drug-, alcohol-, and sex-filled week in Vegas. Readers can decide for themselves how much is based on Thompson's real-life adventures.

The Desert Rose
Larry McMurtry (1983) A bittersweet tale of Las Vegas life beyond the Strip with an aging showgirl and single mother "Harmony," who dances by night and tries to raise a teenage daughter by day.

Beautiful Children
Charles Bock (2008) This Dickensian vision of modern Las Vegas looks at the city that never sleeps from the viewpoint of those who live and work there, from suburbanites to strippers. ■

ABU DHABI

A nascent island metropolis maintaining tradition while forging a new future

A light show radiates from the over-the-top Emirates Palace.

VITAL STATS

- **Average temperature in August** 106°F (41.1°C)

- **Wealth** $773 billion, the value of the state-owned wealth fund, or nearly $1.3 million a person

- **Cost of Emirates Palace hotel, featuring 114 domes and more than 1,000 Swarovski crystal chandeliers** $3 billion

- **Parks and gardens** Approximately 2,000

- **Expatriates** 7.7 million, more than 80 percent of the population

Dreams are built on sand in Abu Dhabi. In the space of just 50 years, oil and imagination have turned a modest Bedouin village into a futuristic metropolis with glinting mega-skyscrapers, sleek shopping malls, and a spectacular Formula 1 racetrack.

LOCAL SECRETS

Grand Birds and Peaceful Waters

Falcons have always had a special place in the Emirates, where the sheiks kept them for sport. You can get close to the imposing creatures at the Falcon Hospital (Al-Raha), an entire clinic devoted to the avian creatures, with tours from Sunday through Thursday.

Locals and visitors make the most of Abu Dhabi's waterside location by heading to the city's many private beach clubs, the most popular ones being Emirates Palace and Hiltonia; the wildly crowded Corniche Beach sees more than 30,000 visitors a month. Wakeboarding, kitesurfing, jet skiing, and paddleboarding are some of the beloved aquatic activities. But if you want to enjoy the water away from the throngs, kayak offshore from the main island to the mangroves. Contact Noukhada Adventure Company (email *info@noukhada.ae*). ∎

Middle Eastern Eats: Tabbouleh to Sea-to-Table

• Middle Eastern fare often means Lebanese, and it's excellent at The Souk in the World Trade Centre (Al Markaziyah), a soaring complex with geometric slats designed by famed British architect Norman Foster. Stuff yourself with silky hummus, eggplant moutabbal, and tabbouleh in its cafés, such as airy Tarbouche al Basha. On the ground floor of the Al Jazeera Tower, Zyara (Corniche St.) appeals to families with its colorful Arab décor and home-style cooking, including pepper steak and fresh mint lemonade (and free Wi-Fi).

• At the Al Mina fish market, the day's catch is laid out before dawn and auctioned off to vendors and restaurants. Choose an exotic pink ear emperor or yellowfin seabream, and have it cooked right there at one of the market stalls. Finz (Beach Rotana Hotel, 10th St.), jutting into the ocean next to a marina, features a wide variety of seafood using traditional and international techniques. At La Mer (Corniche Rd. E.) you can also order from the so-called "fish market," which lets diners choose not only their fish but also how it's cooked. Sayad (Emirates Palace, Corniche Rd. W.), Arabic for fishermen, serves a contemporary take on local seafood with remnants of molecular gastronomy. ■

ODDITIES

Leaning Tower of Abu Dhabi

The sleek 35-story Hyatt Capital Gate Hotel intentionally leans westward at an angle of 18 degrees—14 degrees more than the Leaning Tower of Pisa.

Camel Contest

Every December, Abu Dhabi's camel beauty pageant attracts hundreds of even-toed ungulates from the Gulf region. As in a dog show, the animals are paraded around and given marks on their appearance. Judges are said to look for attractive colors and good posture, as well as broad cheeks, long whiskers, and hunky humps.

Crimes of the Foreign

Justice is not meted out equally in Abu Dhabi, by law. Generally, Muslims charged with a crime are sent to Shariah, or Islamic, court, while foreigners face charges in Criminal Court. ■

Private beach clubs offer relief from the desert heat.

The palatial Sheikh Zayed Grand Mosque

Morocco

MARRAKECH

An exotic maze of markets and mosques against incandescent North African skies

The red stone Koutoubia Mosque is the city's largest.

Browse the two worlds of the city: the Medina, the walled old city, where maze-like streets and bustling souks give way to lush gardens, a vibrant central square, and majestic mosques; and the new town, Guéliz, with its wide boulevards and upscale shops.

À LA CARTE

Finger Food Couscous Plus Moroccan Mains

• Don't leave Marrakech without sampling couscous, a native Berber dish that gives a taste of Morocco's indigenous history. Traditionally, eating is done by hand, which here involves rolling the couscous into little balls. Dig into gourmet couscous at the upscale Restaurant Dar Moha (81 Rue Dar el Bacha) or Al Bahja (Rue Bani Marine) in the Medina.

• Tajine Stews: This must-try classic dish is named for the clay pot in which it's cooked, the tajine, which has a flat bottom and a cone-shaped top. The original (and better) slow cooker, the pot yields tender and flavorful stews: Tajines range from the sweet, like lamb with dates, to the savory, like chicken with chickpeas or preserved lemons and olives. ■

Something for Everyone

Dried spices in the souk

Seeking Hides The Medina's vast array of souks, or markets, features a vast array of leather goods (remember the tanneries!)—belts, bags, *babouche* slippers, *pouf* foot cushions, and smart leather jackets. Browse the tiny leather stalls in the winding alleys of *Souk Cherratin,* or head for upmarket leather shops like *Galere Birkemeyer* (169–171 Rue Mohamed El Beqal).

Magic Carpet Ride Explore the passageways of *Souk Zrabia* (off of Rahba Kedima, Medina), also called *Le Criée Berbère* ("The Berber Auction"), for carpets galore. Give your negotiating skills a workout: Bargaining is expected. Start by slicing the price in half. If hard-core dickering isn't your thing, try an established shop like *Bazar les Palmiers* (145 Souk Dakkakine), where the rugs range from local to High Atlas weaves.

Caftan Cool The psychedelic 1960s introduced the Marrakech caftans to Western fashion that remain popular here today. Designed by some of the city's masterful women tailors, the colorful, billowy gowns are on display at *Femmes de Marrakesh Coopérative Artisanale de Couture* (67 Souk Kchachbia). *La Maison du Kaftan* (65 Rue Sidi el Yamani) offers an incredible array of caftans, as well as pantaloon "harem pants" and *jellabahs* (loose-fitting Berber robes) for men and women. ■

ODDITIES

Hidebound
In the Medina's tanneries, the ancient art of curing animal hides is still in practice, with not much evolution in technology. The process involves removing the hair, soaking and washing the skins, curing them in blood, drying them, and applying dye. Be prepared for very powerful odors.

Wordplay
In Arabic, the city's name is pronounced *mar-raksh,* with an emphasis on the second syllable—a pronunciation that lent European languages the name of the country: Morocco in English, Maroc in French, and Marruecos in Spanish. Marrakech's own nicknames, the "Red City" and the "Ochre City," are inspired by its adobe buildings.

Saved by Fashion
Marrakech is known for its incredible gardens, particularly the Jardin Majorelle (Rue Yves Saint Laurent), a breathtaking landscape of cacti, exotic plants, trees, pools, and fountains. But few realize its creds of haute couture: Fashion legends Yves Saint Laurent and Pierre Bergé bought and restored the garden in 1980, saving it from becoming part of a hotel complex. ■

The Jemaâ el Fna market packs artisans, performers, and perusers into the medina.

THE BEST
Cities for Song

Towns famed for music—and the indelible tunes that pay them tribute.

Spirited tunes in
Salvador, Brazil

Salvador, Brazil

Many consider this port city and its northeastern state of Bahia the heart of Brazilian music. With African and European cultural roots mixed with Latin and contemporary sounds, Bahia is a vibrant, harmonious melting pot of music.

Kingston, Jamaica

Kingston, Jamaica

Reggae first took root in Kingston's poverty-stricken Trench Town district and spread across the globe. Bob Marley's immortal "No Woman, No Cry" reflects his own life in Jamaica's infamous ghetto.

Santiago de Cuba, Cuba

The sultry southern Cuban city is just as hip as Havana when it comes to music. The Chieftains and Ry Cooder explore Santiago's connection to Galician music in the song "Santiago de Cuba."

Freddie Mercury statue, Montreux, Switzerland

Tulsa, Oklahoma

Oklahoma's music city has spawned dozens of songs including "Tulsa Time," Don Williams's no. 1 country hit. The city's Woody Guthrie Center explores the life and times of Oklahoma's legendary singer-songwriter.

Hamburg, Germany

Edith Piaf's emotive "C'est à Hambourg" captures the transient mood of the north German seaport. The city's tuneful heritage also includes the 1930s Swing Kids, the early Beatles, and Germany's best musical theater scene.

Montreux, Switzerland

The lakeside city on the shore of Lake Geneva is famed for its annual jazz festival, held over two weeks each July. But it's also the focus of Deep Purple's classic "Smoke on the Water," which spins the true story of a 1971 rock concert fire that destroyed the city's historic casino.

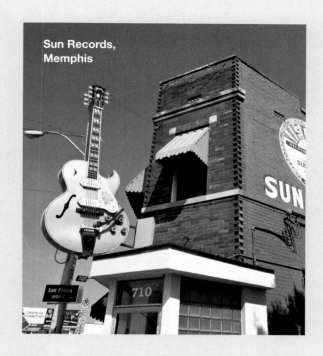

Sun Records, Memphis

Memphis, Tennessee

The subject of the 1991 hit single "Walking in Memphis," the riverfront city is synonymous with two American music legends: the blues, with its heart on Beale Street, and Elvis Presley, whose Graceland has become a place of pilgrimage.

Galveston, Texas

Glen Campbell's 1969 breezy-sounding hit has been adopted as the city's unofficial anthem. Songwriter Jimmy Webb wrote the song, considered an antiwar tune about an American soldier leaving his lover behind in Galveston.

Liverpool, England

The English seaport spawned Merseybeats and groundbreaking groups like the Beatles, Herman's Hermits, and the Dave Clark Five. And Ringo Starr's sweet "Liverpool 8" describes his working-class, pre-Fab Four life in "La la la, la la la, Liverpool."

Nashville, Tennessee

One of the best songs about the capital of country music is "Nashville Cats" by The Lovin' Spoonful, a 1966 tribute to the city's rich musical heritage. Among Nashville's iconic music sights are RCA Studio B and Ryman Auditorium.

Nashville, capital of country music

Norway

OSLO

A booming European hub of world-class enticements with an enduringly Norwegian spirit

Karl Johans Gate is the Nordic capital's main artery.

Oslo, once a small subarctic town, has come into its own. Now capital of one of the richest countries of Europe, the forest-ringed city throbs with booming nightlife, new restaurants sprouting up weekly, and top-notch museums.

À LA CARTE

Haute Oslo's Maritime Menus

• Havsmak (Henrik Ibsens Gate 4), or "taste of the sea," honors the city's maritime heritage with meals like smoked halibut atop risotto. Tjuvholmen Sjømagasin (Tjuvholmen Allé 14) is a raw bar, seafood bistro, and fishmonger rolled into one. Or go straight to the source at Fisherman's Coop (Rådhusbrygge 3), where you can get freshly caught shrimp on a baguette.

• Norwegian haute cuisine at Fru K (Fru Kroghs Brygge 1) is elegantly simple, with dishes like spawning cod from the Arctic Circle paired with bleak roe and oysters. Beautifully presented fares like raw scallop topped with dill "snow" are on show at the Michelin-starred Fauna (Solligata 2). The stratospherically upscale Maaemo (Schweigaards Gate 15) lavishes diners with 26-plate tasting menus of delicacies. ■

The Oslo Opera House

Holmenkollbakken Ski Jump

Norway pretty much invented the idea of strapping on skis to sail on snow, so why not fly too? Holmenkollbakken, a few miles outside Oslo, is the world's premier ski jump hill, giving expert skiers their best shot at flying.

The first competitions at Holmenkollbakken were held in 1892; more than 12,000 people showed up to watch Arne Ustvedt jump 70.5 feet (21.5 meters). Baby steps. By the 1930s, the tower alone was 62 feet (19 m) high. And it all changed again for the 1952 Olympics. Over the years, the jump and hill have been changed 18 times.

Today's Olympians would consider those earliest iterations bunny hills. Now, the jump has a start house 199 feet (61 m) above the ground. On a good day, professional jumpers can sail more than 450 feet (137 m). The thrills are vicarious. Mortals can watch—or just take in some of the best views of Oslo and hang out at the museum. ■

Viking Ship Museum: The Vikingskipshuset

Sailing into some of the roughest seas on Earth in open boats not much longer than a school bus, the Vikings managed to conquer their entire quarter of the world—from France to North America. Perhaps no culture has ever had a better symbol of its power: When Norwegian kings died, they were buried in ships. See three original Viking boats at the Vikingskipshuset. • The museum's most famous boat, the *Oseberg,* was buried in A.D. 834, along with a cargo of jewels, food, 15 horses, six dogs, and two small cows. • The *Gokstad* ship, the best preserved, was built around A.D. 850, and found in 1879 when a couple of bored farm kids started digging into a mound. • Only a bit of the third ship, the *Tune,* built around A.D. 900, has survived. It shows the advanced construction methods the Vikings used, with a clinkered design—strong, flexible, sturdy, and fast. ■

Naked, High, and Dried

Brunost, a caramelized cheese

Huk/Paradisbukta Beach is where you'll find a good part of Oslo's population on a summer day, with bike trails, a beautiful beach, food kiosks, and a lovely fjord to test your cold water tolerance. Parts of the beach are clothing optional.

The **Oslo Opera House,** right at the head of Oslofjord with beautiful views back toward the city, is actually designed for people to get out on the roof and look around in warm weather. But it's not for the faint of heart or the acrophobic; there are no guardrails.

The **Mathallen** is like a farmers market, but the farmers aren't quite offering what you're used to: reindeer sausage fresh from the northern Sami herds; lutefisk, dried and lye-soaked cod, for the truly brave; and brown cheese, an odd Norwegian favorite. ∎

ODDITIES

The Screams
Edvard Munch was never quite happy with "The Scream," Norway's most famous painting, on display at the National Gallery. So he painted four "Screams." That way, when the painting gets stolen (which happened at the museum in 1994 and at the Munch Museum in 2004), there's still an extra version or two around.

Oslo for Peace
All of the Nobel Prizes are awarded in Stockholm, Sweden, except for one: the Peace Prize, which is bestowed in the Oslo City Hall on December 10 each year. It was Swedish founder Alfred Nobel's decision to do things this way, although no one is entirely sure why.

Bottle It Up
Sometimes, the most fun you can have is to visit the heart of obsession. The Mini Bottle Gallery has the largest collection of just that: miniature bottles, more than 50,000 of them— beautifully weird, and proof that you can find something to do even in the longest winter. ∎

Huk Beach on Oslo's Bygdøy Peninsula attracts bathers and baskers.

Hawaii
HONOLULU
The sparkling city that invented world-class beach bumming

Waikiki from Diamond Head State Monument

Waikiki is only the start: Honolulu is the place to try the best plate lunch, take some shave ice (nothing like a snow cone) under a giant banyan tree, shop for anything from the latest fashions to the gaudiest aloha shirt, or drive one of the country's three interstate highway system roads that never sees another state.

SHOPPING CART

Honolulu Must-Haves—From Shirts to Quilts

The Shirt First, buy an aloha shirt. Yes, locals really do wear these. Including for formal occasions. The dozens of *ABC* shops around Waikiki have a good selection of low-cost versions, and any shop in any hotel is ready to sell you shirts full of palm trees and hula girls. But the store of choice is *Bailey's Antiques and Aloha Shirts* (517 Kapahulu Ave.). More than 15,000 to choose from, in prices ranging up to "I need this more than I need a new car anyway."

Koa Collectibles The next step in buying Hawaiian is *Martin & MacArthur* (1815 Kahai St.) for everything koa. A wood that only grows in Hawaii, koa has a dark, beautiful grain that works for a dining room table or the bowls to serve on it. ■

From Tiki and Tropical to Meat and Two

• The Hawaiian staple is the plate lunch: rice, macaroni salad, and some kind of meat. Seven to ten bucks gets you seriously loaded. Try Rainbow Drive-In (3308 Kanaina Ave.) and be ready to wait in line. For something a little less well known, try Aiea Bowl (99-115 Aiea Heights Dr., just past Pearl Harbor)—yes, it's in a bowling alley—or Zippy's Makiki (several locations, including 1222 S. King St.).

• Any grocery store is going to sell fresher pineapple and tropical fruit than you've ever had before, but The Saturday Farmers Market (4303 Diamond Head Rd.) at Kapiʻolani Community College, offers the freshest local produce and ingredients. For real Hawaiian coffee, this is where growers with only an acre or two sell their goods. Also find local honey (try the Christmas berry) and jams (ʻohelo berry), if you strike lucky.

• No visit to Honolulu is complete without at least one visit to a tiki bar. La Mariana Tiki Bar & Restaurant (50 Sand Island Access Rd.) has been around since the 1950s. Catering more to locals than day-trippers, a meal here starts with a very, very stiff mai tai, and moves on to fresh local fish and shrimp. A taste of classic Honolulu. ∎

Beachside shopping along Kalakaua Avenue

Another idyllic day in Waikiki

Scotland

EDINBURGH

Irresistible festivities and a full-on nightlife set amid ancient castles and rolling Scottish hills

At the heart of the capital, Calton Hill peeks over the ancient city.

VITAL STATS

- **Year the University of Edinburgh was founded** 1582

- **Number of historic buildings** 4,500 listed structures

- **Number of shows at the 2013 Edinburgh Festival Fringe** 2,871, by 24,107 artists

- **Number of pubs:** 421, the most in Scotland

- **Percentage of residents over 25 who are college graduates** 48 percent

- **Frequency of rain** 15 to 17 days a month

- **Number of annual festivals** 12. The city's population more than doubles in August as a result.

Edinburgh's ancient streets and entrancing castles are its soul, then its 21st-century flourishes permeate its modern spirit. Top-notch restaurants, a student-energized nightlife, and a roster of festivals that revel in culture high and low fuse its rich past with a pulsing present.

À LA CARTE

Great Scot: Pub Grub and Tea

• Traditional pubs offer a quintessential Scottish dining experience, serving hearty grub like meat pies and haggis (sheep's innards minced with vegetables). The mahogany-lined interiors, cozy crannies, and mood lighting add flavors that are as important to a meal as seasoning and spice. Start your day with a hearty Scottish breakfast, tattie scones and all, at King's Wark (36 Shore); try a bridie, or flaky meat pastry, at Port O'Leith Bar (58 Constitution St.), and end the evening at cozy Last Drop (74–78 Grassmarket) to sample traditionally cask-conditioned real ales.

• It's not just Londoners who enjoy an afternoon of Earl Grey. Spend a day wandering through Edinburgh's tearooms. Eteaket (41 Frederick St.) curates a collection of high-quality loose-leaf teas from sources committed to environmental and social sustainability. ■

A proper Scottish breaky

THEN & NOW

Princess Street

Forming the southernmost boundary of Edinburgh's New Town, Princes Street was already well over 100 years old when the black-and-white image above was taken. Known at the time of the first photograph as the North British Hotel and at the second as the Balmoral, the building's iconic clock has been keeping train passengers—the reason for the hotel's initial construction—on time since it first began ticking in 1902. With the exception of midnight on New Year's Eve, the clock is always set two to three minutes ahead, another way of helping travelers make their trains. ■

Edinburgh Castle towers over the
city's Princes Street Gardens.

Urban and Film Oases

Provisioning at the Edinburgh Farmers Market

Edinburgh's historical industrial heart is now enveloped in nature's greenery. Take a walk or a cycle along the Water of Leith (Conservation Visitor Centre: 24 Lanark Rd.), a newly regenerated, 13-mile (21 km) path dotted with 70 old mills. Once fallen into industrial decay, the trail today winds through banks of wildflowers and riverside otter homes before its grand urban entrance into downtown Edinburgh.

A hotbed for independent and art film, Scotland's capital has been hosting the Edinburgh International Film Festival since 1947. But you don't need to plan your trip around the festival season. Filmhouse (88 Lothian Rd.) screens more than 700 films, from popular hits to abstract art, throughout the year in a renovated church. Century-old Cameo (38 Home St.), one of the oldest cinemas in Scotland with much of its original interior still in tact, focuses on indie screenings and cult classics. ∎

Follow the Water of Leith for a bucolic stroll.

NOVEL INTRODUCTIONS

Edinburgh: Picturesque Notes

Robert Louis Stevenson (1878) Robert Louis Stevenson is best known for masterpieces *Treasure Island* and *Strange Case of Dr. Jekyll and Mr. Hyde.* Turning a magnifying glass onto his hometown, he brings 19th-century Edinburgh to life.

Knots and Crosses

Ian Rankin (1987) The first in a fan-favorite series of mystery and crime thrillers, Detective John Rebus probes the dark corners of Edinburgh and the human race as he struggles to stop murders terrorizing the city.

The Heart of Mid-Lothian

Sir Walter Scott (1818) Once a widely read book across Europe, this story chronicles the journey of dairymaid Jeanie Deans from Edinburgh to London against the historical backdrop of Scotland's rocky unification with England. ∎

Israel
JERUSALEM

Where the sacred, the ancient, and the trendy find joyful coexistence

The Tower of David and the City walls imbue Old Jerusalem with historical gravitas.

My City: Shaanan Streett

My favorite thing about Jerusalem is that it isn't really one city. It's more like three worlds. Three entirely different worlds, speaking different languages, obeying different social laws, and offering all the tension and all the hope imaginable. And the best thing about it? You can easily walk between all three.

Start at Mahane Yehuda Market. Situated in the heart of West Jerusalem, this is the place to capture some authentic Jerusalem vibe. Anything can be purchased here. Anything. But it's probably best to stick to the food. Don't be alarmed by the merchants yelling at you in Hebrew, not caring that you don't understand; they just want to tell you what's on sale. If you want, you can pop into a bar called Casino de Paris (named after a 1930s British establishment with the same name at the very same spot), which I am a part owner of, for a nice house cocktail or a local Shapiro beer.

Once you've recuperated a bit, cross Jaffa Road and within minutes, you'll be in the heart of Me'a She'arim, Jerusalem's ultra-Orthodox Jewish neighborhood. Everything is a trip. The Yiddish signs, the stores, the peoples' attire. It's the familiar hustle and bustle but it's from a galaxy far away that's right under our nose. I like sitting for a beer or coffee at the tiny Espresso Elbaz that offers some good people watching and even an occasional bad boy sneaking an afternoon brew when he should be studying his Gemara. If indeed you make it to Me'a She'arim, don't miss the Museum on the Seam. This small but thought-provoking political contemporary art museum in an old Israeli military outpost was chosen by the *New York Times* as one of the leading 29 art venues around the globe.

Once you're done being artistic, cross Route No. 1 and enter Palestinian Jerusalem. Predominantly Muslim, this section of the city is very different from Mahane Yehuda, and very, very different from Me'a She'arim. I enjoy strolling on Sultan Suleiman Street, trying to understand as much Arabic as I can while walking toward Salah e-Din Street. It would be almost blasphemous to recommend only one hummus restaurant in this hummus heaven we live in, so I'll just say if you decide to walk down the long staircase leading to Abu Ali restaurant, I guarantee you'll be happier when you walk back up.

You've now seen the three worlds of Jerusalem, and you're ready to call it a day. You've taken in an immense amount of information and need a place to relax. A perfect place to chill out and reflect is Beit Hakahava on Yanai Street. This great little café is loosely inspired by Jerusalem's celebrated author Shai Agnon. It offers excellent food and a homey vibe. Like all the other places I've recommended, Beit Hakahava is uniquely Jerusalem.

Shalom, and welcome to my Jerusalem!

Born in Jerusalem, Shaanan David Streett is the lead singer for Hadag Nahash, one of Israel's top musical acts. ∎

Dried fruits for sale at the Mahane Yehuda Market

NOVEL INTRODUCTIONS

The Gospel According to Jesus Christ
José Saramago (1991)
This controversial historical novel by the Portuguese Nobel Prize winner retells the life of Jesus Christ, bringing to life ancient biblical sites.

A Lover in Palestine
Selim Nassib (2007)
This historical novel fills in the blanks about the rumored love affair between Zionist Golda Meir and wealthy Palestinian banker Albert Pharaon. The politics and intrigue of British Mandate for Palestine era serve as the background, with much of the action in Jerusalem.

In the Courtyard of the Kabbalist
Ruchama King Feuerman (2013)
This novel recounts interactions among native Jerusalemites and newcomers, telling the tale of the friendship between New Yorker Isaac Markowitz and the Muslim Mustafa, with much of the story centering on the Temple Mount. ∎

"**Jerusalem is a festival and a lamentation.**
Its song is a sigh across the ages, a delicate, robust, mournful psalm at the great junction of spiritual cultures."

—David K. Shipler, former Jerusalem bureau chief for the *New York Times*

The Temple Mount Complex

The Temple Mount complex is the most visible and controversial of Jerusalem's holy sites, significant to all three major Abrahamic faiths. Its religious origins began as the site where Abraham is thought to have prepared to sacrifice Isaac to God in circa 2000 B.C. King Solomon is said to have built the First Temple here after his father King David established Jerusalem as the capital of his empire. • Destroyed by the Babylonians in 586 B.C., the temple was rebuilt only to be wrecked by the Romans in A.D. 70. • Christian legend states baby Jesus was presented here soon after his birth. • The blue-tiled and gilded Dome of the Rock is the shrine where Muslim tradition states Prophet Muhammad ascended to heaven in 632 B.C. Nearby Al-Aqsa Mosque is the third holiest site in Islam. • The Western Wall at the temple's western foot is the holiest site in Judaism. It is all that remains of the Second Temple. ■

Jerusalem Checklist—From Spirit to Body

A Passover Seder plate

Holy Shopping High-quality religious souvenirs of Israel, from handmade crosses to menorahs in materials ranging from olive wood and ceramic to silver and even Jerusalem stone, are some of the Holy Land's best gifts. *Gans Jerusalem Gifts & Judaica* (8 Rivlin St.) has Seder plates, mezuzah cases, and many other objects crowded into its shop.

Ancient Beauty The Dead Sea's special powers over beauty and health have been legendary since ancient times. Head to *Sea of Spa* (28 King George St.) for a vast array of locally made Dead Sea products from creams to soaps to facial scrubs. (You can also get a spa treatment.) The *Dead Sea Gift Shop* (Yoel Solomon St. 19) offers products from several Dead Sea cosmetics companies, including Premier Dead Sea and Sea of Spa Black Pearl.

Market Finds If you're traveling with children, you can pick up a veil-covered *Fulla doll*, the pious Arabic version of Barbie, available from many of the vendors in the Arab Market along *Via Dolorosa*, where Christian legend says Jesus made his way to the Crucifixion. ■

The Arab Quarter of Jerusalem's Old City

Holy City Hummus and Destination Kosher

Abundant chickpeas mean hummus and falafel heaven in Jerusalem.

• Jerusalem is heaven for hummus lovers. Don't be put off by the broken tables at Abu Shukri (63 al-Wad Rd.), near the Damascus Gate; the lines of locals waiting for hummus, spiced ground chickpeas, certainly aren't. Abu Ali (Salah e-Din St.), in a windowless basement, isn't the prettiest place either, but it's the fresh hummus that counts. For late-night hummus cravings, head to Ben Sira (3 Ben Sira St.) in West Jerusalem, along with all the others snacking during their bar crawls.

• Of course, kosher is king here. At Heimishe Essen Restaurant (19 Keren Kayemet St.), you'll find home-style dishes served from old Ashkenazi, or eastern European Jewish, recipes. Delights include chopped liver, gefilte fish, and chicken soup. Montefiore Restaurant (Yemin Moshe at HaBreha Sts.), overlooking the walls of the Old City and under a giant windmill, specializes in Italian- and Mediterranean-style dishes, with an emphasis on seafood. It's one of the best places in town for Roman-Jewish–style artichokes. Scala Restaurant (7 King David St. in the David Citadel Hotel) is one of the city's best restaurants. Chef Oren Yerushalmi mixes traditional and local ingredients with French flair. A large selection of kosher wines and unusual desserts like tahini ice cream are on the menu. ∎

Walk on Walls and Find Religions

Built in 1538, the two-and-a-half-mile-long (4 km) walls around Jerusalem are a relatively recent addition, considering the city's nearly 5,000-year-old history. A pleasure for locals and tourists is walking on the walls and seeing the Old City from their heights.

Tradition and archaeological evidence cites Jerusalem's Temple Mount as the site of the First and Second Temples, now the location of the Al-Aqsa Mosque. However, Samaritans, who practice a form of Judaism and live in Nablus in the West Bank, believe the temples were on Mount Gerizim overlooking that city.

Pontius Pilate was famous for his role in the execution of Jesus Christ, but he also is thought to have built the Mamilla Pool in today's Independence Park as part of the Herod-era city's waterworks. Supplied by spring rains, it teems with crabs, frogs, and other aquatic life.

Although Judaism, Christianity, and Islam are considered the three major Abrahamic faiths, they are not the only religions. About 200 Druze, a monotheistic, secretive religion rooted in Islamic principles, also live in Jerusalem. ∎

The Citadel, part of the Old City wall

A Bedouin bride in her elaborate wedding veil

THE BEST
Walled Cities

Ancient ramparts built to bar invaders now invite visitors to play, explore, and marvel.

Toledo, Spain

Toledo, Spain

The ancient Spanish gem and UNESCO World Heritage site dates to the Bronze Age. It later became a peaceful, multicultural home to Christians, Muslims, and Jews. Fun fact: The striking settlement is said to be the inspiration behind the expression, "holy Toledo!"

Quebec City

Quebec City, Canada

After the British conquered France in 1759 to gain control of northern Canada, they fortified what is now the only walled city north of Mexico. The ramparts and four remaining gates are now beloved city landmarks.

Itchan Kala, Uzbekistan

This sand-colored town with crenulated walls has earned international fame for its ancient Islamic architecture with towers and minarets, and its 19th-century palaces.

Harar, Ethiopia

This holy Islamic city sits at a crossroads of the Horn of Africa. Its ancient history writ largely in myth and tradition, the settlement is still surrounded by 13-foot (4 m) ramparts. It's also home to packs of urban hyenas that are fed nightly for tourists.

Medieval wall

Carcassonne, France

This remarkably preserved fortress city in the south of France, which pre-dates the Romans, still looks impenetrable. With a drawbridge, towers, and gatehouses, it's easy to imagine soldiers protecting the frontier outpost, now a World Heritage site, which has watched over an important trade route for millennia.

Óbidos, Portugal

Visigoths and Moors later occupied this pristine Roman settlement north of Lisbon. Every summer, the city gets in touch with its medieval side, hosting a raucous two-week festival with parades, jousting, and public feasts.

Pingyao, China

This nearly 3,000-year-old city with 39-foot (12 m) walls is one of the best preserved ancient cities on the planet. Built with six gates, it is nicknamed "Turtle City" because its outline resembles the reptile's shape.

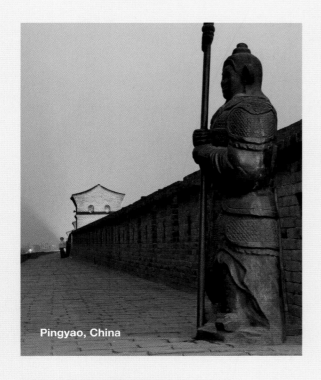

Pingyao, China

York, England

A two-mile (3.4 km) path tracing the city's Roman-built walls takes visitors through nearly 2,000 years of history, past gates that defended against marauding Vikings and rapacious revolutionaries. The fortified gatehouse at Walmgate Bar makes it clear these walls weren't just for show.

Galle, Sri Lanka

Called "the best example of a fortified city built by Europeans in South and South-East Asia," by UNESCO, old Galle and its fort offer a striking mixture of Portuguese, Dutch, and Asian influences. The European-built fort thrives with kite flyers, cricket players, and couples out for a stroll.

Dubrovnik, Croatia

With a panoramic view of red-tile roofs backed by the azure Adriatic Sea, it's hard to imagine a more magnificent city setting than the one welcoming visitors from the top of the city's towering stone ramparts.

Dubrovnik's handsome ramparts

Nova Scotia, Canada

HALIFAX

Atlantic Canada's youthful capital of breezy coastal living

Boardwalk bistros along Halifax's naturally deep harbor

VITAL STATS

- **Year the Old Town Clock was installed** 1803, and still ticking

- **Number of *Titanic* victims buried in Halifax** An estimated 150

- **Number of college students** Approximately 81 per 1,000 people, three times the Canadian average

- **Year Halifax-Dartmouth ferry service started** 1836, making it the oldest continuous saltwater ferry service in North America

- **Number of lighthouses** 25

Haligonians celebrate a roster of year-round pleasures. Winter offers sleigh rides, maple harvests, ice wines, and ice-skating. Come summer, this coastal city blossoms into a hub for vibrant shopping, nightlife, and dining.

À LA CARTE

Halifax's Hoagies and, Yes, Wines

• Raise a toast to Nova Scotia's growing wine industry. The small province is home to more than 70 grape growers, producing rustic wines, plus notable ice and sparkling wines. Try some at Obladee Wine Bar (1600 Barrington St.) and stock up on Benjamin Bridge and Jost Vineyards bottles at Bishop's Cellar (1477 Lower Water St.).

• The doner kebab is a quintessential Mediterranean dish; the donair is a uniquely Haligonian variation on the classic. It replaces the traditional spit-roasted lamb with spiced beef and adds a sweet secret sauce, diced tomatoes, and diced onion, all wrapped up in pita. The place to go for donairs is its 1970s originator, King of Donair (original location: 6420 Quinpool Rd.), which parlayed the sandwiches' popularity into a well-loved franchise. ■

Haligonian Must-Haves—From Tartans to Treasure of the Sea

Find nautical antiques in this port city.

Read All About It The 40-plus-year-old *Atlantic News* (5560 Morris St.) is, it proudly boasts, "Halifax's original newsstand." If you cannot find it here among its thousands of magazines and newspapers, Haligonians aren't reading it.

Skirting the Issue Scottish heritage runs so deep in Halifax that the city sports a kilt shop. The *Plaid Place* (1903 Barrington St.) features an array of tartans and kilt accessories. If you're not quite ready to buy, it also offers a Highlands dress rental package, including a men's kilt in choice of three tartans, hose, and a Prince Charlie jacket. Bagpipe not included.

For a modern take on tartan, meet with Halifax designer *Veronica MacIsaac (veronica macisaac.com)*, whose collections have won raves around the Celtic world, and beyond.

Anchors Away With its strategic location on the edge of the continent, Halifax has always looked to the sea. It's no surprise, then, that it's an excellent place to find maritime antiques. Set sail for *Finer Things Antiques & Curios* (2797 Agricola St.), which offers a beguiling selection of vintage sea captain accessories, including anchors, octants, and cutlasses. Neighboring *McLellan Antiques & Restoration* (2738 Agricola St.) also offers a wide range of collectibles, lamps, and furnishings. ∎

What's in a Name?
They're neither "Halifax-ians" nor "Halifaxers." The proper demonym for residents is "Haligonians," which some believe comes from the Latin for the city, "Haligonia." You can also call them "Bluenosers," a centuries-old nickname for the people of Nova Scotia that is even less understood.

Dead Men Tell No Tales
Halifax has a rich and spirited pirate past. In 1844, the crew of the British ship *Saladin* was found shipwrecked with a loot of silver bars and coins taken. The Royal Navy tried six of the sailors for the murder of their captain and crewmates. Four were convicted and executed, the last pirates hanged in Canada's history.

Oh, Christmas Tree
Before Halifax lights its Christmas tree each December, it donates one of the region's majestic white spruce trees to Boston Common. The tradition of the "Nova Scotia tree for Boston" began in 1918 as a thank-you for Boston's assistance following a tragic Halifax cargo ship explosion in 1917 that killed some 2,000 people. Each year, a series of public celebrations marks the departure of the tree. ∎

Sommeliers at Obladee Wine Bar pour Canadian specialties like ice wine.

VENICE

An unequalled world gem with a timeless luster

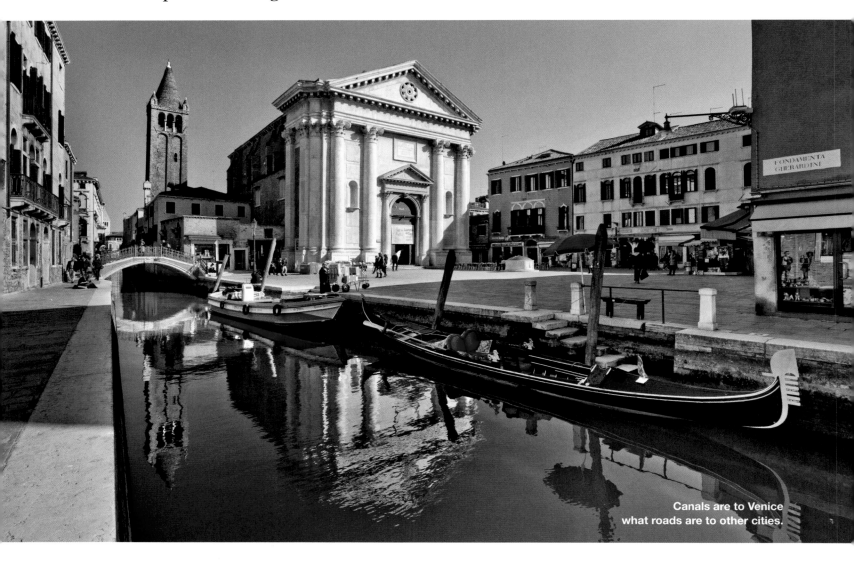

Canals are to Venice
what roads are to other cities.

VITAL STATS

- **Pigeons living in St. Mark's Square** More than 100,000

- **Number of gondolier licenses issued annually** 3 to 4

- **Bridges** 416

- **Canals** 177

- **Islands** More than 118 make up the city's archipelago

- **Length of the Bridge of Sighs** 36 feet (11 m)

My City: Roberto Zammattio

Venice is a treasure chest filled with secrets unveiled to only those who love Venice. You need to live in Venice (at least a few days) to understand, to taste, and to experience the cacophony of the voices and sounds that make the city unique, with its own distinctive pace, continuously changing like the tides that allow the city to breathe.

It is important to begin with understanding the element of water. This is where Venice was founded, and it has always been the city's stronghold.

There are days—the best way to really relish this trip is to wake up at dawn—when I board an almost empty *vaporetto* (water bus) and sail through the Grand Canal, admiring its splendid palaces.

Every neighborhood has its own sites where you can literally "get lost," or stop for a break.

Time is not chaotic in Venice, so when I find myself near the Accademia Bridge, I let myself be transported into the San Samuele area, near Palazzo Grassi, where I slip into narrow streets and boxed-in little squares where the perfume of washed laundry drying in the sun makes me feel like a child again.

If I'm at Rialto, I emerge myself into the noise of the bustling and spectacular fish market and the greengrocers stands, where I can eat a *cicchetti* snack, and drink an *ombra,* a small glass of wine, at All'Arco, one of the few authentic remaining *bacaro,* or little bars. After, I venture into the more silent yet fascinating area known as the Carampane, behind Albrizzi Square, where one of the best restaurants of the city, Trattoria Antiche Carampane, is located.

The neighborhoods of Cannaregio and Castello are still residential areas where "real" Venetians live. Here you can still see a part of Venice that is slowly disappearing: women sitting in front of their homes chatting; children playing soccer in the square; fishermen returning from the lagoon in their low but fast boats.

A perfect day would include strolling through the Jewish Ghetto, walking along the Fondamenta Nuove, and turning along Calle del Fumo toward the Church of Miracles (Chiesa dei Miracoli) and Sts. John and Paul Square (Campo Santi Giovanni e Paolo), then walking down la Barbaria dele Tole until you reach the Arsenale.

Venice is fascinating if you allow yourself to be led by curiosity and see things in a different perspective. For example, the way high tide tends to flatten the city's horizon, or the way low tide changes the form of the palaces reflected in the canals so they appear higher. Or how the sun and the shadows play hide-and-seek and transform the streets into a kaleidoscope of various colors and reflections.

I love getting lost inside this splendid and protective city. And I never forget to raise my eyes toward the sky to savor another part of Venice.

Roberto Zammattio, who owns Pensione Guerrato, has lived in Venice all his life. ∎

Castello, home to Venice's ancient shipyard, provides a quiet refuge.

ODDITIES

The Maze
Despite the twist of waterways and walkways, Venice only has three official canals and two streets. All the rest are *rio* for the waterways or a wide variety of names—*calle, ruga, salizzada*—for the walkways. Still, the best way to see Venice is to simply start walking until you're lost, which won't take long.

The Original Ghetto
Shakespeare's *Merchant of Venice* is set in the Jewish Ghetto of Venice, near San Marcuola Church. The term "ghetto" originally relates to smelting and making iron. The local island where the ironworks were located was also the Jewish neighborhood, once the heart of the city's shipping.

No Bike Zone
Bicycles are against the law in Venice. Except for the occasional child on a bike, the only wheels you'll see are the hand trucks used to get goods from the canals to the shops. ∎

> **"As the world goes, this city is the eye's beloved.**
> **After it, everything else is a letdown.**
> **A tear is the anticipation of the eye's future."**
> —Russian author Joseph Brodsky, *Watermark* (1992), who spent winters in Venice

The sinuous Grand Canal curves around the city's many palaces.

St. Mark's Basilica

A tribute to the incomprehensible amounts of money that once flowed through these islands, St. Mark's Basilica, standing watch over its namesake square, is the soul of Venice. From the unicorn horn by the rood screen to the way sunset on the lagoon glimmers in the golden mosaics of the facade, St. Mark's is, yes, tourist central. But it's also the heart of this beautiful city of bridges. • The cathedral (which began as a palace chapel) was begun in A.D. 829 to house relics of the Apostle Mark the Evangelist that a group of Venetian businessmen had stolen from Alexandria, Egypt. • The four bronze horses that are a symbol of the cathedral were taken from Constantinople in 1204. • The 323-foot (98 m) bell tower collapsed during an earthquake in 1902 and took 10 years to rebuild. • Some believe the mummified remains under the altar actually belong to Alexander the Great. ∎

Irresistible Venetian: Glass, Masks, and More

Vibrant Murano glassware

Behind and Above A *carnivale mask* is the closest you'll come to feeling like you're on the canals again. Masks are for sale everywhere. *Papier Mache* (Castello 5175) mixes the modern and the traditional in its colorful creations. For those with a bigger budget, Venetian *chandelier shops* abound, selling everything from pure elegance to gum ball machines gone wild.

Artful Paper The other must-have from Venice is *paper:* As the end of the Silk Road, Venice has been selling handmade paper notebooks since paper first made it to Europe. Try *Rivoaltus,* on the Rialto Bridge—family run, in a shop not much bigger than a closet, with beautiful leather-bound journals, photo albums, and more.

Gorgeous Glass Murano, a *vaporetto* ride from Venice proper, has been fine glass central for centuries. Today, it's the place to go for glass butterflies, elephants, and vases in colors that exist nowhere else in the world. *Abate Zanetti* (Calle Briati 8/b) offers top-quality work, and even a school where you can try the ancient techniques yourself. A warning: Serious Murano glass has a serious price tag; make sure you're getting the real thing with a certificate of authenticity. ∎

Masquerade madness for the Venice Carnival

Consummate Venetian Eats: Starting with *Cicchetti*

Cicchetti, like tapas, are for eating with vino and sharing with **amici.**

• For classic, old Italian fare, Cantina do Mori (San Polo 429) near the Rialto Market, has been pleasing patrons for over 500 years. An enormous selection of wines, *cicchetti* (like tapas), and *tramezzini* (to call them sandwiches is to insult them) means this place is always jammed. Another good cicchetti option is Cantina Do Spade (San Polo 860), which has been around for more than 500 years.

• For something more sit-down, Bistrot de Venise (Calle dei Fabbri 4685), a favored locals' hangout near San Marco, serves classic Venetian food with a modern twist; try the *figa' de vedelo a la venexiana* (a traditional calves' liver dish) or fresh seafood. Small rooms with only a few tables each make for an intimate setting, or grab an outside table for the best people watching. Trattoria Ai Cugnai (Centro Storico piscina dei Forner 857) goes for pure Venice comfort food: lasagna, gnocchi, or simply trust the day's special.

• Or take an outing for the absolute best: Trattoria da Romano (S. Martino, DX 221, Burano). Catch a vaporetto to the colorful, quiet outer island of Burano. The destination restaurant is widely recognized as serving the best seafood risotto— or seafood, period—in Italy. ■

Venice: Hidden and Exposed

You could spend a lifetime in Venice and not run out of masterpiece paintings to see. But for the best of the guy who truly painted the city, the unassuming Scuola Grande di San Rocco (Campo San Rocco, San Polo 3052) is the place to go. Tintoretto, Venice's homegrown master, spent 24 years creating more than 50 paintings of history that glow like stained glass.

Instead of St. Mark's, those in the know hit the rooftop breakfast buffet at Hotel Danieli (Riva Schiavoni 4196) for great views. Those really in the know cross the lagoon and climb the bell tower of San Giorgio Maggiore, the church that caps the Grand Canal. The church itself has some of the best art in town, but from the tower, you get to look back at the entire sweep of the city.

At the far end of the city's reach is the island of Torcello. Here you'll find the Venice of the deep past, when it was nothing but water and stone and beauty. Torcello's basilica contains some of the best Byzantine mosaics in Italy. ■

The fresco-filled interior of Scuola Grande di San Rocco

Cafés in the Piazza San Marco offer front-row views of the Basilica.

Switzerland
GENEVA

An expatriate oasis set against glassy Lake Geneva and the towering Alps

A city rich in natural beauty, with Alpine vistas and a sparkling lake

VITAL STATS

- **Number of watches at Bucherer** 1,300, possibly the largest selection in the world

- **Age of the site of St. Pierre's Cathedral** Approximately 1,600 years old

- **Working-age population that is not Swiss** 45 percent

- **Length of bench on the Promenade de la Treille** 400 feet (122 m), probably the world's longest

- **Length of the second hand on the Flower Clock** 8 feet (2.5 m), the world's longest

Known as the United Nations' European headquarters, a financial capital, and the site of flight layovers, Geneva in fact boasts much more, from breathtaking views of the lake and mountains to gorgeous parks and fine shopping.

SHOPPING CART
What Else? Watches and Chocolates

Wind Up Geneva is known for its centuries-long history of fine watch craftsmanship, and the legacy is visible along Rue du Rhône. Stop in at *Piaget* (No. 40), *Marconi* (No. 53 Rue), a boutique with colorful watches on offer, and *Bucherer* (No. 45), which offers an enormous selection of Rolexes. Cross the Rhône to Rue du Mont-Blanc, another treasure trove of watch sellers, including Bucherer's second Geneva location (No. 22 Rue du Mont-Blanc), *Espace Temps* (No. 13 Rue du Mont-Blanc), and *Swatch* (Rue du Mont-Blanc 19).

Sweet Dreams Geneva's homegrown chocolate makers include *Du Rhône Chocolatier* (Rue de la Confédération 3) and *Confiserie Ducret* (Rue Hoffmann 6). Established in 1826, *Favarger Chocolat* has both a boutique in town (Quai des Bergues 19) and factory tours in lakeside Versoix. ∎

Juste à Genève: Ride, Escape, Reflect

Cruise like a Genevan on a lake ferry.

Avoid the crowds by cycling the lakeside bike route to La Belotte and hopping a ferry back to the city center. Genève Roule Association (three locations) offers free loans during the summer, while Rent a Bike at the Gare de Cornavin (7 Place de Cornavin) hires a variety of pedal-powered transport, including tandems and child trailers.

Join the locals in their green retreats. Mont Salève in Geneva's backyard has hiking trails with breathtaking views. The waterfront Parc des Eaux Vives (Quai Gustave-Ador) renders postcard vistas of the lake and Jura Mountains, as well as an 18th-century chateau transformed into a modern hotel and restaurant. The Plainpalais Cemetery (10 Rue des Rois), also known as the "Cemetery of Kings," is not only where notables from Fyodor Dostoyevsky's daughter to Jorge Luis Borges are buried—it is also a lush oasis.

From the Palais Wilson (original home of the League of Nations) to the "Broken Chair" monument for victims of land mines, Geneva offers varied peace symbols. None is more poignant than the U.N. High Commission for Refugees Visitors' Centre (94 Rue de Montbrillant), which illuminates the plight of refugees around the globe. ∎

Parc des Eaux Vives wows with its regal vistas and elegant mansion turned hotel.

THE BEST
Spa Cities

These legendary urban retreats offer the ultimate escape from hectic lives.

Thermal baths in Vichy, France

Vichy, France

The volcanic mineral water of this belle epoque resort town is said to have relieved many prominent visitors, including Napoleon III. Drench yourself at Le Célestins (111 Blvd. des États Unis), which claims to be the original home of the many-nozzled Vichy shower.

Spa, Belgium

Spa, Belgium

The namesake for the very word, lush Spa is known for its healing springs—so healthful that the water is sold across Europe for drinking. Soothe your joints at the hilltop Thermes de Spa (Colline d'Annette et Lubin).

Fez, Morocco

Experience history in this 1,200-year-old city's ancient bathhouses like beautifully restored Seffarine Hammam (inside the medina) where your spirits will soar as high as its domed ceiling.

Truth or Consequences, New Mexico

Before it adopted the name of the popular TV game show in 1950, T or C, as it's known, was Hot Springs, named after the mineral wells around which the town grew up. Today, its downtown spas have some 50 soaking pools and tubs.

Zen ingredients

Edipsos, Greece

Hugging the Evia Island coast, Edipsos boasts 80 hot springs and a client list that stretches back 5,000 years (to battle-worn Hercules, legend has it) and includes Winston Churchill.

Hot Springs, Arkansas

When you tire of trout fishing, water sports, hiking, and horseback riding, poach yourself at Buckstaff Bath House (509 Central Ave.), the only operating spa inside Hot Springs National Park.

British Columbia's Harrison Hot Springs

Harrison Hot Springs, Canada

On gleaming Harrison Lake with a view of snowcapped mountains, the British Columbia town boasts a Public Pool (101 Hot Springs Rd.) where you can even paddle in its thermal water. No wonder it's known as the "Spa of Canada."

São Lourenço, Brazil

In this town four hours outside Rio de Janeiro lies the Parque das Águas (Water Park), bragging nine soothing varieties of mineral waters in its art deco buildings. At the balneário (Praça João Lage), or hydrotherapy spa, take a load off with a soak, a sauna, and a massage.

Sapareva Banya, Bulgaria

Lest you forget what this Bulgarian town is about, a steamy natural geyser in the center of town shoots six stories high every 20 seconds. The 103°F (40°C) water might just be the perfect après-ski treat after slaloming down the northern slope of nearby Rila Mountain.

Daruvar, Croatia

A rejuvenating retreat for more than 2,000 years, the city by the verdant Papuk Mountain is famous for its healing resorts like the Daruvar Thermal Spa (Julijev park 1) and wineries—a perfect place for a sybarite.

Calming gardens at Daruvar Thermal Spa

North Carolina
ASHEVILLE

A mecca of awesome mountain scenery, bohemian art, and high southern cuisine

A relaxed hub of artists and foodies folded into purple mountains' majesty

VITAL STATS

- **Size of Biltmore Estate, America's largest privately owned house** 178,926 square feet (16,623 sq m)

- **Artists' studios** 250

- **Waterfalls** More than 250 in the area

- **Size of Historic District** An estimated 170 buildings, including one of the country's greatest assemblies of art deco architecture

- **Craft breweries** 11

Situated at the foot of the breathtaking Blue Ridge Mountains, this laid-back town draws a funky mix of artists, nature lovers, and professional foodies. The restored Grove Arcade, a giant market built in 1929, anchors a downtown gleaming with art deco treasures.

À LA CARTE

Foodie Destinations with Southern Flair

• Asheville's exuberant foodie scene is all about fusion and updated southern favorites. Zambra Wine & Tapas (85 Walnut St.) has an evolving menu that features Carolina seafood with Spanish and North African flair; try the bluefish and rice croquettes with charred tomato mojo. Salsa's (6 Patton Ave.) skillfully blends Mexican and Caribbean in its jerk chicken with ginger carrots, and chipotle, or Cuban mojo steak.

• In the specialized world of barbecue, western North Carolina emphasizes slowly cooked, pulled pork shoulder with a thick tomato-based sauce. Try out Asheville's finest at Luella's Bar-B-Que (501 Merrimon Ave.) or 12 Bones Smokehouse (3578 Sweeten Creek Rd.). ■

Zippy Views and Bauhaus at Its Best

The modern facade of the Asheville Art Museum

Glide like a bird above the treetops at Asheville Zipline Canopy Adventures (1 Resort Dr.), whose easy-access, graduated-height course offers gorgeous views of the Blue Ridge Mountains and Asheville's skyline. The family-friendly adventure park also offers climbing, jumping, and rappelling. Ranked among the best in the country, the more challenging zips of Navitat (242 Poverty Branch Rd., Bernardsville) are in exhilarating locations with big sky bridges and artfully designed platforms built into the upper reaches of giant oaks.

Josef Albers, a German artist and color theorist, was a student and instructor at the acclaimed Bauhaus school of architecture and design in Germany. When the Nazis shut it down in 1933, Josef and his wife Anni, a textile designer, moved to Asheville to teach at the experimental Black Mountain College. The Asheville Art Museum (2 S. Pack Sq.) has a permanent exhibition of the Albers' canvases, including Josef's celebrated "Formulation" series of delicate, geometric shapes and Anni's bold abstracts. ∎

ODDITIES

Kudos, Please

Clearly, Asheville is different things to different people. Either it's the "New Freak Capital of the U.S." *(Rolling Stone),* an "Appalachian Shangri-La," *(The New York Times),* the "Most Romantic Place in the U.S. and Canada" *(About.com),* or the "Happiest City in America" *(Self).* Or perhaps all of the above?

Clear to Partly

Asheville is home to the National Climatic Data Center, the world's largest archive of weather data. Details flow in daily from weather stations, balloons, ships, buoys, radar, and satellites. The NCDC's banks store over six petabytes of data (with 15 zeros, a petabyte amounts to a million billion).

Believe It or Not

Ripley's meets Jack Kerouac at The Odditorium (1045 Haywood Rd.), a quirky performance space with music, poetry slams, and open-mic comedy nights. Glass cases display creepy dolls, stuffed animals, and freak-show items collected from around the globe. ∎

Mountain biking, camping, zip-lining, hiking . . . Asheville is an adventurer's dream.

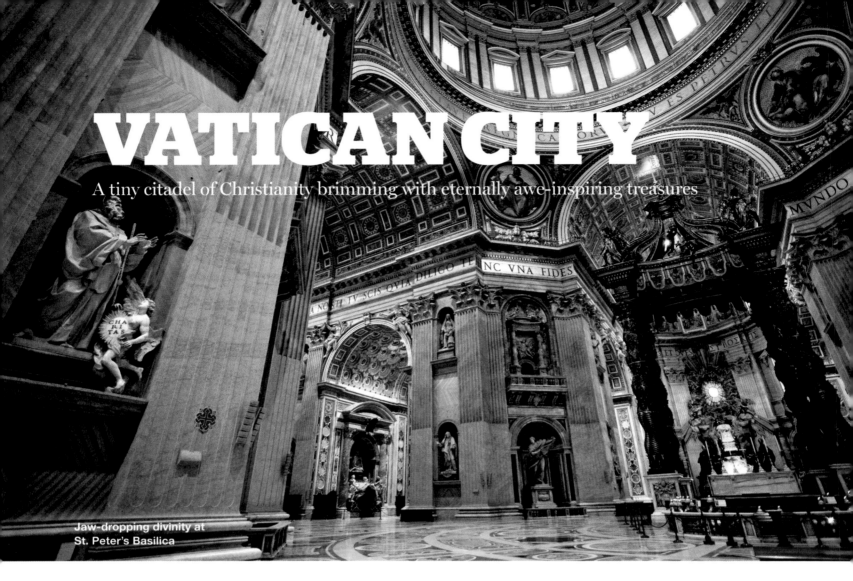

VATICAN CITY

A tiny citadel of Christianity brimming with eternally awe-inspiring treasures

Jaw-dropping divinity at
St. Peter's Basilica

Popes have wielded enormous influence for centuries from their bastion of Vatican City, the world's smallest state and the center of Roman Catholicism. While devotees flock to St. Peter's, the priceless artifacts and artworks of the Vatican Museums entice pilgrims of all kinds.

SHOPPING CART

Very Vatican: From Papal Blessings to Coins of the Realm

Philatelist Alert Vatican City has its own post office, with two branches in St. Peter's Square on either side of the basilica, and issues its own *francobolli* (stamps). Stamps frequently feature former popes, famous Roman citizens, and religious miracles. Buy a few to mail letters from the Vatican with a rare surprise.

DIY Blessing There's no gift more holy than one blessed by the pope himself. Skip the specialty shops near the Vatican that offer preblessed items and do it yourself: Bring a rosary, cross, Bible, or other object of religious devotion to the Sunday or Wednesday papal appearances, and hold it up when the pope blesses the crowd.

Coins of the Realm When purchasing items in Vatican City, take a close look at any change you get back. The Vatican issues its own currency and mints euros embossed with an image of the pope's head. Very few coins and no notes are issued. They're worth much more than their face value and are highly sought by collectors—so if you find one, hang onto it. ∎

St. Peter's Square

Thousands of horse-drawn carts cluster in St. Peter's Square for the papal benediction in 1860. At the time, Italy wasn't a unified country—it was divided into different states, with the pope ruling over Rome. As the nation marched toward unification, the papacy refused to recognize the new Kingdom of Italy proclaimed in 1861. The kingdom's invading army broke through Rome's ancient Aurelian Walls with cannon fire and finally wrested the city from the pope's control in 1870.

In response, Pope Pius IX declared himself a "prisoner of the Vatican," and for almost 60 years popes refused to leave their stronghold and submit to the Italian government's authority, until Vatican City was granted its sovereign independence in 1929.

On March 13, 2013, Argentinian Cardinal Jorge Mario Bergoglio became the 266th pontiff and the first pope from the Americas. The newly elected Pope Francis I greets cheering multitudes from the central balcony of St. Peter's Basilica. ■

ICON

Sistine Chapel

The Vatican's Sistine Chapel is the work of several Renaissance artists, but Michelangelo's masterpiece ceiling, completed in 1512, is its crowning jewel. The frescoes, painted in bright colors so as to be visible from the floor below, took the artist four years to complete. • Michelangelo's ceiling has lost only one

piece in 500 years. In 1797, an explosion from a nearby gunpowder depot caused a chunk of sky in "The Great Flood" to fall to the floor. • More than 350 figures are portrayed on the ceiling, including families with children and angels and demons, some of them wearing the faces of Michelangelo's contemporaries. •

Contrary to popular belief, Michelangelo did not paint his masterpiece flat on his back—he was supported while leaning backward onto scaffolding that he cleverly engineered. • Michelangelo painted 20 muscular men, *ignudi,* whose bare bodies scandalized Pope Adrian VI. He wanted them painted over. They weren't. ◼

Holy Sneak Peeks!

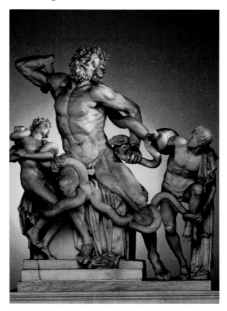

"Laocoön and His Sons," in the Vatican

Upon entering St. Peter's Basilica, peek into the first chapel on the right. Standing proudly is the "Pietà," Michelangelo's famed statue of the Virgin and the only sculpture he ever signed. Look for "Michael. Angelus. Bonarotus. Florent. Faciebat" (Michelangelo Buonarroti of Florence created this) on the strap across the Virgin's body.

St. Peter's Square, the grand elliptical piazza with 284 columns laid out by Bernini in the 17th century, features an intriguing optical illusion. Stand on the white marble disk labeled "Centro del Colonnato" between the central Egyptian obelisk and each fountain and look at the colonnade: The four columns seem to slide into one.

In the Octagonal Court within the Vatican Museums, seek out the Laocoön, a rare classical marble sculpture group that was excavated in 1506 on Rome's Esquiline Hill. Attributed to first-century B.C. sculptors from Rhodes, the figures represent Laocoön, a priest of Apollo, and his two sons, who were killed by serpents sent by Athena and Poseidon to keep them from warning the Trojans about the wooden horse. ∎

Tuscan colonnades fringe St. Peter's Square.

Young at Heart
Despite centuries of history, the Vatican state itself is less than 100 years old. Italian dictator Benito Mussolini granted Vatican City its sovereign independence in 1929 with the signing of the Lateran Treaty.

Narrow Escape
A once secret passageway connects the Vatican with the Castel Sant'Angelo, a fortress on the banks of the Tiber River that was originally built as a mausoleum for the Roman Emperor Hadrian in the second century. The Passetto, a half-mile-long (805 m) passage, was built as an escape route for popes in danger.

What Lies Beneath
St. Peter's Basilica is built upon what appears to be the actual tomb of St. Peter, the first pope. Excavations in the mid-20th century revealed the bones of a man between 60 and 70 (about Peter's age) with ancient purple and gold threads, colors used to wrap people of high standing. In 1968, Pope Paul VI declared that the bones were most likely those of St. Peter. ∎

The Tiber River, cradle of the mighty Roman Empire

INDEX

Boldface indicates illustrations.

ILLUSTRATIONS CREDITS

Front Cover, Iakov Kalinin/Shutterstock; Back Cover, (UP, L to R): SIME/eStock Photo; Fraser Hall/Corbis; SIME/eStock Photo; Andersen Ross/Blend Images/Corbis; (LO), Andrew Mace; 1, Antonino Bartuccio/eStock Photo; 2-3, S. Borisov/Shutterstock; 4, Luigi Vaccarella/eStock Photo; 7, Paolo Giocoso/eStock Photo; 10, shirophoto/iStockphoto; 11, TORU YAMANAKA/AFP/Getty Images; 12 (UP), Old Japan Picture Library 2007; 12 (LO), Torin Boyd; 13 (UP), Iconotec/Alamy; 13 (LO), woojpn/iStockphoto; 14-15, SIME/eStock Photo; 16 (UP), Richard Taylor/4Corners/eStock Photo; 16 (LO), John Lander/Alamy; 17, Michael Runkel/Robert Harding World Imagery/Corbis; 18 (UP), Jess Kraft/Shutterstock; 18 (LO), Ocean/Corbis; 19, Günter Gräfenhain/eStock Photo; 20 (UP), Alberto L. Godoy/National Geographic Creative; 20 (LO), Melissa Farlow/National Geographic Creative; 21 (UP), John Mitchell/Alamy; 21 (LO), David R. Frazier Photolibrary, Inc./Alamy; 22 (UP), Olha Insight/Shutterstock.com; 22 (LOLE), Jerome Levitch/Corbis; 22 (LORT), Andrey Pronin/NurPhoto/Corbis; 23 (UP), Jerry Cooke/Corbis; 23 (LO), Ragnar Singsaas/Getty Images; 24, Luigi Vaccarella/eStock Photo; 25 (UP), Matteo Carassale/eStock Photo; 25 (LO), Qilai Shen/The New York Times/Redux Pictures; 26, Günter Gräfenhain/eStock Photo; 27 (UP), imageBROKER/Alamy; 27 (LO), Dinodia Photos/Alamy; 28, Scott S. Warren/National Geographic Creative; 29, Stefano Amantini/eStock Photo; 30-31, Rudy Balasko/Shutterstock; 32, Danny Lehman/Corbis; 33 (UP), Gary Gershoff/Getty Images; 33 (LO), Adam Macchia; 34 (UP), Richard Levine/Alamy; 34 (LO), Marmaduke St. John/Alamy; 35, Susan Seubert/National Geographic Creative; 36 (UP), Massimo Borchi/eStock Photo; 36 (LO), Sean Gallagher/National Geographic Creative; 37 (UP), C.H. Graves/Corbis; 37 (LO), Macduff Everton; 38, Luigi Vaccarella/eStock Photo; 39 (UP), Megapress/Alamy; 39 (LO), Rolf_52/Shutterstock.com; 40 (UP), elnavegante/Shutterstock; 40 (LO), dijkgraaf/Hollandse Hoogte/Redux Pictures; 41 (UP), Bettmann/Corbis; 41 (LO), Bernardo Galmarini/Alamy; 42, REUTERS/Marcos Brindicci/Corbis; 43 (UP), Jon Arnold Images Ltd/Alamy; 43 (LO), Yadid Levy/Alamy; 44, Renato Mariz/

National Geographic Your Shot; 45 (UP), Ryzhkov/iStockphoto; 45 (LO), Ingolf Pompe 57/Alamy; 46-47, Cesar Okada/iStockphoto; 48 (UP), Migel/Shutterstock.com; 48 (LOLE), Anna Webber/The Hell Gate/Corbis; 48 (LORT), Richard Maschmeyer/Robert Harding World Imagery/Corbis; 49 (UP), Doug Pearson/JAI/Corbis; 49 (LO), AFP/Getty Images; 50 (UP), SIME/eStock Photo; 50 (LO), Ashman, Laura/the food passionates/Corbis; 51, Günter Gräfenhain/eStock Photo; 52 (UP), NG Creative; 52 (LO), Pavel L Photo and Video/Shutterstock; 53 (UP), RIA Novosti/Alamy; 53 (LO), Richard T. Nowitz/Corbis; 54, Della Huff/Alamy; 55, AXEL KOESTER/The New York Times/Redux Pictures; 56, Helen King/Corbis; 57 (UP), Catherine Karnow/National Geographic Creative; 57 (LO), Poketo // Poketo.com; 58 (UP), Gary Friedman/Los Angeles Times; 58 (LO), Ambient Images Inc./Alamy; 59, nito/Shutterstock.com; 60 (UP), TheYok/iStockphoto; 60 (LOLE), MARKA/Alamy; 60 (LORT), James Steidl/Shutterstock; 61 (UP), Nigel-Spiers/Shutterstock; 61 (LO), Design Pics Inc./National Geographic Creative; 62, Anna Serrano/eStock Photo; 63 (UP), Kerem Uzel/NarPhotos/Redux Pictures; 63 (LO), Frank Heuer/laif/Redux Pictures; 64-65, Anna Serrano/eStock Photo; 66 (UP), Anna Serrano/eStock Photo; 66 (LO), Wolfgang Kaehler/Corbis; 67, Siegfried Stolzfuss/eStock Photo; 68, SIME/eStock Photo; 69 (UP), John Hopkins/Alamy; 69 (LO), Abdallah Adel/NurPhoto/Corbis; 70, Richard Nowitz/National Geographic Creative; 71, Ian Shaw/Alamy; 72-73, thinkomatic/iStockphoto; 74, tomy/Shutterstock; 75 (UP), Brian Jannsen/Alamy; 75 (LO), Charles Lupica/Alamy; 76 (UP), Ed Alcock/eyevine/Redux Pictures; 76 (LO), Chris Lawrence/Alamy; 77, Günter Gräfenhain/SIME/eStock Photo; 78 (UP), Michael Ventura/Alamy; 78 (LOLE), Brandon Bourdages/Shutterstock; 78 (LORT), bonchan/Shutterstock; 79 (UP), Christopher Groenhout/Lonely Planet Images/Getty Images; 79 (LO), Eros Hoagland/Redux Pictures; 80 (UP), Holger Mette/iStockphoto; 80 (LO), ppart/Shutterstock; 81 (UP), Maynard Owen Williams/National Geographic Creative; 81 (LO), Robert Harding World Imagery/Alamy; 82, Paul Harris/JAI/Corbis; 83 (UP), Simon Reddy/Alamy; 83 (LO), Prashant Panjiar/Anzenberger/Redux Pictures; 84, SIME/eStock Photo; 85, Neil Setchfield/Alamy; 86-87, Justin Foulkes/4Corners/SIME/eStock

Photo; 88, compassandcamera/iStockphoto; 89 (UP), tony french/Alamy; 89 (LO), SIME/eStock Photo; 90 (UP), Steven Poh/Shutterstock; 90 (LO), Justin Kase z12z/Alamy; 91, SIME/eStock Photo; 92 (UP), Abilio Lope/Corbis; 92 (LOLE), Caro/Alamy; 92 (LORT), Michael Jenner/Alamy; 93 (UP), Hemis/Alamy; 93 (LO), Emi Cristea/Alamy; 94, Paul Chesley/National Geographic Creative; 95 (UP), olyniteowl/iStockphoto; 95 (LO), NORMA JOSEPH/Alamy; 96, Lissandra Melo/Shutterstock.com; 97, Michael S. Williamson/The Washington Post via GI; 98, Songquan Deng/Shutterstock; 99 (UP), LEGO is a trademark of the LEGO Group of companies, used here by special permission. © 2014 The LEGO Group; 99 (LO), John Van Hasselt/Corbis; 100 (UP), Achim Multhaupt/laif/Redux Pictures; 100 (LO), John Kernick/National Geographic Creative; 101 (UP), Bettmann/Corbis; 101 (LO), Landon Nordeman; 102, Bruno Morandi/SIME/eStock Photo; 103, Gavin Hellier/Robert Harding World Imagery/Corbis; 104-105, Tim Draper/ 4Corners/Sime/eStock Photo; 106 (UP), W. Robert Moore; 106 (LO), Steve McCurry; 107 (UP), Lucas Vallecillos/VWPics/Redux Pictures; 107 (LO), Hub/laif/Redux Pictures; 108 (UP), Massimo Borchi/SIME/eStock Photo; 108 (LO), PAUL YEUNG/Reuters/Corbis; 109, Tibor Bognar/Corbis; 110 (UP), OPIS Zagreb/Shutterstock; 110 (LOLE), John Warburton-Lee Photography/Alamy; 110 (LORT), prochasson frederic/Shutterstock; 111 (UP), Horia Bogdan/Shutterstock; 111 (LO), SIME/eStock Photo; 112 (UP), Walter Bibikow/Getty Images; 112 (LO), Bon Appetit/Alamy; 113 (UP), NG Creative; 113 (LO), Radius Images/Corbis; 114, Richard Nowitz/National Geographic Creative; 115 (UP), Soren Egeberg Photography/Shutterstock.com; 115 (LO), UIG via GI; 116 (UP), Susan Seubert/National Geographic Creative; 116 (LO), foodfolio/Alamy; 117, SOPA/eStock Photo; 118, Pietro Canali/SIME/eStock Photo; 119 (UP), Mike Paterson/National Geographic Your Shot; 119 (LO), Rosemarie Stennull/Alamy; 120, SIME/eStock Photo; 121 (UP), Photolibrary/Getty Images; 121 (LO), Travel Pictures/Alamy; 122-123, MasterLu/iStockphoto; 124, SIME/eStock Photo; 125 (UP), Thomas Cockrem/Alamy; 125 (LO), SOPA/eStock Photo; 126 (UP), imageBROKER/Alamy; 126 (LOLE), Aurora Photos/Alamy; 126 (LORT), boryak/iStockphoto; 127 (UP), age fotostock/Alamy; 127 (LO), Jason Hosking/Corbis; 128 (UP), John

Greim/LOOP IMAGES/Corbis; 128 (LO), William Manning/Corbis; 129, Richard Nowitz/National Geographic Creative; 130 (UP), Clifton R. Adams and Edwin L. Wisherd/National Geographic Creative;130 (LO), JJM Stock Photography/Alamy; 131 (UP), Raymond Patrick/National Geographic Creative; 131 (LO), Raymond Patrick/National Geographic Stock; 132, SIME/eStock Photo; 133, SONNET Sylvain/Hemis/Corbis; 134, Boris Stroujko/Shutterstock; 135 (UP), ITAR-TASS Photo Agency/Alamy; 135 (LO), JOHN KELLERMAN/Alamy; 136 (UP), Martin Sasse/LAIF/Redux Pictures; 136 (LO), Andrew Koturanov/Shutterstock; 137, SIME/eStock Photo; 138, SIME/eStock Photo; 139, Richard Taylor/Getty Images; 140-141, SIME/eStock Photo; 142, David Ball/Alamy; 143 (UP), AWSeebaran/iStockphoto; 143 (LO), Amer Ghazzal/Demotix/Corbis; 144 (UP), Nick Green/Photolibrary/Getty Images; 144 (LO), Photolibrary/Getty Images; 145, SIME/eStock Photo; 146, SOPA/eStock Photo; 147 (UP), Ruaridh Stewart/ZUMA Press/Corbis; 147 (LO), Matt Propert/National Geographic Creative; 148 (UP), Danny Lehman/Corbis; 148 (LOLE), Bates Littlehales/National Geographic Creative; 148 (LORT), Stan Rohrer/Alamy; 149 (UP), David R. Frazier Photolibrary, Inc./Alamy; 149 (LO), Richard Nowitz/National Geographic Creative; 150 (UP), Brook Mitchell/SIME/eStock Photo; 150 (LO), Andrew Watson/Photolibrary/Getty Images; 151 (UP), Bettmann/Corbis; 151 (LO), Allan Symon Gerry/Alamy; 152, Johanna Huber/SIME/eStock Photo; 153 (UP), Tim Draper/Sime/eStock Photo; 153 (LO), Gerard Walker/Lonely Planet Images/Getty Images; 154, Pietro Canali/SIME/eStock Photo; 155, Design Pics Inc./Alamy; 156-157, Susan Seubert/National Geographic Creative; 158, jiawangkun/Shutterstock; 159 (UP), David Giral/Alamy; 159 (LO), Stacy Gold/National Geographic Creative; 160 (UP), Lee Brown/Alamy; 160 (LO), Stacy Gold/National Geographic Creative; 161 (UP), Chesterfield & Mclaren/National Geographic Creative; 161 (LO), Richard T. Nowitz/Corbis; 162 (UP), Massimo Borchi/SIME/eStock Photo; 162 (LO), Annie Libby/Alamy; 163, col/Shutterstock; 164, Lisa Seaman/Aurora Photos/Corbis; 165 (UP), Randy Duchaine/Alamy; 165 (LO), Alastair Balderstone/Alamy; 166, Orhan Cam/Shutterstock; 167 (UP), Envision/Corbis; 167 (LO), Jenny Kallenbrunnen/dpa/Corbis; 168-169, Massimo Borchi/

World's Best Cities
Celebrating 220 Great Destinations

Published by the National Geographic Society
Gary E. Knell, *President and Chief Executive Officer*
John M. Fahey, *Chairman of the Board*
Declan Moore, *Executive Vice President; President, Publishing and Travel*
Melina Gerosa Bellows, *Executive Vice President; Publisher and Chief Creative Officer, Books, Kids, and Family*
Lynn Cutter, *Executive Vice President, Travel*
Keith Bellows, *Senior Vice President and Editor in Chief, National Geographic Travel Media*

Prepared by the Book Division
Hector Sierra, *Senior Vice President and General Manager*
Janet Goldstein, *Senior Vice President and Editorial Director*
Jonathan Halling, *Creative Director*
Marianne R. Koszorus, *Design Director*
Barbara A. Noe, *Senior Editor*
R. Gary Colbert, *Production Director*
Jennifer A. Thornton, *Director of Managing Editorial*
Susan S. Blair, *Director of Photography*
Meredith C. Wilcox, *Director, Administration and Rights Clearance*

Staff for This Book
Lawrence M. Porges, *Editor*
Carol Clurman, *Project Editor*
Elisa Gibson, *Art Director*
Nancy Marion, *Illustrations Editor*
Meg Weaver, *Researcher*
Carl Mehler, *Director of Maps*
Mapping Specialists, *Ltd. Map Research and Production*
Mark Baker, Larry Bleiberg, Karen Carmichael, Amy Fabris-Shi, Dana Facaros, Thomas Fuller, Conner Gorry, Jeremy Gray, Graeme Green, Jessica Gross, Michael Luongo, Jenna Makowski, Ed Readicker-Henderson, Emma Rowley, April White, Joe Yogerst, *Contributing Writers*
Sophie Massie, *Picture Legends Writer*
Marshall Kiker, *Associate Managing Editor*
Judith Klein, *Production Editor*
Lisa A. Walker, *Production Manager*
Galen Young, *Rights Clearance Specialist*
Katie Olsen, *Production Design Assistant*
Rose Davidson, Hannah Lauterback, *Contributors*

Production Services
Phillip L. Schlosser, *Senior Vice President*
Chris Brown, *Vice President, NG Book Manufacturing*
Nicole Elliott, *Director of Production*
George Bounelis, *Senior Production Manager*
Rachel Faulise, *Manager*
Robert L. Barr, *Manager*

The National Geographic Society is one of the world's largest nonprofit scientific and educational organizations. Founded in 1888 to "increase and diffuse geographic knowledge," the member-supported Society works to inspire people to care about the planet. Through its online community, members can get closer to explorers and photographers, connect with other members around the world, and help make a difference. National Geographic reflects the world through its magazines, television programs, films, music and radio, books, DVDs, maps, exhibitions, live events, school publishing programs, interactive media, and merchandise. *National Geographic* magazine, the Society's official journal, published in English and 38 local-language editions, is read by more than 60 million people each month. The National Geographic Channel reaches 440 million households in 171 countries in 38 languages. National Geographic Digital Media receives more than 25 million visitors a month. National Geographic has funded more than 10,000 scientific research, conservation, and exploration projects and supports an education program promoting geography literacy. For more information, visit www.nationalgeographic.com.

For more information, please call 1-800-NGS LINE (647-5463) or write to the following address:

National Geographic Society
1145 17th Street N.W.
Washington, D.C. 20036-4688 U.S.A.

For information about special discounts for bulk purchases, please contact National Geographic Books Special Sales: ngspecsales@ngs.org

For rights or permissions inquiries, please contact National Geographic Books Subsidiary Rights: ngbookrights@ngs.org

ISBN: 978-1-4262-1378-6

Printed in the United States of America

14/RRD-CML/1